QUEER ITALY

Intersections
in Communications
and Culture

Global Approaches and Transdisciplinary
Perspectives

Cameron McCarthy and Angharad N. Valdivia
General Editors

Vol. 18

PETER LANG
New York • Washington, D.C./Baltimore • Bern
Frankfurt am Main • Berlin • Brussels • Vienna • Oxford

Miguel Andrés Malagreca

QUEER ITALY

Contexts, Antecedents and Representation

PETER LANG
New York • Washington, D.C./Baltimore • Bern
Frankfurt am Main • Berlin • Brussels • Vienna • Oxford

Library of Congress Cataloging-in-Publication Data

Malagreca, Miguel.
Queer Italy: contexts, antecedents and representation / Miguel Malagreca.
p. cm. — (Intersections in communications and culture:
global approaches and transdisciplinary perspectives; vol. 18)
Includes bibliographical references.
1. Gays—Italy. 2. Homosexuality in motion pictures. I. Title.
HQ76.2.I8M35   306.76'60945—dc22   2006022883
ISBN 978-0-8204-8816-5
ISSN 1528-610X

Bibliographic information published by **Die Deutsche Bibliothek**.
Die Deutsche Bibliothek lists this publication in the "Deutsche
Nationalbibliografie"; detailed bibliographic data is available
on the Internet at http://dnb.ddb.de/.

Cover design by Joshua Hanson

The paper in this book meets the guidelines for permanence and durability
of the Committee on Production Guidelines for Book Longevity
of the Council of Library Resources.

Table of Contents

ᴄ⅁ **Preface** ᴇᴏ

By the time this book is published, the conditions under which queer persons in Italy live may have changed forever. Of course, it is also possible that very little indeed may change. The truth is that in trying to make queer sexuality, politics, and culture speak to each other, this book (and its author) embarked on a daunting project, based on the premise that these are conditions subject to great instability and are in constant flux. Just after the manuscript of *Queer Italy* was finished and submitted to the editors, a new page appeared to have been turned in Italian (queer) history. During the first months of 2007, a new project for the recognition of cohabitation (including same-sex couples) was presented to the Council of Ministers. Usually called DICO, it stands for *diritti e doveri delle persone stabilmente conviventi* (or, rights and duties of stable, cohabiting people). The intention of this brief preface is not to describe the DICO extensively, for indeed my book (as the introduction and first chapters make clear) is not a chronological presentation of every historical or legal landmark in the history of queer sexuality in Italy; neither does this study center its attention on statistical analyses of the way queer life is changing in Italy. While all these and many other approaches are not only interesting but absolutely vital for the study of queer issues in Italy and Europe in general, the point that this manuscript seeks to make is quite another: that a critical understanding of queer subjectivity needs to move beyond fixed scholastic delimitations to resemble as much as possible the very personal, playful, unfixed, sometimes chaotic, and oftentimes (and sadly) threatened life of queerness. The significance of proposals such as the DICO is, however, incontrovertible, and readers of this book deserve a brief comment on it and on its adjacent cultural circumstances.

Curiously, the drafting of the DICO (a proposal that, at the time of writing this preface, remains to be passed) reinforces a general observation made in this book. When I started my research for this project, the proposal of PACS (see below, in particular chapters 4 and 5 and the conclusion) was the

Master signifier that prompted profound and thorny debates about the weak status of queers in Italy. For this reason, proud as I am about the idea of a project like PACS (or any similar one) being passed in Italy, the book discusses it in a critical light, making the point that, no matter how important it might be, it needs to be considered a point of departure for queer rights in Italy—not a point of arrival. PACS, the homophobic mind imagined, represented a threat to the sanctity and civility of the Italian nuclear, heterosexual family. Today, debates over PACS continue, and queers are as strong and probably as united as ever before; we are defending our right to see our relationships protected and—let's say it loud and clear!—*respected* and *humanized*. This is a shout for freedom and deference, the firing of a shot that cannot and will not be silenced. Yet, at the same time, the question of PACS has been eclipsed by the DICO. Added to the questions that I raise about PACS in this book (including, for example, the problem of parenthood), the most problematic aspects of the DICO are that it does not institute a marriage or a civil union, it does not guarantee extensive civil rights to cohabiting partners, and, on some issues, it only becomes fully effective progressively, after the couple has demonstrated stability for a number of years. Moreover, the document demands up to nine years of cohabitation to fully guarantee a partner the right of inheritance in the event of the death of his/her partner, it does not grant citizenship to a foreign partner, and in the case of one member of the couple being hospitalized, the DICO leaves entirely to a public health institution the choice of recognizing a partner as a proper family member or not.

As I try to clarify in the pages of this book, the relevant question here is not whether we are for or against proposals of this type—and one can almost hear the super Ego shouting, "Didn't you want to be legal? Then enjoy this piece of Law!" This is the moment when the realm of the Symbolic Law is in danger of falling prey to the immediate effect of the imaginary. It all appears as if, finally, queer couples could be on the verge of attaining exactly what they have been seeking for so long. Then why the grievance? Why the protest?

Indeed, protests have taken place. In March 2007, for example, Rome was once again the city where some 80,000 people gathered, marched, and expressed their solidarity with one of the most debilitated queer communities in Western Europe. What was expressed this time was not only the urgency of making a document respond to the concrete demands of an informed society, but also a deeper and more sophisticated awareness about the law: that legal instruments can be extremely effective in prescribing and ordering subjectivity, and that they command the suffering body to adjust to and bend to the weight of grand signifiers. The risk is that in some cases these can become signifiers that try to get hold of difference, so as to codify and degrade the unlimited human diversity to the particularistic capriciousness of the small mind. It is against the small mind that we rise and march.

This preface would be incomplete if I did not mention in passing that during the same period when the DICO was presented and when the march in Rome took place, the new film by Ferzan Özpetek, *Saturno Contro*, was released. From a Lacanian perspective, this might be the film in which the director interweaves most successfully the issues of loss, the question of the object (petit a), and the issue of enjoyment. Unfortunately, while I mention the movie briefly in chapter 6, an analysis of its plot and cultural significance will have to await another opportunity.

ෆ Acknowledgments ෨

I would like to thank all the people who were in some way involved in this project and continuously offered their support: Cameron McCarthy, Nancy Blake, Pat Gill, and Robert Rushing of the University of Illinois, and Juan Jorge Michel Fariña of the University of Buenos Aires. I would also like to thank the kind staff of Peter Lang for believing in the potential of this project and Marco Pustianaz for his feedback on the manuscript.

This book was finished at the same time I was granted Italian citizenship, and I therefore offer it as a symbolic acknowledgment of the struggle of all queer emigrants to/from Italy, including my grandparents and parents.

The book is dedicated to D., *vita ed amore.*

Finally, grateful acknowledgment is hereby made to copyright holders for permission to use the following material:

An earlier version of some fragments of chapter 1 appeared in my article "Psychoanalytic Theory and Everyday Cultural Politics: A Critical Reading of the Argentinean Crisis of 2001." *Kaleidoscope* 2, 1, pp. 1-12, and in *Human Architecture. Journal of the Sociology of Self-Knowledge* 6, (Summer 2006), pp. 187-204.

An earlier version of some fragments of chapter 2 appeared in my article "Lottiamo Ancora. Reviewing One Hundred and Fifty Years of Italian Feminism." *Journal of International Women's Studies*, 7, 4 (May 2006), pp. 69-89.

An earlier version of some fragments of chapter 4 appeared in my articles "Ominous Impunity." *Rocky Mountain Communication Review Journal*, 2, 1 (Summer 2004), pp.19-30, University of Utah; and in "Rethinking State Terrorism in Argentina, Twenty Years After the Return of Democracy." *Global Media Journal*, 4, 6 (Spring 2005).

An earlier version of some fragments of chapter 5 appeared in my book review article, "Des Parents comme les Autres: Homosexualité et Parenté." *Contemporary French Civilization*, 29, 1, 188-191.

An earlier version of some fragments of chapter 6 appeared in my article "Queer Kinships in Italian Cinema." *Genre Journal*, 25, pp. 42-59.

⚕ **Introduction** ⚕

I would like to begin with two brief comments, one about the 2000 World Gay Pride Parade held in Rome, Italy, and another, more personal one, about being a migrant (and queer) person in Italy. First, the year 2000 marked a moment in history when Rome, the Eternal and Sacred City, was reclaimed and remade by thousands of transsexuals, bisexuals, gays, lesbians, transgender persons, and queers (hereafter GLBTQs). The 2000 World Gay Pride Parade was perhaps the most remarkable queer activist performance in decades in Italy. Rome was chosen as the host city for an international queer parade that would transcend all national and cultural frontiers, bringing visibility to GLBTQs in Italy (see Luongo, 2002; Cestaro, 2004). Metonymically, Rome stands for a millennial empire. It is also associated with the Catholic "eternal city," and it evokes images of world fashion, design, refined arts, and culinary traditions. Michael Luongo's (2002) analysis of the parade suggests that by choosing Rome to host the event, a number of international and domestic gay associations were stimulating GLBTQ activism: the very same year that hundreds of queers visited the capital city of the Italian peninsula, thousands of devout Catholics from all corners of the world traveled there to celebrate the new millennium. Indeed, just as the jubilee signaled the renewal of Catholic faith, the parade also renewed hopes for queers in Italy, who expected to contest the legal state of affairs regarding sexual orientation and to challenge heterosexist ideologies and institutions long present in the country (Luongo, 2002; Cestaro, 2004).

Without doubt, as Cestaro (2004) suggests, the World Pride celebration was the site to contest material and symbolic forms of hostility toward the Italian gay community. Hundreds of queers, including female-to-male/male-to-female, transsexuals, leathers, bears and bisexuals, butch and fem lesbians, fag hags, non-heterosexist straights, drag queens and kings, brought visibility to one of the most vibrant acts of political and communal action in years, shaking old stereotypes and myths about gender that have been immortalized in media images about the *uomo mediterraneo* and the *donna romana*. We learn with Luongo (2002) that the assortment of groups, political affiliations, voices, and colors presented a diversified yet united queer community that marched from an obscurantist past toward an assertive present. Among the groups, a number of gay and lesbian parents marched with their children, representing associations of gay parents who struggled for the right of queer couples to adopt. Right beside them, it was not unusual to see posters exhorting Parliament to pass a law providing for domestic partnerships and legal equality in the workplace (see Luongo, 2002). The gay community that marched in the streets of Rome may have had the positive effect of showing the existence of queer as pure diversity or Otherness.

Accounts of the parade show how a variety of cultural, tourist, religious, and activist groups participated in World Pride, creating a kaleidoscope of political aims. Allegedly, this kaleidoscope mirrored the existence of a new Italy characterized by "cultural diversity." This multiculturalism, mapped by other authors in other social contexts, can be imagined as a grid. It takes for granted the existence of fixed, pre-consolidated identities that have the potential to participate democratically and rationally within an emergent political dialogue, a view that assumes that there are cultural and subjective identities constituted before the fact (see Rapisardi, 2003a, 2003b). As I will demonstrate in chapters 4 and 5, this has been for some years now the implicit political assumption of some Italian gay movements. While I will try to show in what ways this politics might present advantages over previous forms of gay activism, my hope is to also show in what ways this politics needs to be more critically anchored, particularly every time sexual identity is reduced to a vague notion of individuality or difference that masks the problems of race, gender, region, and class inequality within the country.

The second comment I would like to make is illustrative of what such ordered and rational mapping might imply. As soon as I came to Italy with my partner, I began the process of obtaining Italian citizenship. While my partner is Italian, and while we registered our partnership some time before coming to Italy, our affiliation is not recognized by the Italian state. Therefore, I had to start a *pratica*, or legal exercise, to live and work in Italy. Little did I know at that point that this *pratica* would consume enormous amounts of time and resources, and involve several bureaucratic steps. It all started with the very first step. It was around 5:00 in the morning when I arrived at the office of immigration, and my eyes could not believe that the queue already extended around the corner from the entrance. I suddenly felt relieved that I was not the only one, but my initial fears of not being understood by the police morphed into anger and dismay as I discovered, in talking to other immigrants, how many times this procedure would be repeated. The queue to obtain a *permesso di soggiorno* moved slowly. That day, I returned home at 4:00 P.M.

As the *pratica* became more prolonged, we grew more and more tense and tired. Many of us protested the procedures and the way in which we were treated, which included being shouted at by police officers. One officer, carrying a gun in his uniform, addressed a group of North Africans by stating that although we demanded rights, we seemed to be unable to stand in a queue in order. This incident made me think that our presence in a public office constituted a performance against a totalizing order. In some way it crashed bureaucracy, abruptly exposing a symbolic divide. While an immigration office aims at regulating the entrance of immigrants to a country, and while it might help immigrants by providing them with documents, there is an inescapable component of anxiety involved in the process. This component of anxiety cannot be fully regulated. It derives from the presence of Otherness, which cannot be fully absorbed by any normative system. The Otherness I am describing here should not be mistaken with the strangeness that some might experience when meeting someone from a different ethnic or racial background, although this strangeness might be involved in the uncovering of Otherness. Otherness, then, is neither external nor internal to personal psychology, and it does not belong to either me or you. Instead, the Otherness I am referring to with the example of the immigration office, appears to me as the tearing off of an imaginary connecting "tissue" that is supposed to be at the basis of social interaction. It is this unexpected Otherness that our bodies suffer from, for it cannot be completely regulated or anticipated in the functioning of a social institution. Nevertheless, what was most interesting for me about this experience was the realization of a "queer" synchronicity, the understanding that most probably there were other thousands of people queuing in similar offices all around Italy as well as in other Western European countries. It also struck me that at the same time these "parades" might take place almost every day throughout the West, but are nevertheless hardly ever considered a compelling performance of love, life, and bravery. It is rare that these "parades" make it to the front pages of newspapers, and yet they are an act of pride for those of us who choose or are forced to remake our lives in a new nation.

Being queer and being an immigrant are definitely two different social phenomena, but they do share some characteristics that are worth exploring. More important, and what will be treated in parts of this book, are the intersections between queer and migrant: intersections that our bodies—bodies of suffering and bodies of pleasure—dare to speak about when our voices are silenced or ignored.

Defining the Limits of PACS

On October 16, 2005, Italians had the opportunity to vote for a candidate from the center-left coalition to represent them as President of the Council during the next national elections. For weeks, the press and television focused on the coverage of this political event. Among other issues central to the media coverage of the elections were presentations to Parliament regarding a Pact of Civil Unions (hereafter PACS), together with considerations about the 1989 and 1994 resolutions of the European Parliament regarding the rights of transsexuals, the situation of sexual minorities in the country, and the laws banning discrimination based on sexual orientation (Arcigay, 2005).

The position of each candidate on these issues was scrutinized, analyzed, and often trivialized on television and in newspapers. Anticipating the confusing media coverage of the issues at stake, major GLBTQ organizations publicly pressed candidates for a clear statement either in favor or against the project of civil unions, so as to inform the public and make clear the electoral choice. Interestingly, some candidates, including Romano Prodi, the main candidate for the left who would eventually win the election, responded to these letters showing support for the rights of GLBTQ persons (see Arcigay, 2005).

These fascinating political events took place only months after Arcigay had issued to Parliament a Project for PACS—the fourth project defending the rights of queers in Italy, but the first one with a reasonable chance of being discussed and passed in Parliament following years of intense negotiations and struggle among activists, politicians, and religious authorities. If passed, this document might change Italian civil society drastically. To understand the current plea for civil unions in Italy demands situating it contextually across the specific history, religion, politics, and the material symbolic of the country. Indeed, this book illustrates that the current conundrum of the Italian GLBTQ population is that the appeal to the state is a necessary instrument of struggle, the logical result of international and domestic transformations. Consider, for example, the findings of recent research that indicate that 68.7 percent of Catholics in Italy are sympathetic toward a PACS project, and 65.6 percent approve of divorce ("Eurispes," 2006). Following the works of authors such as Berlant and Warner, but situating my argument within the context of Italy, I contend that petitioning the state to legitimate same-sex unions is, however, a highly problematic movement. It potentially reifies the already existing exclusion of a large section of the population that does not conform to the normative labeling of intimacy. Legalizing civil unions is a practical yet dubious movement that might require surrender to the state's power to sanction certain relationships, symbols, sexual practices, and morals, while constructing at the same time a fantasy of queerness as the shadow of an Otherness that lies beyond the law.

Defining Queer

> **queer** . *agg.* **1** strano, bizzarro, eccentrico; capriccioso / *he is a - fish*, (*fam.*) è un individuo eccentrico / *to be in Queer Street*, (*antiq.*) avere debiti;. . .**queer** *v. tr.* (*sl.*) **1** mettere in ridicolo **2** ingannare; rovinare / *to - s.o.'s pitch*, rompere le uova nel paniere a qlcu. [to break somebody's balls] **queerish** *agg.* alquanto strano, piutosto bizzarro. (*Online Dictionary English-Italian Garzanti Linguistica*; my emphasis and bracketed translations)

Since this book examines the meaning of the term *queer* within the context of Italian culture, it is important to clarify the use I make of this signifier. For some years now, the term *queer* has been appropriated in Italy in a variety of ways, but oftentimes without carrying some of the connotations that the history of GLBTQ politics lent to this expression in English. While *queer* names sexual identities or practices that do not align with heterosexism and that transcend fixed binaries (such as homosexual/heterosexual or gay/straight), quite often it is used in non-academic Italian contexts as a trendy synonym for *gay*. Although the word *queer* is perhaps not as frequently used in Italy as in France or Spain, Italian political organizations are making a transition toward use of the word, although national groups like Arcigay or Circolo Mario Mieli are usually identified simply as gay and lesbian activist groups. In some Italian literature, *queer* might be used as a synonym for homosexual, or gay and lesbian. Cultural studies works in Italian that document the whole history of the Italian GLBTQ movement are few. Two comprehensive books are Rossi Barilli's (1999) and Consoli's (2000), texts that were fundamental in this project and to which I refer the reader. Italian cultural studies scholarship regarding Italian transgender or transsexual identities was scarce at the time I began this study. There are Italian writers who, nevertheless, discuss non-heterosexual subjectivities that do not fit within the gay identity (see chapters 4 and 5), and so they prefer to use the word *queer*.

In this book, I take the liberty of playing with signifiers and shifting several times from queer to gay, from *we* to *I* or *they*, from "gay and lesbian" to "GLBTQ" or other denominations to avoid securing meaning to signifiers. On the contrary, I make one important distinction between the terms *queer* and *heterosexism* or *heterosexist* to underline sexual, political, and ethical differences between social actors or social practices. To be sure, whenever I use the word *straight*, I am referring to heterosexist individuals and not to heterosexuality *per se*. In my view, heterosexism is a system of meanings, moral values, and behaviors contrary to the unfixed and always political nature of human desire. In this sense, heterosexual individuals who are not heterosexist can be *queer* as much as gay persons can act in accordance with heterosexism. This means that queerness has little to do with either a form of being or a form of sexual orientation. Instead, it implies an ethical/political/personal perspective about desire that will unfold in the course of my analysis. Although I agree with historians that the term *queer* cannot be mechanically applied to the Italian context, I still prefer its use to terms like *gay*. In Italy, the term *gay* is as foreign as *queer*, but the word *gay* might sometimes reify essentialist view of identity. Finally, I prefer the word *queer* because it resonates with postcolonial theory's notion of hybridity, which is crucial in my discussion of migrant, borderline, or nomadic subjectivities.

Regarding the debates on essentialist and anti-essentialist identities, queer theory authors have been elaborating on the poststructural notion of difference to include aspects of sexuality and subjectivity that are central to GLBTQ politics. Judith Butler (1997a), for example, uses Derrida's philosophical work to analyze in conceptual and political terms the meaning of "context." Butler interprets Derrida's analysis of written texts by highlighting the idea that context is not a definite, stabilizing reference but is instead a notion that is never fully determined. Since much of my book deals with the historic, political, and symbolic contexts surrounding PACS, I borrow from this line of queer theory the idea that any context is always an unstable category of analysis that surpasses the intention of the enunciator. According to this view, the intention of any subject or speaker cannot govern the meaning of any communication; instead, meaning is a product that exceeds the speaker's sphere of rationality. The speaker does not rule over the communication because any utterance is always polysemic; in other words, the linguistic context goes beyond the speaker's agency (see Michalik, 2001; Romano, 1999; Smith, 2001; White, 1998).

According to the line of thought initiated by Butler (1993) and reinterpreted by other queer theory writers (see Lehr, 1999; Wilchins, 2004), sex might not be something that exists independently of gender; masculine and feminine distinctions are constructions, although ones that appear naturalized *a posteriori* or resignified under the effect of social interactions. Butler (1993) teaches that sexual bodies are in fact as much a cultural product as gender is. There is only partial significance in defining gender as the operation of social interpretation of sex, because sex is already a constructed category that might assume dissimilar values within different cultural realms. Following this line of interpretation, Butler (1993) suggests that it is possible to develop a strategy that complicates the understanding of sex and body, criticizing deterministic or biological considerations. Instead, it is possible to empower the recoding and reinterpretation of corporeal categories, of gender and of sexuality. Gender identity, Butler seems to suggest, is a set of gestures, words, performances, and desires that produce the imaginary effect of a reality, but this totalizing gestalt, one would say, never completely reveals the mechanisms of its own organization. Butler (1993) calls these acts "performative." She proposes to unfold quotidian gender performances and the subjects they imply through parody gestures that unveil and destabilize the performative character of gender. Therefore, Butler appears to support a politics of resistance, based on parody aesthetics that would demonstrate that identities are always fictional. Opening the space to these parodies would make alternative, multiple, non-normative identities emerge from the restrictive space to which they are usually confined (see Kirsch, 2000; Lehr, 1999; Wilchins, 2004).

In examining the history of feminist and gay politics (chapters 2 and 3) and in studying the activism of Italian GLBTQ organizations and their plea for civil unions (chapters 4 and 5), I also found it useful to draw indirectly on

Butler as well. For instance, in her essay on kinship, Butler (2002) posits that
the (French) argument for PACS[1] can in fact work in combination with
normalizing family relations, and might not overturn the phallocentric power.
Although she does not seem to directly reject the French model, Butler (2002)
interprets it as a symbol of a dilemma faced by queers: that the desire to
constitute legalized families or civil unions by requesting an intervention by
the state makes them subject to excessive regulation in the domains of
intimacy, elective families, and friendships. For Butler, legal instruments like
PACS reveal that cultural constructions on family deploy systems of representations that provide allegories about the nation, race, and class composition. Similarly, without disapproving of the Italian PACS, I claim in this
study that the struggle for same-sex unions in Italy should not neglect other
possibilities for intimacy. Under current circumstances, individuals choosing
to love or live outside the purview of legal unions—including non-
monogamous couples and multi-parenthood families—would not be considered in their power to contribute to and challenge the symbolic. In addition,
even when PACS is, in principle, a union independent of the gender or
sexual orientation of the participants, transsexuals and intersex individuals
are less likely to be represented in a ritual similar to marriage, whose history
in Italy reifies the language of binary gender and heterosexual marriage.

Politics and Performativity. According to Butler's (1993) model, performativity is at play when individuals create identity, and this creation implies the
elaboration and articulation of multiple discourses. She also argued, however,
that subjects misunderstand the constitutive role of these discourses in the
process of identification (Lehr, 1999). Both identity and its recognition are
related to power structures:

> Thus every insistence on identity must at some point lead to a taking stock of the
> constitutive exclusions that reconsolidate hegemonic power differentials, exclusions
> that each articulation was forced to make in order to proceed. (Butler, 1993, p. 118)

According to this model, the usefulness of the notion of parody is that it
draws attention to the symbolic and imaginary practices of resistance,
conflict, and compromise that are necessary to build identity positions. In
this light, the notion of parody suggests that there are no "before the fact"
essences. In the same way, Lacanian psychoanalysis teaches that the working
of language—and, more specifically, the power of the signifier—is retroac-

tive. The linguistic potential of the performative to structure meaning is derived from the logical organization of language around a fundamental *lack*: language cannot name everything. The symbolic order is an incomplete order.

Tim Dean (2000) and Slavoj Žižek (1999) have both discussed Butler's notion of the real as a *pre*-symbolic order. They remind the reader that the Lacanian real is *extra*-symbolic and resists symbolization; it is what sets a limit to the efficacy of the symbolic and not something that is *previous* to it. It derives from this criticism that the idea that gender identity is achieved through the repetition of contingent social practices implies, perhaps, a conception about human sexuality that emphasizes the imaginary. Indeed, important to Butler's (1993) model is Foucault's account of subjectivity, but this is crucial to understanding that it is through the performativity of disciplinary practices that the subject becomes interpellated into the order of things. However, because the Foucauldian subject is not the Lacanian subject, as these authors have shown, the movement from subjection to norms to the problem of sexual identity that Butler attempts is not easy. The subject of the unconscious is neither a subject formed by an aggregate of cultural experiences nor a sociopsychological formation that expresses an existential void within the human being. A suggestion that cultural practices eventually become internalized or coagulated in gender identity seems to refer more to the Lacanian imaginary: the Ego as a place of identifications (see Dean, 1987, 2000, and 2003). The symbolic in Lacan, however, holds the subject because it structures a conjectural fiction limited by the contingency of the real, which I explore in several chapters.

Unlike other studies on Italian culture, mine does not begin by assuming the existence of regular, preexisting identities that are distributed within the cultural map of a nation. Instead I apply a perspective that does not regard Italy as an object or essence, inhabited by groups of people whose nationality defines their cultural identities (e.g., the *Italians*) or groups of people whose sexual choices define who they are (e.g., the *homosexuals*). Against this position, and following Argentine writers Flavio Rapisardi (2003a, 2003b) and Silvia Delfino (1998), I explore *contexts* (historic, political, and representational) where there are unequal and hierarchical identity positions. These identity positions are not stable, but instead are the result of a regime of configuration and production that operates through antagonism and difference within each of the contexts explored (see Rapisardi, 2003a, 2003b; Delfino, 1998). Notice that this theoretical choice is also a political one, for it engages a discussion about subjectivities that escape the historic or current distribution of roles and identities imposed from afar. My intention is to show that this way of thinking of identity allows subjects to articulate a number of claims and statements in their political struggle for representation, although in doing so they do not propose homogeneity. Instead, identities are in part the result of the interplay of power and meaning in specific historical and cultural settings. In this understanding, my study criticizes any romanticized version of a homogeneous queer community in which individuals need to adapt their desires and subjectivities to conform to a preexistent map. Instead, following previous works related to queer theory, I place emphasis on social inequalities derived from class, gender, racial, and political antagonisms (see Rapisardi, 2003a, 2003b; Delfino, 1998).

This book is the result of an inquiry into the contexts surrounding the struggle of Italian queers to be granted a law for civil unions. The main claim of my work is that this struggle must be understood dialectically: it is culturally specific, and, at the same time, it is analogous to similar demands that have already materialized in other Western countries. In Italy, however, twenty-five years after a queer movement made the first demand to the government to legitimize same-sex unions, negligible positive changes have been seen in the legal sphere. It is my aim in this book to explore the main contexts that explain such opposition to change and to discuss how we can move forward in our quest for human and social rights. This is an exploration of the most relevant contexts in which to understand the current status of queers in Italy: the historical, the personal, the political, and the symbolic or representational.

Italian Homosexuality in History

In the first two chapters of this book, I trace the historical roots of the Italian GLBTQ movement. These chapters cover a period of 150 years, from the unification of the country in the 1860s to the present day. In this introduction, however, I would like to make some brief observations about early same-sex relations. Undoubtedly there is a strong tradition of research that explores this issue. The studies that I consulted represent a variety of perspectives, alternating between Foucauldian writings (stressing the existence of same-sex practices but also challenging the claim that there were homosexual subjects before modernity) and historical inquiry that evidences earlier forms of same-sex relations that involved neither masculinizing nor feminizing roles.

Of course, same-sex relations may always have existed. For example, some paintings in Val Camonica dating back over eight thousand years show men having sexual intercourse. Further, historian Stephen Murray (2000) suggests that at a very early stage in the formation of the Roman Empire, Romans followed the sexual traditions of the Etruscans. A source from that time expressed that for them "it is no disgrace. . .to be seen doing anything in the open, or even having anything done to them, for that is the custom of the country. . .they consort very eagerly with women, but find more pleasure with boys and young men" (Athenaeus, cited in Murray, 2000, p. 112). Murray also suggests that the Etruscan influence on Romans was central to the early organization of the city. As the empire grew, however, Romans also assimilated elements from Greek culture, including the practice of same-sex intercourse. Anal penetration and intercrural[2] intercourse were not uncommon between some Romans, although they did not always conform to the highly aesthetic or pedagogic Greek model. These practices, historians reveal, increased as the Romans expanded the limits of the empire and enlarged the number of slaves. By 31 B.C. there were more than two million slaves in the territory known today as Italy. Those slaves who were particularly beautiful were treated as objects of lust and pleasure, and most of the time they were forced to enter into intimate relations with their masters and their masters' guests: "Their plenitude made the role of slavery within Roman same-sex relations far more salient than it was in Greece" (Murray, 2000, p. 117).

Because subsequent chapters will discuss the terms passive/active in the context of sexual relations in Italy, it is interesting to notice that in Rome, the slave/master dichotomy did not align with feminine/masculine, but it did imply hierarchical roles between the penetrator and the penetrated. Historians seem to agree that, as a consequence, same-sex relations were restricted within the Roman army in order to protect group symmetries. Interestingly, contrary to the Greek model of citizenship, the first and most important role of a man in Rome was that of head of the family, not that of citizen. For this reason, the Greek model of pederasty as a state-building practice did not prosper in Rome. Later in the Roman Republic, a tradition of exaltation of young, masculine, male bodies (*puer delicatus*) developed; male bodies were carefully chosen, shaved, and groomed for the pleasure of other men (see Crompton, 2003; Murray, 2000; Norton, 1997).

While male same-sex desire in Rome has been largely explored, there are fewer studies on female same-sex relations, although there is some evidence of practices similar to gender crossing between women (Murray, 2000) and in early Sicilian art (Crompton, 2003). Like sex with freeborn males, adultery, seduction of virgins, and female same-sex activity violated the authority of the *pater familias* and was severely punished. Several family traditions that developed on the Italian peninsula furnished mothers with agency, giving them more authority and longer control over their sons' lives than in Greece (Crompton, 2003), although they remained subordinated to their husbands.

Although sexuality was used as a form of dominance or conquest of a male enemy through rape, the Roman emperors invented the first same-sex unions in the West. Nero, for instance, is believed to have married two male couples in two different wedding ceremonies (Crompton, 2003). Moreover, John Boswell (1994) found evidence of same-sex unions in ancient Rome: in the seventh century, roman officers and lovers Sergius and Bacchus were tortured to death for their refusal to worship Roman gods. Bacchus died from severe torture. Sergius resisted and cried for his partner. Later, he was beheaded. They became saints that Boswell (1994) takes to represent the tolerance of early Christianity toward non-marital same-sex unions.

Medieval and Renaissance Italy. In medieval Italian society, new forms of trade and agriculture flourished, and a taste for Greek culture revived in the elites. However, historians have provided evidence that the papal city fiercely imposed its rule across Europe in an attempt to repudiate the Islamic world, which had influenced several regions until 1000 A.D. In central Italy, Catholics condemned sodomites with the help of the administrative powers distributed throughout the disaggregated peninsular territory (see Crompton, 2003; Murray, 2000). Similarly, in the fourteenth century, Dante Alighieri's conception of a unified linguistic and geographical area served to oppose influences from France by creating a unified linguistic identity.[3] John Dickie (2001) suggests that in the *De Vulgari Eloquentia*, Dante Alighieri proposed that the vernacular Italian could be a vehicle for bringing the different regions into unity; furthermore, in *La Divina Comedia*, Dante illustrated the usefulness of Florentine as a literary medium to reach out to the populations of the peninsula. Interestingly, *La Divina Comedia* has also raised intense debates about homosexuality. It is not easy to ponder Dante's position: while

Inferno's cantos 15 and 16 seem to condemn sodomites to the seventh circle of hell, some commentators argue that none of the men mentioned in the book had been associated with homosexuality. In addition, there is not a single comment on their erotic life or anything related to the medieval sodomite (see Crompton, 2003).

Italian scholarly work on homosexuality is more abundant and better detailed when it applies to the Italian Renaissance. Giovanni Dall'Orto (1989), perhaps the most important Italian historian in the field, claims that although the birth of the homosexual as a species occurred in the eighteenth century, homoeroticism was present throughout the Italian Renaissance in the form of *amor socraticus*, which he characterizes as the relationship closest to contemporary homosexual love. *Amor socraticus* was not always condemned by law, although the Italian Catholic Church prohibited same-sex relations as sinful acts or the result of devilish mania.

Curiously, although the Renaissance is generally imagined to be the re-birth of classic aesthetics and morals, it was a virulently punitive period. As the Inquisition burned sodomites alive in Spain, in cities like Florence and Venice the sexual life of men and women was closely monitored. Between 1400 and 1700 the number victims of homophobia in Italy was larger than in the Middle Ages, and the form of punishment these victims experienced was taken as a model by other countries such as France and Spain (Crompton, 2003). Beginning with Bologna in 1259, many cities across the territory imposed the death penalty for sodomy: Rome in 1363, Cremona in 1387, Lodi in 1390, Milan in 1476, Padua in 1329, Bassano in 1392, Carpi in 1351, Parma in 1494, and Genoa in 1556. Several other *comuni* (city-states) adopted serious punishment and fines against sodomy (Crompton, 2003). Among other torments, a person suspected of sodomy was first subjected to interrogations by local authorities. Then the individual could be exposed naked in a public square awaiting confession, mutilated, or burned (Crompton, 2003). There is evidence, however, that same-sex love relationships not only survived but also resisted this brutal rule. An example of the interesting relationship between punishment and resistance is the *Bernesque* poetry of Francesco Berni, a Tuscan poet from the sixteenth century whose witty poetry initiated a genre that used words with double meanings and homo-erotic metaphors understandable only to trained readers (Norton, 1997).[4]

While literature concealed and coded homoerotic desire, the fine arts created a visual sensibility for highly erotic, beautiful male bodies. Donatello's, Boticelli's, Leonardo's, and Caravaggio's homoeroticism have been largely discussed (see Bennet & Wilkins 1984; Clark, 1956; Rocke, 1996). Perhaps Donatello's most homoerotic sculpture is his soft-looking, handsome *David*, which he represented as a naked young hunter wearing military boots. Unlike Donatello, Boticelli and Leonardo were accused of being sodomites. The three of them, however, shared an almost activist repulsion for marriage and exalted the beauty of young male bodies (see Crompton, 2003).

Omosessualità Mediterranea. At this point, it might be useful to discuss briefly the notion of *omosessualità mediterranea* (Mediterranean homosexuality), commonly associated with some Mediterranean Christian and Islamic cultures. According to Dall'Orto (2004b), there are distinctive features of male homosexuality common to several societies along the Mediterranean coast. Central among these features is the repetitive existence of age-asymmetric relations. Different ways of naming these relations are the Greek *kìnaidos*, the old Roman *mollis mas,* and the Italian *ricchione* for the male penetree.

Dall'Orto (2004b) suggests that the first description of a *ricchione* can be traced to 1586 in the literature of Giovanni Battista Della Porta (1538?–1615), who described the life of an adult Neapolitan man who disguised himself and talked as a woman. The *ricchione* contrasts with the *sodomite* of the Renaissance, insofar as the *ricchione* is a man who adopts a feminine position, while the *sodomite* can alternate sexual behavior: the "passive" adolescent is penetrated by an older man but, eventually, grows up and reproduces the "active" behavior with a younger man (see Dall'Orto, 2004b). Marzio Barbagli and Asher Colombo (2001) show historical evidence of legal cases in Renaissance Florence in which charges were pressed against "passive" adults in a same-sex relationship. To be sure, what characterizes the *omosessualità mediterranea*, research suggests, is a distinction between the two individuals in the homosexual relationship. One of the individuals takes on a passive sexual role while the other one assumes an active sexual role. Only the first one, however, is the *omossesuale* or *invertito* (meaning homosexual, but also implying deviant or inverted). Terms like *arruso* or *recchione* or *ricchione* all indicating the passive, non-transvestite, male homosexual, and words like *femminiella* (one who cross-dresses) are still used in Italy (see Barbagli & Colombo, 2001; Dall'Orto, 2004b; Rossi Barilli, 1999).

Dall'Orto (2004b) explains the implications of the continued use of the term *Mediterranean homosexuality*. First, he indicates that the masculine/feminine or active/passive dichotomies are meant to soothe the subversive or scandalous element of homoerotic desire while making one person in the relationship guilty of seducing the other (the "passive" acts feminine, seducing or confusing the virile, "active" male). Second, the popularization of terms like *ricchione* or *inverted* actually serves to deny the existence of a homosexual identity, mainly in the sense that these terms mock or denigrate homosexuality and trivialize the act of coming out. In addition, by forcing homosexual identity into secrecy, society profits from its implicitly double-standard morality. The historian suggests that at the same time that this morality condemns homosexuality, it may forgive a manly man who, in a state of transitory confusion, has sex with an *inverted* man. In providing manly men with a means of channeling their sexual energy, the *inverted* is the scapegoat who stabilizes the moral functioning of a society that worships female virginity. Ultimately, the *inverted* was a metaphor for Italy's asymmetric gender relations and the imperviousness of heterosexual marriage. As a matter of fact, Dall'Orto (2004b) indicates a close connection among homosexual desire, shame, and the heterosexual mandate to marry:

> The alternative proposed to society is clear: on the one hand, one can live an exclusive and open relationship with one's desires insofar as one accepts being a grotesque being, the *checca*. On the other hand, one can live one's desires and also maintain the privileged role of being a male, if one accepts the mandate of not living according to such desires. To demonstrate his manliness, a man must marry and produce offspring. The adherence to the institution of marriage is the price one pays to live one's homosexual instincts [sic] without being stigmatized. (p. 3; my translation)

As the passage implies, the institution of marriage has a social function that serves to regulate sexual life while forcing the individual to adapt to the social rule. This research suggests that the *ricchione* seems to have played a socially useful role for societies in which virgin women were closely watched and segregated from men until their marriage. Being active in an occasional homosexual relationship was considered a minor sin even for Catholics during the eighteenth century in some parts of the country (Rossi Barilli, 1999). Indeed, it was much more accepted than a sexual transgression with a forbidden female virgin. In 1860, when the Piedmont's criminal code extended to the recently conquered southern Italy, Article 425 (which penalized homosexuality) was crossed out in southern cities. As Dall'Orto (2004b) states, authorities preferred to give in to homosexual acts rather than to eradicate an entrenched and extensive practice.

Italian Queers, Family, and Europe

While queer theorists and historians like Dall'Orto and Rossi Barilli are rewriting the private history of Italy, activists are remaking the nation on a grassroots level. This remaking has been related to larger transformations in postmodernity, and in confrontation with deep-rooted traditions (Laviosa, 2003). At the beginning of this introduction, I mentioned the relevance of the 2000 World Pride Parade as an unprecedented political event. Further, in chapters 4 and 5, I explore in detail the transition to a global market economy and the impact of this transition on queer politics. Changes in Italian society are more visible in primary social institutions like the family. The *change* in family and intimacy that I am describing should not be equated with radical metamorphosis. Instead, I use the term change to mean the continual re-coding of experience or reworking of the symbolic (and the sphere of norms, rituals, and representations) that can occur when the relation between social agents and social institutions is altered. Indeed, there has never been a *one and only* or essentially typical Italian family, and that this knowledge is beneficial for queer activism.

Social change includes the emergence of a new vocabulary used to describe the plurality of family arrangements present in Italy today. Flavia Laviosa (2003) describes some of these newly coined words:

> The *famiglia unipersonale* is the smallest unit. It consists of a single person, of any age, living alone. It is often an option open to individuals who are without children and have never married, or are divorced, or widowed. The *famiglia monoparentale* offers a solution to a single parent who finds him/herself in a situation of independent single parenthood, *monogenitorialitá*. The recent wave of couples without children constitutes an example of the micro-nuclear family, *famiglia micronucleare*. (Laviosa, 2003, p. 542)

In light of this evidence, while families change constantly, it is the appearance of new terms for naming relationships that is worth noting. Some of the words that express family changes, according to this line of research, are *famiglia lunga*, with more than two generations living in the same *famiglia lunga*, with more than two generations living in the same household; *famiglia impresa*, where members of the family create self-sustaining networks that provide economically and emotionally for larger units with intergenerational differences. Words like *genitori sociali* (social parents) are challenging assumptions about paternity, while terms like *famiglia ricosti-tuita* (reconstituted families), *famiglia allargata* (enlarged family), *famiglia aperta* (open family), or *famigliastra* (stepfamily) denote the new family (Bonaccorso, 1994; Laviosa, 2003). A family vocabulary like this one denotes the interdependence of a large number of individuals. They cohabit and share everyday jobs to care for and support the younger members, and distribute their responsibilities among all the adults: "The effort to function as an operational family in a new kind of kinship is the challenge that contemporary Italian society faces" (Laviosa, 2003, p. 542).

Demographic data about Italy provide more information about family change. According to journalist Alessandro Cecchi Paone (2004), while in 1970 the number of children per woman was 2.43, it dropped to 1.25 in 2001 and became the lowest in the region. In 2001 there were only 535,000 newborns, compared to 900,000 babies born exactly thirty years earlier. In these thirty years, the expense of raising a child rose 22 percent for a work-ing-class family, and it continues to increase by 2 percent each year. The number of children adopted is higher now than ever before, this evidence suggests. Curiously, Italians adopted more than one million children from abroad in 2002.

Cecchi Paone (2004) also indicates that families dependent exclusively upon the economic support of a female member are less than 1 percent in Italy, compared to 11 percent in the United States. In 2002, the portion of the state budget designated for family programs was 3.8 percent, compared to 12 percent in France and Scandinavia. The data from his research and the European Institute of Statistics, or EUROSTAT, indicate that Italy spends 0.5 percent of its gross national product on family assistance, while the average of the European Union is 1.4 percent and reaches up to 2.6 percent in Scandinavia. This research also reveals that while funds for family assistance increased to an average of 36 percent in the European Union in the last decade, Italy's funds for family assistance increased 28 percent, includ-ing a nominal 5 percent of assistance in cash funds to deprived family units. Curiously, there were 260,940 marriages in Italy in 2001–20,000 fewer than in the year 2000. Twenty percent of marriages end in divorce before they reach their fifth anniversary. The average length of marriage is thirteen years and, in 2004, there were 50,051 divorces, as compared to 40,573 in the previous year. From 1995 to 2004, separation rates increased by 40 percent in Italy; by the year 2050, 34.4 percent of the population will be sixty-five years of age or older, and many of them will be divorced, separated, or widowed (see Cecchi Paone, 2004; Ginsborg, 2003).

While these demographics indicate social adjustments to postmodern life, I suggest that it is the demand on the Italian state to pass a law that legitimates civil unions that is the most visible indicator that Italy is being changed on a grassroots level. According to the International Lesbian and Gay Association of Europe or ILGA-Europe (2004), civil unions are forms of officially registered partnership and/or cohabitation that give heterosexual or same-sex couples specific rights, responsibilities, and legal recognition.

In this study I move away from naive defenses of PACS to embrace instead critical and interpretive methodologies that situate the different aspects of a problem in constant flux. I construct a detailed, intertextual, and contextual investigation that allows queers in Italy to take into account issues of sex, subjectivity, race, class, history, politics, and representation that have been minimally present in previous cultural studies of Italy.

This is not to suggest that I discard the advantages of a law allowing civil unions. I have advocated a similar project in Buenos Aires, Argentina, where civil unions have been legal since 2000. However, there is a pressing need to clarify that civil union is not a panacea for the ostracism and alienation that challenges the lives of queers every day. Moreover, it is essential that scholarly work enters the space of activism (and vice versa) and that it promotes critical conversations among queers that dissent with the partially normative language of PACS. Passing a law like PACS will help thousands of couples who want and need a legal instrument that legitimates their relationship. In this respect, the legal benefits that come with the right to form a legally recognized couple are undoubtedly many and also well deserved. Nevertheless, basing queer politics on one single strategy is counterproductive in that it limits the scope of politics. As Warner (1999) has shown, by demanding from the state its approval of our relationships, we may take for granted the structure and role of the state, we may assimilate it and we may perform self-censorship on other areas of queer life. There are many other legal issues, forms of relationality, and social and human rights that demand equal attention. From adoption to citizenship for immigrant partners, from anti-discrimination laws to worker unions, and from laws on reproductive technologies to laws for the legalization of prostitution, the struggle is far from ended: indeed, it has just begun.

A symbol of the need for queers to remain vigilant of our struggles is the choice of Joseph Ratzinger as the new Catholic leader. Far from accepting an open dialogue with queers, Ratzinger has turned out to be the new icon of homophobic discourse in Italy. In July 2003, he issued a correspondence exhorting the parliaments of the world to exercise the right to veto any form of same-sex union or marriage on the basis that, he claims, it is an immoral act that goes against the basics of human organization. Regarding the adoption of children by same-sex couples, the document asserts that "to insert children within a homosexual union through adoption implies an act of violence which profits from the child's natural status of weakness and introduces them within an environment that is unfavorable to the human development" (Vaticano, 2003, s/p; my translation). Ratzinger's comments probably come late to an Italy whose younger generation is moving quickly into new forms of intimacy and more liberal morals. For example, much before Ratzinger's letter, Rossi Barilli (1999) comments, Paolo Hutter defied the administration of Milan in front of hundreds of families and participants who came to witness the marriage of ten couples in Piazza Scala, a public park (Rossi Barilli, 1999).

Organization of This Work

The first part of this book, *Contexts of Queer Italy*, includes an auto-ethnographic narrative that positions me as the author and, in part, as the subject of this study. In this vein, chapter 1, "Writing Queer in the Confines," makes the point that queer subjectivities can be understood as sexual, ethical, and epistemological identities different from heterosexism. The term *confines* is a complex signifier that condenses the idea of borderline, limit, transition, margin, and confinement. Here I draw on Anzaldúa's (1987/1999) notion of borderland: "Borderlands are physically present wherever two or more cultures edge each other, where people of different races occupy the same territory, where under, lower, middle and upper classes touch, where the space between two individuals shrinks with intimacy" (p. 3). By using an interpretive framework, I am able to situate my concurrent foreignness and belonging to Italy. This simultaneous cultural/sexual borderland identity provides richness to my book, offering a vantage point to examine the situation of queers in Italy. In addition, in this chapter, as in others, I integrate borderland and psychoanalytic theory, in this case the notion of *transitional space* as developed by Donald Winnicott, to explore the meaning of living within a queer sexual, ethical, and epistemological identity. This exploration anticipates my discussion of the current plea for gay unions, for it criticizes the idea that queers need to incorporate heterosexual practices in order to validate their lives. It is in this chapter that I also discuss my own understanding of queer theory and its relationship to cultural studies.

Part Two, *Antecedents of Queer Italy,* consists of two chapters oriented toward constructing a contesting history of queer Italy. The first chapter, "Women's Voices, from the *Risorgimento* to Civil Unions," explores the relationship between Italian feminism and the queer movement in terms of century-long struggles to achieve legal and symbolic parity. In addition to my discussion of civil unions, I pay close attention to the interplay of gender parity and difference within the family and the domestic sphere. Starting with the unification of Italy, this chapter studies the historical victories of Italian feminism in transforming deep-rooted beliefs and practices of gender roles in Italy. I specifically focus on the legal, political, and symbolic levels and document biographies of women who became founders of the feminist movement. Next I examine the emergence of new feminist groups and their involvement with protests of the late 1960s. I then briefly explore the issues of divorce, labor, and family laws during the 1970s and 1980s. Finally, I describe the reasons why the current queer movement is fundamentally indebted to feminism. In chapter 3, "Gay and Lesbian Activism, from Homophiles to Arcigay," I investigate the origins of gay and lesbian activism in Italy. What concerns me in this chapter is the specificity of the Italian gay movement; at the same time I explore its similarity to other GLBTQ movements in Europe and the United States. For this reason, I do not take for granted the applicability of notions such as *homosexual, homophile, gay,* and *lesbian,* but evaluate them critically. In addition to the interpretive and historical inquiry, chapter 3 also discusses such notions as gender and sex in light of prominent Italian queer authors like Mario Mieli. Finally, I concentrate my attention on Mieli's *politics of the transsexual* because I find it a provocative and radical framework that, as early as the 1970s, dared to criticize the assimilation of queers within the heterosexuality that is presently embodied in several political perspectives regarding civil unions.

The third part of this book is devoted to discussing the *Politics of Queer Italy*. In chapter 4, "From Fragmentation to Unification," I analyze the rhetorical and political strategies used by Italian queers to create a movement that would achieve parliamentary representation and social visibility. These strategies alternated between fragmentation and unification and led finally to the formation of a nationwide network of organizations and groups with significant differences. In particular, I explore the case of Arcigay, because it is a major gay national organization. Chapter 4 is also a detailed exploration of the political and cultural forces that favored a transition from radical queer politics that advocated the subversion of the family, to more mainstream gay politics in the 1980s and 1990s that advocated the legalization of gay unions. Some of the reasons for this shift are the AIDS pandemic and the rise of neoliberalism and a global market economy. Chapter 5, "Redefining the Meanings of Marriage and Family," deepens this query by looking at alternate, emergent meanings for marriage and family in Italy. Combining demographic, ethnographic, and psychoanalytic notions, I perform a critique of the ethics implied in PACS and advocate other, more radical alternatives that would preserve the diversity of the queer community.

This study of the contexts of queer Italy would not be complete without looking into the realm of the material symbolic, and so that is the aim of Part Four in this book. Although throughout the first five chapters I do include many references to films, literature, theater, and theory, it is in chapter 6, "Inversion, Defiance, and Activism in Italian Film," that I concentrate more comprehensively on representations. At this point, I want to explain the particular use of film in this book. Although one could argue that insofar as I examine movies then I perform *film analysis*, I do so in a very limited way that might not satisfy the exigencies of some film-studies scholars. The whole purpose of my use of films is to say something about identity or sexuality, but not to explore the films themselves or the relation between cinema and industry. As much as I am not a historian, I am not a film-studies scholar either, and I cannot claim that my research performs film or historical analysis. Whenever I comment on a film—either at length or briefly—it is for the purpose of relating the domains of politics, history, sexuality, and representation. My approach to films combines queer theory and Lacanian psychoanalytic theory to explore a number of films—with particular attention to the work of director Ferzan Özpetek—in which the issue of queer relationships and families stands out. What these films have in common is a recodification of sexual identity that suspends any universal, objective knowledge. They are also forms of political and cultural intervention. In this case I agree with Cameron McCarthy (2004) that sometimes the aesthetic of the art itself can anticipate and challenge the work of theory criticism; for this reason I want to situate cinema at the same level of importance and political commitment as theory, politics, and auto-ethnography.

It is also imperative that I comment here about my position as a person who carried out research about queer Italy. The richness, contradictions, and depth of Italian culture(s) makes it difficult for any author to pursue research on a country and people that are alive and always changing. To this difficulty one should add the relative scarcity of academic sources relating to queer culture in Italy. I concentrate here on a limited number of sources that I consulted in Argentina, Italy, and the United States between the years 2002 and 2006. As I grow as a writer, I hope to increase my references and perspectives to represent my topic of research as well as possible. Nevertheless, I believe there is a difference between academic knowledge and *experience*. Whereas the first one tends to be represented in books and classes, the second one is a more personal, intimate relationship with the subject/object of study. In this sense, I identify with Renato Rosaldo (1993) in his postmodern anthropological work, in which he focuses on the process of doing fieldwork and incorporates his personal experiences in the research process. Like him, I value the process of understanding and writing about another culture as a process in which one is transformed oneself. With Norman Denzin (1992), I strongly believe that this form of writing is "an ensemble of social practices, social forms, social relationships, and technologies of representation which construct definitions of reality" (p. 98). He also adds: "They do so in concrete historical moments, to produce particular ideological, emotional, and cultural meanings which are connected to the lived experiences of interacting individuals" (p. 98). Perhaps as a result of this understanding my study will be bordered by discovery and uncertainty, but such are the borders that I cherish the most.

Part One

Contexts of Queer Italy

ℭ૪ **Chapter 1** ૪ઝ
Writing Queer in the Confines

A question that I have often been asked while carrying out research on *Queer Italy* is how I could possibly speak for Italians, not being Italian myself. This is neither a naive nor a critical question. Unlike other Ph.D. candidates, I did *not* write my dissertation to obtain a job in the United States. In contrast to other foreign students at a North American university, I neither wanted to remain in the United States nor planned to continue my work in Argentina, the country where I was born. Unlike most of my Argentine colleagues in Urbana-Champaign, my research would probably be considered marginal for Argentineans—not because my work was not relevant for them, but for the exact opposite reason: Argentina is still deeply imbued with homophobic laws, attitudes, and institutions, including the university. On top of that, although mine was a dissertation in communications, my writing contravenes more orthodox communication studies scholarship.

Notice that in the last paragraph I emphasize the negative form of the verbs and phrases that I use, although I could have highlighted, using affirmative sentences, who I am. Undoubtedly, had I chosen to start this project by accentuating this line of thought, I would have been stressing commonalties with others who might share similar concerns for identity, or with those who position themselves similarly in their enunciation. (A parallel point can be found in Kirsch [2000].) Indeed, many times in my work I stress forms of affiliation and mechanisms of identification with others, particularly when trying to give a voice to some segments of the queer Italian community. In highlighting negativity, however, the aim is to question the limits of what Lacanians call imaginary identifications, thus questioning the stability or unity of the self. In this light, one of the best definitions of the *I* continues to be Freud's classical claim: the I is *not* the master of its own house.

While the erosion of a fixed identity is familiar to cultural studies in some of its manifestations (Lacanian, queer, and postcolonial studies among others), it has been little explored in Italian cultural studies. Interestingly enough, however, the question of national and cultural identity within Italy remains a problem demanding further examination, for the wide range of regional, linguistic, and historic diversities found in that Mediterranean peninsula has always been regarded with utmost awe. While illuminating all the aspects of this problem is beyond my scope here, by highlighting the limits of identification (what I am *not*), I hope to give voice to a sector of Italy that is nominally audible: Italian queers, for most of history, have *not* been allowed to be. By being a *non*-Italian writing about Italy, I hope to defy the borders of social alienation, familial secrecy, historical erasure, Catholic cursing, communist rejection, fascist execution, university segregation, parliamentary refusal, political misrepresentation, and everyday panic.

Donald Winnicott's (1951) notion of "transitional space" illustrates some of the qualities of this borderline/transitional zone that I am trying to describe. According to Winnicott, the outer and inner realities are not the only existing domains. There is a third, transitional space that develops quite early in life, before the choice of sexual object is completed during the oedipal complex. This zone is a transitional border not because it is "in the middle" or irreal or less important, but for just the opposite reasons: it is all real, crucial, and acts as a bridge between the diverse stages of psychical development. Nevertheless, Winnicott's research suggests that, once created, the transitional space never disappears, but remains as a zone of creation, dreams, and life projects. The transitional border/zone/space and objects are functional in times of despair and crisis. It is a zone that does not belong to any individual in particular, that is, it is not personal but ontologically *relational*; it makes the encounter of an embodied subject with Otherness possible. Within this transitional space, a creative act can occur, for role-plays, illusions, contradictions, and paradoxes can coexist inasmuch as they have a real existence in the unconscious; distinctions between fantasy and reality are challenged, the rules of logic are not valid, and "you" and "me" do not have much value as discretional, fixed, or essential identities, but as creational and changing definitions. The transitional space, I believe, is the first locus for the creation of an ethics of solidarity; it is the space for co-constructed, shared, and interchanged symbols.

Notions of transitional space, *frontera* identities, and cultural boundaries function as the background for my writing about queer Italy. To be sure, my intention in this study is not to *neutrally* describe or contextualize the current situation of queers in Italy, but instead to deploy the position of an explorer who, situated in the borderlands, constructs a narrative, transitional space. Within this space, the reader will find passages from Italian history, biographies, autoethnographic pieces, and short scenes from films, newspaper articles, dialogues, and other textual and symbolic materials that I integrate in a system of meaning. For example, I include fictional narratives that do not correspond to single interviews, but that are assembled from dialogues with characters, internal or external to my own self, that emerge from different stories that I heard, or that refer to my own experience, and which I combine into a new, fictionalized synthesis.

To a positivistic mind, this stress on a negative form of identification might be strange. How does this negativity, after all, voice more genuinely the struggle against heterosexism in Italy? The point that I wish to make here is that any positive form of identity creates boundaries with others that, while useful in some circumstances, might be manipulated to pursue surveillance and control of bodies and pleasures. Instead, the examination of negative or border or queer identities brings to light forms of speaking and doing that are reclaiming multiple nationalities, sexualities, enunciations, and spaces at the same time. What makes this reclaiming interesting is not the idealizing of sexual or cultural *laissez-faire*, but exactly the opposite: the interplay between the fantasy of total enjoyment in the queer image of identities unhooked versus the symbolic constraints of history, class, language, or race. Words like negativity, third space, or border illustrate the dialectic tension between these two split ends. In this sense the current struggle of many queer Italians to achieve the legal recognition of their unions is a paradigmatic case. On the one hand, it is clearly high time that the Italian government granted us equal social, legal, and civil rights. On the other hand, we need to remain critical and observant of what representations, values, and norms our claims might reify.

Queuing for Hope

I first learned about the Italian PACS while queuing at the Italian embassy in Buenos Aires, Argentina, the most southern country in America. As part of an epiphany that dislocated my sense of inner/outer geographies, I was reading the news about PACS while listening to Canadian singer Alanis Morissette, who, from almost the extreme opposite end of the hemisphere, made me realize how ironic life can be. Indeed, it was ironic that although I was born into one of the numerous Italian families that came to Argentina to escape famine and war in Italy and that today my whole family (including my partner) is Italian, the Italian authorities in Argentina delayed to grant new citizenship to any Argentine after the 2001 economic crisis that boosted emigration of Argentines *back* to Italy. What was most ironic, however, was that the Italian PACS generated by my own peers, queer activists in Italy, did not ease much the union of an immigrant and an Italian person, limiting the possibilities for remaking the meaning of identity and family in Italy.

Turin, Italy

"Let's stay in *our* home in Turin," my partner suggests while revising our plans for our first trip to Italy together. "What home are you talking about?" I reply. "Sorry, I meant my parents' home." It is infuriating when possessive adjectives have the power to impassion the transitory nature of human experiences. I still refer to my parents' home in similar ways; I call it *mi casa*. *Our* home is also the home my partner and I made in Illinois, where we met while pursuing our graduate studies. Other times, *nostra casa* is our future home in Turin. Over the years we have created varieties of emotional languages that redo our meaning of cultural belonging. These intimate languages juxtapose the grammatical borders between Rioplatense Spanish, self-taught Portuguese, Piedmont Italian, primitive French, and some bizarre English. At first we would just mix our native languages in the heroic virtue of surviving as our national selves. After a while we allowed ourselves to play with neologisms and rules of syntax. Sometimes my partner speaks to me in his beautiful *Torinese*, with open vowels and endless s's, and I reply with my strong y's (as in the words *Yerba*, *Yo*, or *Lluvia*) and my fainting plurals, so typical of the working class's Rioplatense Spanish. Language is our middle ground; it expresses mutual affection and commitment. Our hybrid language is a shelter from the heterosexist storm, similar to the tongue built by Chicano communities. This linguistic middle ground includes verbs conjugated in Spanish directly derived from Italian, like *guardare* (to see, instead of the Spanish *ver* or *mirar*): *Te estoy guardando, amore* (I am looking at you, my love; instead of *Te estoy mirando, mi amor*). Words like *cartas* (letters) have been transformed in neologisms like *letras*, a mix of the Italian *lettera* and the plural form of the Spanish word *carta*. We always remember playing Scrabble in Café Pekara on a sunny autumn Saturday. We would start each round by picking a letter-tile from the bag of tiles. The letter determined the language we had to use in making the next word on the board: English, Spanish, Italian, French, or the *mix* of all of them. At the same time, it determined the language we were to speak during the round. In the café there was a Tibetan monk who was visiting the city, and he approached our table in silence. He found Tibetan words displayed in our board, accidentally—his smile was that of a surprised child who articulates a word for the first time. We master identity when we master language. In creating a conversation combining phonemes and words from different languages we defy law, for there is no other law than the law of language.

This form of invented communication derives, I suggest, from the peculiar state of being constantly exposed to identity limits, both as queers and as foreigners. Whenever we confront heterosexism and queer panic, or sense that we are pushed to invisibility (the *not*), then we create alternative ways *to be*. For instance, we usually code-shift when we do not want somebody to know of our relationship because it would be potentially harmful to either of us. This care of oneself and the other complicates our sense of what "coming out" really means. Undoubtedly, more than simply identity rigidity, *coming out* implies particular ethics that bind us to each other's secrets and truths. When I went to the United States, rights and possibilities that I had taken for granted became questioned and identified as artificial constructions that privilege only some individuals. Sometimes my partner and I disagree about the extent to which we are affected by cultural homophobia: He invites me to a party held at his college. "Will I be able to hug and kiss you if I want to?" Silence. "Then I won't even bother."

Other times we negotiate and accept the fallibility of language. "Ok, let's stay in *your* home in Turin," I finally agree. We would stop first in Paris to say "hi" to his friend Marie on her birthday; immediately afterward we would take the TGV to Turin, stay two days, unpack, and start our tour, going all the way south from Turin to Messina. Since traveling to the land of our ancestors had been a lifelong dream of my parents and sister, Italy appeared to me not only as a dream come true but as a land that was undeserved and forbidden for me as the youngest sibling and the least related to Italy. Indeed, before meeting my partner, I had rejected learning Italian or attending the celebrations at the Club Italiano; I thought I would never be touched by any sort of nostalgia for *La Terra Madre* (motherland); I believed my generation had brought nostalgia to an end.

Five years after leaving Argentina, I became a fluent Italian speaker, became a devoted Italian cook, wrote on Italian gay culture, and was once chosen vice-president of the only Italian student association in Champaign, Illinois. Throughout this time, my identity as Argentine did not dissolve but became more complex and less solid. It is from this particular identity formed by the intersections of my identity with space, law, and desire that I write of *queer* Italy, an Italy that is usually ignored even among Italians. Indeed, my trips to Italy made me aware of the peculiarity of my cultural identities. To stress negativity again, I am *not* (exclusively) Italian in the same sense that I am *not* (exclusively) Argentine, and I am in part American even if my passport will never tell you so. This is probably one of the strongest motivations to keep writing about Italy, the United States, and Argentina at the same time. Being an Italian-Argentine writing in English and looking into Italian culture has exceeded my expectations of finding my own academic voice; indeed, it has given me the opportunity to *produce* a new self altogether.

Buenos Aires via Cadiz

"Carmen locked the door to her room and never looked back at her small Cadiz [Spain]." Any time my mother told my sister and me a story about our great-grandmother Carmen, she would start somewhat that way. Little was ever spoken at home about Carmen's departure to Argentina. Other things were said about her instead. All I know about her decision to emigrate is that she had been struggling with "bones and blood" to make ends meet after my great-grandfather Abraham, a strong Jewish Moor, passed away. My great-grandmother was an early feminist not easily intimidated by war or economic hardship. However, with two children to feed and no money to pay the rent, she decided to leave Spain and try a new life in Argentina, where her sisters had already emigrated and would help her settle.

My great-grandmother, Carmen, left a particular mark on my mother. Carmen was a free woman of cheerful spirit living as an immigrant in the land of tango and *compadritos*. At the age of sixty, and blind from diabetes, my great-grandma would ask my mom to guide her lovers to the main room, where they would wait for her while she prepared her skin with honey and perfumes. While my mother believes I inherited Abraham's eyes, big and profound, I always thought that I had inherited some of my great-grandmother's appreciation for the care of the self. The subject of anecdotes and jokes, she is still remembered today in our Christmas Eve family tales as a defiant, sexual woman. In times when sexual pleasure was forbidden for a Catholic widow, she settled in Buenos Aires and never had to work again: lovers, friends, and agnostics, many of them affluent land owners, provided for her until her last days. By then my grandmother, Josefina, had already grown into a beautiful young woman: unlike most girls from her native Andalusia, she was fair-haired and had green eyes. In Argentina, Josefina met Andrés, a southern Italian emigrant and a worker in the general markets of Buenos Aires since he was ten. His family had escaped famine and the horrors of war. They married in the Catholic rite, although Carmen disapproved, of course. Grandmother Josefina gave birth at home, cared for by her mother and friends from the house. After she was married, she left Carmen's big house and moved to a *conventillo*—a big, multi-bedroom household unit inhabited by several families at the same time. In good times, they would all live peacefully as one big family. In times of gossip or quarrel, however, they would be loud and fight with each other to the ire of everybody. There were few private issues. On the bright side, they could rely on each other: they had an organized network of relationships that differed from the Argentinean middle class in the traditions they kept, in the shared economies they arranged, in the language they spoke (a mix of Italian, Castilian Spanish, Jewish, and Creole), and in the emotions they shared.

My mother, María, was the second of the three children raised by my grandparents. As a child she was rebellious and was nicknamed *marimacho* (mannish girl) because she would fight with her fists to defend her beliefs. She defended my uncles when they played with my grandmother's clothes: apparently, they dressed up not because they were *maricas* (fags), as their friends believed, but because they wanted to rehearse how to behave and what to say on their first date.

Across the neighborhood lived José, my father. He was the twelfth son of a large family of fishermen from Catanzaro, in the south of Italy, who moved to Argentina at almost the same time my grandmother did. José's mother, Concetta, and his father, Michele (or, later on, Miguel), also worked in the general markets of Buenos Aires, where they befriended Andrés, and introduced my parents to each other on their first day of work: they were ten years old.

My parents have known each other for almost fifty years and have spent almost every day of their lives together. Predictably, through so many years of being together, they went through several ups and downs. They never finished primary school, but they managed to visit Disneyland once; they changed jobs dozens of times but still do not own a house; they lost money repeatedly in all the memorable Argentinean crises; they once sold their wedding rings to pay the rent; they recovered and started all over by selling homemade clothes in the neighborhood. They argued but were never disrespectful to one another. They had two children, my sister Sandra and me. They taught us how to survive during the 1976-1983 dictatorship by keeping a low profile at school, or covering our books in newspaper so as to not to attract the attention of the agents in buses and in the streets, or giving us the addresses of friends who could rescue us and send us to Madrid if they were captured. My parents were engaged at the age of eighteen and got married at the age of twenty-four, saw my sister living with her fiancé before marrying him, and welcomed my partner to their home in 2002.

In Argentina, in my parent's generation and class, issues like divorce, cohabitation, and civil unions—let alone same-sex couples—were not part of their language, at least until the return of democracy to Argentina. Two of my uncles had divorced in Uruguay, but it was definitely something you did not talk about in family meetings. When divorce was finally introduced in Argentina in the mid-1980s, it came with a series of rapid cultural changes that accelerated during the next twenty years.

Because the last totalitarian government in Argentina repressed groups and associations, tried to indoctrinate youth, and instilled panic and an ultra-orthodox Catholic sense of obedience to the family, the redefinition of intimacy has been at the center of the cultural transformations undergone by Argentina since the return of democracy. Two comparatively crucial events signaled the beginning and the continuation of this transformation: on the one hand, the Abuelas de Plaza de Mayo's now three-decade-old struggle for recovering the identity of illegally abducted children; on the other, and more recently, the law allowing civil unions (including same-sex unions) that, thanks to the struggle of the Comunidad Homosexual Argentina (Homosexual Community of Argentina) was passed in Buenos Aires in 2001. The changes in law have been reflected in recent cultural changes. For instance, in 2005, for the first time in the history of the country, a lesbian couple from the central province of Córdoba together registered their baby, who was conceived as a result of artificial insemination. These two events illustrate a radical recoding of what constitutes intimate, nourishing family relationships.

Crises

Before 2001, Carlos Menem's administration had promised a productive revolution in Argentina. Instead, it dismantled the national state, sold out public reserves to transnational corporations and private individuals, and amplifyied the gap between rich and poor Argentineans to comply with the dictates of the International Monetary Fund and the Bush and Clinton administrations. These actions resulted in one of the deepest economic disasters ever experienced in Argentina. The next administration did not perform much better, despite pledging democratic renewal and social justice. The new president was Fernando De La Rua, whose brief and inefficient administration was halted shortly after taking power, following the vice-president's resignation. In December 2001, a series of interlinked political events led to De La Rua stepping down. Political unrest, muggings, street chaos, anxiety, and brutal police repression followed. Several international banks closed their doors and froze the bank accounts. Companies closed down, leaving thousands of people without jobs. A handful of provisional presidents, one after another in the course of a week, could not control the crisis. Finally, after a year and a half, on May 18, 2003, a new democratic administration was elected.

Personally, I remember December 2001 as the time when I turned a page in my biography, for I "came out" to my sister, my closest friend, at the same time that I came out into the streets to march with other protesters. Their challenging of social oppression offered me a metaphor for understanding the political implications of my own "coming out." It seemed that I was not the only one for whom coming out into the streets in December 2001 served as a metaphor for discussing with one's family the question of sexual identity. In a country like Argentina, marked by a profound and deeply held hetero-sexual, white, middle-class value system, this coming out is particularly significant. In a certain way, many in Argentina were also coming out; they came out, albeit for different reasons, into the streets, into organized unions, into their neighborhoods, at the workplace, and in classrooms. What could be understood as being redefined in these circumstances was our sense of family and intimacy. It was a fertile repositioning or redefining experience that challenged familiar meanings, values, and experiences; it was an instance of self-defined truth that broke the imaginary unity of many families for a moment. Heroic acts transcend time: just a moment suffices to rearticulate difference through communal action.

A Country in Flames

During the first months of 2002, it was virtually impossible to stroll down some of the most beautiful avenues in Buenos Aires. The intersection of Marcelo T. de Alvear Street and 9 de Julio Avenue, for example, looked like a campsite. This is the corner where the Italian embassy is situated. People slept in tents or mattresses in the street, or remained standing for days. The hundreds of people lining up every day at the front door of the embassy were desperate. I was one of them. We were the children or grandchildren of Italians who had lost their savings and hope and wanted to start all over again, abroad, in the land of their ancestors. We wanted to change the empire. Contradictory as it might seem, we also wanted to be a part of it.

Since 2001, some Italian consulates in Argentina have delayed issuing Italian citizenships to Italo-Argentines without commenting on the reason for or the extension of this measure. Contrary to the intention, this has not acted as a deterrent to emigration, but has only augmented the number of illegal Argentines seeking a new beginning in the land of their grandparents.

Although my hope of reclaiming my Italian citizenship vanished at the entrance to the embassy, I was, without knowing it, closer to Italy than ever before. At the beginning of 2002, I was granted a Fulbright scholarship to pursue my Ph.D. in the United States, which would lead to my research on Italian culture and my relationship with my partner. Leaving Argentina was more painful than I expected. In one of the pre-departure workshops organized by the Fulbright Commission, I looked around trying to discover if anybody else had a sense of being invaded, like me, by a mixture of competing feelings, including social guilt, anxiety, pride, and hope. During the crisis, some grantees had lost all the money they had saved for an experience that would probably save their professional careers. Others had lost their jobs and did not expect to reconstruct their work careers in the ensuing years.

Neighbors in *mi barrio* learned that I was leaving for the United States through my father, who invited them for a celebration at home. Two days before my departure, they brought *alfajores de maizena con dulce de leche*, long letters, and dedicated photos for their own daughters and sons, who were living in Chicago. They wanted me to deliver them, because the cost of postal service had tripled in one month during the crisis. It was just for a second, but I looked at them in awe, fearing that they would somehow *taint* me: a wind of hate crossed my mind, whispering *"tu no estás para lavar los platos de los Yankees."*

Shame. Privilege.

The look I gave to my neighbors was exactly the same that others had given me and my grandmothers and my parents and my sisters and brothers in the past; it is the gaze of the *colonizador* stepping onto the land of the *desposeído*. The look I gave to my neighbors reflects the lamentable fact that I, too, am in desperate need. Being the first person in my family to pursue graduate-level education meant an opportunity to redeem a past of famine and emigration for my family.

Who could heal the open wounds of *America Latina*?

At that time I did not know I was to bring to my family other hungers, other languages, and other foreign landscapes. One must embrace the past to enable the present to happen.

Zen in Urbana, Illinois (United States)

One day my sister wrote me an email. She said:

> The phrase [for the book] is beautiful. Besides, it is really useful for me the explanation about gay relationships. How silly I might look to you, right? I'm not worried for you two or for you in particular anymore, simply because I feel you are doing great. I see you opening your heart, smiling. And that is the way I want to see you. I would like you both to stay together forever. But that is your decision, and whatever it is that you decide to do, it will always be accepted and respected.

In our weekly electronic correspondence, my sister and I spend hours remembering childhood experiences, trying to recode their meaning, or smiling today about something that seemed so painful in the past. This meditation about what has been and what could have been is typical of immigrants. In her study of immigrant lesbians, Olivia Espin (1997) stresses that as an immigrant, one crosses geographical, psychological, and emotional boundaries with a body that houses anxieties and ruminations about the past, or thoughts nagging at the corners of one's mind about a parallel present that could have been, had one not emigrated. Emigrants try to construct new cartographies of identities.

Sometimes we fail.

When I passed my preliminary examinations, I wrote an email to my sister, sharing with her a sentence I wanted to use to open my dissertation. I also explained to her how my partner and I understood the term *family*, and how difficult I believed it was for a heterosexist, straight person to under-

stand that the way queers and heterosexists *know* or make sense of the world
might not be exactly the same. My sister replied to me, apologizing for not
knowing enough about gay relationships. I'm not sure about that, actually,
but it was funny that she would like my partner and I to stay together forever.
That sounded like a piece of advice for a married straight couple. I now
reread the phrase "stay together" as meaning "care for each other." She
meant well, undoubtedly.

Love cannot be measured using discrete time and space units. In the
queer framework in which I write, to "stay together" has nothing to do with
the place where one lives or the amount of time spent with a person. Staying
together has to do with loyalty and care of the self and care for the other.
And freedom. Living in the borders of sexuality and nationality implies
confronting the transitory nature of identity or desire, and a responsibility to
improve one's life and the life of the ones we love in the deep understanding
that nothing belongs to us or remains the same at any time. This implies a
continuous creative yet unsafe state of doing and speaking, a form of
conocimiento siempre parcial, as Anzaldúa would have put it.

Zen.

To some heterosexists, this epistemology can sound dangerous, for it
challenges more stable attachments to the self, to the body, or to the nuclear,
monogamous family. Reading Valery Lehr's (1999) work about queer
families was most inspirational for me. I learned that the framework I write
about is suspicious of these values cherished by middle-class, white heterosexist matrimony; it is critical of morals of faithfulness, unity, or sameness.
Most important, it assumes that queerness is not a new form of solid being,
but a fragile way of speaking and doing. In this vein, queerness is an image
or metaphor for a larger way of knowing that is incomplete and transitory.

Zen.

Before Crossing the Borders

As my partner walked into gate 4 heading to the Mediterranean Sea, I
wondered: "Will I ever see him again or will I succumb to nostalgia?" What
sort of reality will I have in a land that, although belonging to my family,
continues to be foreign territory to me? And if I decide to join him after all,
will I ever regret the path I could have taken by staying somewhere else?
How will it feel to inhabit a geography where buildings and streets are
anonymous? Will I be able to make this geography speak to me? I realized

suddenly that these questions were not new for me. For a moment—as in many other moments in my life—I had lost my body, the link to reality. I was, after all, in an American airport. I had made Urbana my home, as in the past I had made my *barrio* in Argentina home, even if I had not grown up there as a child.

Wherever I am, I am an immigrant, and wherever I go, I make it home.

Sometimes I cannot avoid passing judgment that my claims on identity are simple wishful thinking; a part of me is trying to assure myself that time and experience are reversible, that I can go back anytime I want to, that nationality is as fluid as sexuality. The fallacies of a memory crisscrossed by the workings of the unconscious make us slaves wishing we could go back somewhere and recover a mythical Thing, land, self, time.. . .Having already left one land, I have not yet arrived at a final destination, probably because there is no final destination. Being alive is just a parenthetical moment of life, basking around the infinite moment before we are born and the infinite time after we are dead.

My choice was to travel to Italy and create a home with my partner.

Piazza di Spagna, Rome

Though I am writing this paragraph four years after I started this research at a café located at the center of Piazza di Spagna, I can still feel the frantic pace of life that inundates that square at any time during the day. Despite the intoxicating heat, the square was crowded: all around me were European entrepreneurs wearing fine clothes; housekeepers sale-shopping swimsuits made in Pakistan, Paris, or Taiwan; international and domestic vacationers from the *Mezzogiorno*; and street merchants offering illegal copies of music CDs to clergymen heading to Vatican City. Not New York or Paris, but Rome's Piazza di Spagna appeared to me as the ultimate center of the world, past and present. Designed in the 1720s, its old architecture embraces the finest fashion designers, several of all the Italian dialects, and a diversified cacophony of classes and tourists. Nobody is an invader here. Everybody is, as Charly Garcia would sing it, a passenger in transit.

Everybody brings to this piazza a share of cultural capital. Tourist guides are meaningless in their anodyne descriptions of this Roman epicenter of wealth and tourism. I let myself be captured by the intoxicating coexistence of parallel, alternative, and anti-cultures formed by the lower class bargaining in small shops, North African and Latin American immigrants selling knockoffs of fashion items in the streets, and the working girls streetwalking at daylight. I was at home; oh, yes I was.

I was sipping a hot, dense *espresso doppio* next to my partner, mimicking a typical tourist pose and pretending it was perfectly normal to pay €4 for a tiny cup of coffee. To avoid paying for a hotel room, we had dozed on the night train to Rome and skipped a restaurant lunch. After walking for hours around the city center, dinner was the only thought that consoled our vagabond souls. The decent meal would not materialize until nighttime, when we would meet Fabio—a friend we had met in Urbana during our first year in the United States, and who kindly hosted us. It was 2:00 P.M. when we finally found a place for me to scribble some notes and for him to retreat from the role of tour guide. I felt honored to be in Rome guided by my Italian lover. He was sitting at the table, talking to me in the dialect of Rome, a fast-paced jumble of expressions he imitates quite well.

When I put the espresso cup down, the mid-afternoon sun exposed the wrinkles on the palm of my hand; I could see the thickness of my dry skin stretched across and along and through my fingers like all the roads of a One World, stretched without boundaries—an imaginary Oneness, whether I was ready or not, rested invincibly in the palm of my hand. I was lagging behind the frantic pace of globalization, and definitely on the periphery of the market.

A street seller stopped nearby with replicas of Gucci purses and Armani belts. He was from Naples, my partner said. "How do you know?" I asked. "Neapolitans are the best street sellers in the whole world. I *have to take you* to Naples. The whole South is like this. Sellers enter into the train carriage where you are, with boom boxes, MP3 players, and computers that might never really work." "How can you speak of the South in this way?" I asked. "Because my parents are southerners. I am an infiltrator in the North. I am a southerner myself." I do not really know why I was so surprised about my partner's comments. I am a southerner, too.

Whenever I took the Linea B train in the Victorian-style Retiro station in Buenos Aires, the platform was flooded with voices and accents from Córdoba, San Luis, Catamarca, and Capital Federal. A wholesaler of sports goods, my father moved his whole life from north to south. Just as my partner does now, my dad would *take me with him* on his trips. I was eleven years old, and trips fell during my school vacations. I had to learn to travel on my own, because "that is what you expect from a daring man," he would say. In these male trips, my father and I would travel for hours chatting little, enjoying the landscapes of silence. Eating regional foods from *Pastelitos de Membrillo* to *Empanadas Salteñas* or *Pan Caliente con Chipá*, and buying *Alfajores Santafesinos* for mother, was the perfect excuse to pretend that we talked the language of masculinity. Similar to all the languages I could listen to around me in Piazza di Spagna, my father's explanations about sexuality were a perfectly strange dialect for me as well, a chain of words lacking ties to my desire. When he was talking about his trips, his language was dense and his words were silky; even if he never finished primary school, he narrated like a trained folktale writer. His descriptions of the female anatomy were hesitant, yet his acquaintance with the country's anatomy was mesmerizing. I remember with emotion his tales of dry cities in the north of Argentina, his fascinating reports of whale-watching in Patagonia, and even his portrayal of the south of Italy as a land of fishermen with salty skin.

In my father's imagination there are two languages and two nationalities working in unison. His identity, as my own, is hybrid, *bi*, mixed. His veins are wide-open canals for the endless journey of the human race. "All traveling happens in your imagination," my father would say. "The best trip of all is the trip without destination."

❧ **Part Two** ❧
Antecedents of Queer Italy

Women's Voices, from the *Risorgimento* to Civil Unions

The queer movement is indebted to feminism. Feminism provided the first and most influential theoretical models to explore the intersections of gender and sexuality, and it advanced political strategies adopted in the defense of gender and human rights (see Barker, 2004). Contemporary debates on gender construction, hybrid identities, gender emancipation, subjectivity, and sexual desire were first raised by women like Rosi Braidotti, Teresa de Lauretis, Adriana Cavarero, Luisa Passerini, and Oriana Fallaci, among others. Central to the original Italian feminist project was a critique of the country's patriarchal family structure. Feminism's continuous struggle against gender subordination has granted women formal legal and civic equality, while it has also meant the transformation of informal structures and everyday relations within social institutions like the family, the university and, to a lesser extent, the church (Passerini, 1996).

Although Italian feminists are currently divided into several groups, feminist critiques of gender have immense value for Italian queers. Feminism demonstrates that gender is not a secondary category of analysis but a pivotal axis of political activism and social living. Gender is wholly cultural (Barker, 2004): its intersections with issues of class, sexual orientation, ethnicity, and nation demonstrate that gender is material and symbolic at the same time.

Gender is, indeed, a fundamental symbolic system of signs and performances used to interpret ourselves and the world. Gender analysis should be considered central to queer theory as it is an invaluable framework to complete the theoretical criticism of the cultural workings and making of sexuality and the self. In this sense, a queer movement uninformed of gender activism is highly deficient and might risk being male-normative. In chapter 3, indeed, I discuss the consequences of founding a gay movement centered mainly on gay male politics and eroticism; moreover, in chapter 6, I stress the need to move from homosexual/heterosexual divides to the notion of genderqueer, which I take from activist Riki Wilchins (2004). This notion situates gender at the center of queer politics. In this chapter, however, my intention is to introduce the critique of gender construction and patriarchy performed by early feminism, because it is extremely useful for evaluating the advantages and limitations of the current GLBTQ movement's plea for civil unions (see chapter 5).

Family as a Construction

Anthropological and sociological evidence (see Weston, 1991) shows that the term "family" describes a hypothetically universal phenomenon entailing an alliance or marriage, the results of which are descendants or children. In Western European countries, the making of a family traditionally implies not only the union of a man and a woman, but also a non-specific number of behaviors and beliefs, such as the enactment of sexual difference, the roles and functions ascribed to each sex, and the duties and responsibilities derived from gender division. Lévi-Strauss observed in 1956 that the creation of the family also presupposes the existence of other families within the social system (Roudinesco, 2002). Lévi-Strauss's observations suggest that the stability of the social domain depends on a coordinated interchange of individuals that guarantees the continuity and reproduction of kinship structures. For instance, one family presents the man, while another offers the woman. Then, the social domain is responsible for sanctioning (naming) the man as a husband and the woman as a wife—or any other terms that symbolize their union. In this case, both families participate in a highly regulated, culturally specific and ritualized interchange[1] that permits social regeneration. The parties that present a man and a woman in matrimony are endorsed as families by the social domain or any of its legitimate agencies. Every time there is a ritual of matrimony or union, this whole social structure is present, participating in the naming of the new union.[2] The power of institutions like the state to confer legitimacy on certain relationships and not others has not remained without criticism in Italy. A wide range of Italian feminists have criticized the belief that there is one traditional family by questioning gender divides and, more recently, the general heterocentrist culture in which this model prospers. In this sense, and as Roman writer

Tomasso Giartosio (2004) suggests, Italian feminism is in *blood relation* with the Italian queer movement—and the pun could not be more apt.

To be sure, from many feminist perspectives, the heterosexual family that appeared in Western countries—what Judith Stacey (1996) calls the "modern family"—is a recent, transitory phenomenon.[3] The modern heterosexual conjugal family is neither a universal nor a *de facto* formation that was mechanically installed and invariably assimilated within all Western cultures. In Italy, the family has undergone multiple variations. For centuries, several oftentimes contradictory types of family arrangements have coexisted, from multiple-family household units in Tuscany to Sardinian matriarchal conjugal aristocratic families (Kertzer & Saller, 1991). These dissimilar family arrangements could be found throughout the *bel paese*[4] before, during, and after its political unification.

Indeed, family arrangements depend on the political history of Italy: events like the unification, fascism, industrialization, and the more recent incorporation into the European Union are in fact consubstantial to family transformations. As I anticipated earlier and further discuss in chapter 5, fluctuations in birth rates, family members, living arrangements, cohesion, and cohabitation render the monolithic model of the family an assumption, at its best a "privileged construct" (Weston, 1991) that has shifted enormously throughout history. The reasons for family change in Italy are complex and must be assessed on a number of bases. Central to these, the convulsive process of Italian modernization implied a shift in gender relations, marital traditions, and parenthood. More generally, industrialization and urbanization triggered enormous changes in family life throughout the nineteenth and twentieth centuries everywhere in Western Europe. There was less and less need for extended families, nuclear units shrunk, children started to be invested emotionally as their value as workers diminished, and marriages for life were no longer a reality for an increasing number of couples, probably as a result of a lengthened life span and decreased economic dependencies (Zelizer, 1985).

Subject to these trends, Italians witnessed the transformation of families later and more slowly than other nations on the northern coast of the Mediterranean (Barbagli & Colombo, 2001). Specific to the Italian modernization of the family were the large waves of internal migration, the liberalization of sexual habits, the shift in gender roles starting in the 1950s, and the struggles, in the second half of the twentieth century, for changes in laws concerning divorce and abortion. Following Luisa Passerini (1996) in this chapter, I discuss the importance of feminism and its struggle for transforming deep-rooted gendered beliefs and practices in Italy since the late nineteenth century, paying attention to two levels in dialectic relation with each other. This relation is manifested in a movement toward parity expressed in the domains of law, norms, and institutional functioning, and a movement toward differentiation expressed in literature, politics, and psychology (Passerini, 1996). I first provide a brief description of the historical formation of Italian feminism and its relation to literature and political visibility. Second, I examine the emergence of what Sharon Wood and Joseph Farrell (2001) call New Feminism, its materialization during the late 1960s, and its impact during the following decades. I include here a comparison of two different short stories from the 1980s that I regard as illustrative of cultural reallocations typical of these decades. These stories offer an excellent way to explore some of the many ways a linear, developmental version of history can be disrupted, or challenged. Finally, I briefly explore divorce, labor, and family laws that were subject to similar legal transformations during these same decades.

While the direct achievements of Italian feminists on legislation cannot be overemphasized, their influence on challenging the cultural status quo has also been remarkable. In a country where tradition has sometimes meant structurally grounded male patriarchal power, the history of Italian feminism is revealing and inspiring. Although this history has been characterized by internal strife, heterogeneity of political aspirations, and a competing range of strategies, Italian feminists shared, for some years, the belief that women should act as essentially interconnected individuals (Passerini, 1996). Groups such as Unione Donne Italiane (Union of Italian Women, officially created in 1944), for example, were a hybrid coalition of militant communists, socialists, Roman Catholics, and laity. In abbreviated form, however, and as Andreina de Clementi (2002) suggests, the history of Italian feminism can be divided into two parts—early and contemporary—separated from each other by a long period of compulsory hibernation during fascism.

The specificities of Italian feminism must be discussed by taking into account the wider European emergence of feminism that functioned as context and sometimes horizon for the Italian movement. Whenever distinctions are made among feminist groups or movements, it is important to stress that these distinctions are based on practical reasoning, and can only partially reflect the complexity of a constituency whose history has alternated between fragmentation and unification (Passerini, 1996). Accordingly, although some authors choose to discuss at least six branches of feminism in general—liberal, difference, socialist, poststructural, black, and postcolonial feminism (Barker, 2004)–influential Italian film critic Teresa de Lauretis prefers to look for commonalties as characteristic of the Italian context. She terms these commonalties *comunità* (community) "in the sense that everything is intrinsically unstable and contextual, not based on the identity of components or their natural bond, but a community that is the result of work, of struggle, of interpretation" (1999, p. 3; my translation).

Early Italian Feminism

The antecedents of Italian feminism can be traced back to the Renaissance, in the literary work of upper-class, well-read women like Isotta Nogarola and Laura Cereta. During the Enlightenment, other European writers like Mary de Gournay and Joespha Amar provided further inspiration to these educated women, who opposed misogyny and resisted in their own way the subordination of women to men and their political advantage (Ballarin et al., 2004). The idea of a truly feminine politics—at the root of the term *feminism*—usually defines a more homogeneous political movement, however, one that originated in France as a social doctrine attempting to grant women rights generally reserved for men. Early collective declarations in France inspired the formation of women's republican clubs during the revolutionary period, embracing the ideals of the French Revolution based on universal, natural, and political equality (see Ballarin et al., 2004). This antecedent is important in understanding the feminist plea for equality. At the time of the unification of Italy, European feminism was calling for the emancipation of women, promoted especially through the struggle of the suffragists, particularly British suffragists. These feminists thought that granting women the right to vote would allow them to participate in political decisions and to pass laws against gender inequities (see Ballarin et al., 2004).

Italian feminism emerged in the nineteenth century, later than in Britain or France, and was represented by women such as Princess Cristina Trivulzo Barbiano di Belgioioso—heroine of the Italian unification because of her nationalistic politics (Forgacs, 1997). During the 1870s, early feminist philanthropic interventions such as di Belgioioso's founding of charitable institutions, aimed to improve the standard of education for girls and battled against illiteracy in the recently unified peninsula. Situated in the political disjunction between a monarchical liberalism and a democratic republicanism, these interventions supported Giuseppe Mazzini's ideals of shaping Italy as a republican democratic state (Forgacs, 1997). Mazzini defended an abstract notion of culture and the role of a literary education that Antonio Gramsci explicitly blamed for being instrumental in the passivity of the *Risorgimento*[5] (Cento Bull, 2001)—that is, unable to develop a political culture relevant for the peasant masses. Also notable from this period is Anna Maria Mozzoni's *La Donna e i suoi Rapporti Sociali in Occasione della Revisione del Codice Italiano* (Woman and Her Social Relationships on the Occasion of the Revision of the Italian Civil Code). Regarded a founder of the Italian women's movement, Mozzoni became internationally famous for her focus on legal reforms and her critique of Italian family law (Wood and Farrell, 2001).

In their speeches and interventions, early Italian feminists like Mozzoni addressed the poor working conditions of women textile workers who entered the market during the 1890s. In the same period, the first women's magazine was edited (*La Donna,* or Woman, founded by Adelaide Beccari in the 1860s); Matilde Serao's novel *Fantasia* (Fantasy) was published in 1883; and the term "feminism" was introduced very gradually into the vocabulary of the northern aristocratic elites. The word, which was to be re-elaborated by feminist writers, was meant to signify an aspiration toward universalism, the improvement of women's education, and women's access to liberal professions (Amoia, 1996; Wood and Farrell, 2001). Ironically, however, in order to voice their claims, early feminists had to rely on a universal, usually asexual and generally ahistorical conception of the human subject (see Barker, 2004). Italian feminist Adriana Cavarero (1987) refers to this when she says that, for a long time, women did not have a language of their own, but had to use that of the other—that is, they had to utilize a patriarchal symbolic framework. Throughout history, however, some feminine voices resisted. In the following section I examine as an example the life of Anna Kuliscioff, a political activist whose work reveals the early existence of a radical feminism in Italy.

Anna Kuliscioff. Italian industrialization coincided with the rise of the left and anarchism, and women workers rebelled against the exploitation they were subject to, both in the domestic sphere and in the workplace (see Wood and Farrell, 2001). In this sense, the life of Anna Kuliscioff is illustrative of the politically overwhelming end of the nineteenth century in Italy. Her life illustrates the complicated links between achieving parity and creating a space for differentiation (Passerini, 1996). Also known as *La dottora*[6] [sic] *dei poveri* (the doctor of the poor people), Anna Kuliscioff was born Anja Rosenstein in Crimea under the regime of czarist Russia. She became a vigorous feminist thinker and an energetic activist. According to Paola Mocchi (2004), she was persecuted for her anarchist political ideas under the order of the czar and emigrated to Switzerland. She participated in rebellions in France, from where she was also deported in 1878, and in Florence, Italy, where she was arrested under the charge of anarchic conspirator. She had a daughter with political writer Andrea Costa before they separated because of political differences. Back in Italy, she became an advocate for socialism and befriended the president of the Socialist Party, Filippo Turati. Although she was ill with tuberculosis, she traveled back and forth from Switzerland to Italy, where she finally graduated as a physician in Naples, specializing in gynecology at the Universities of Turin and Padua. During her practice, she discovered the bacterial origin of puerperal fevers, opening the way for the treatment of a disease that had killed millions of women in the past. Her nickname *la dottora dei poveri* goes back to her work in the poorest districts of Milan, where she treated women who were victims of domestic violence, poverty, and disease (Mocchi, 2004; Wood and Farrell, 2001).

Paola Mocchi (2004) explains that Kuliscioff never abandoned clinical practice while she continued her active political involvement. She became the first woman lecturer at a Milan university on April 27, 1890, discussing the subject of women-men relationships. Her talks, termed "The Monopoly of the Men," argued that male dominance was intrinsic to Italian social dynamics, structurally reifying women's subordination.

Kuliscioff was far from naïve. Mocchi shows that she reproached women for conceding power to men, hence remaining slaves of the domestic sphere. Kuliscioff believed that social and work equality would lead women to achieve freedom, dignity, and respect, while marriage and family life would always humiliate them: "[T]he married woman is the being most worthy of commiseration" (cited in Mocchi, 2004, paragraph 16). For Kuliscioff, Italian women still had not developed the sense of solidarity that would subvert oppressive structures, the clergy, and the Socialist Party. In later speeches, Kuliscioff disputed Pope Pius X's 1907 encyclical *Pascendi*

Dominici Gregis, on the doctrines of the modernists. She also referred to the regressive political agenda of Italian socialism, which would not battle for women's suffrage. Her position was founded, perhaps, in the belief that granting women the vote would have been "considered politically too dangerous, a move which might not only hand votes to less progressive parties, but which might also be greeted with less than enthusiasm by Socialist supporters" (Wood and Farrell, 2001, pp. 143-144). Specifically concerned during her last lectures with the untenable situation of women amid changing patterns of work triggered by the development of the industrialized Italian infrastructure, her radical position, eloquence, and rough personality render her today an icon of Italian feminism (see Mocchi, 2004).

Italian Feminism during the Giolittian Era. Feminist political activists hoping to win women the right to vote often encountered the ambivalence— and frequently the explicit rejection—of political leaders like Turati, head of the Socialist Party (see Wood and Farrell, 2001). This opposition put women's suffrage in doubt until after the first decade of the twentieth century. Women's emancipation from patriarchal structures like the traditional family was at risk of fading to an echo, as the industrial workers' struggle for better wages vindicated the same family that Kuliscioff had criticized years before (see Mocchi, 2004). This oscillation for and against the family—a real love-hate relationship with what is probably the cornerstone of Italian culture—is repeated several times in the history of Italy.

As historians have suggested (see Cento Bull, 2001; Dickie, 2001; Wood and Farrell, 2001), in 1913 the Giolittian[7] administration expanded the right to vote through a new electoral law that was strategically set up as a concession to the Socialist Party first and with the Catholics later, in the hope of ending a succession of boycotts that threatened his administration. Through these pacts, almost-universal male suffrage was introduced, but women were still not granted the vote. The so-called Giolittian Era lasted until the Great War, and was characterized by substantial industrial growth. New industrial conglomerates appeared in Turin, Milan, and Genoa, which would remain cities of development and wealth in the following decades. Nevertheless, the concentration of industries in the North increased economic imbalances, plunging regions in the South into poverty (Cento Bull, 2001; Dickie, 2001). This modernizing, asymmetric industrial growth identified the Giolittian era with increasing labor mobility across national boundaries (Dickie, 2001).

Before and during the Great War, emigration from southern Italian areas like Calabria, Puglia, and Sicily increased as people looked for better opportunities across the Atlantic Ocean. The economic imbalance between the North and the South had several repercussions, one of which was reflected in the way regional societies arranged their social structures: emigration might have made many families shrink in size, for example. At the same time, they remained attached to more traditional values, while the Northern centers were probably more exposed to new traditions, modernization, industry, and cultural interchange with other parts of Europe.

Changes in society during this period were examined by writers who emerged in response to the reluctance of socialism to support women suffragists, as well as in reaction to the division of the Italian political landscape among Catholics, nationalists, and socialists. Some of these writers, like Anna Maria Mozzoni and Sibilla Aleramo, might be called feminists in the sense that they reclaimed an original position that contested the gendered locus offered by the discourse of the literate establishment. According to Wood and Farrell (2001), Mozzoni argued in favor of the absorption of women into a more progressive state, in particular through rural and urban educational programs, work, and the struggle to attain the right to divorce. She translated John Stuart Mill's *On the Subjection of Women* and contributed to the feminist magazine *La Donna,* although it could be argued that she remained attached to the male universal subject advocated in Mazzini's ideals of universal humanity and equality (Wood and Farrell, 2001). In contrast, Aleramo brought awareness to the middle-class female consciousness of the limitations of domestic roles, wrote about sexuality, had female and male lovers, and was not timid about homoerotic themes (see Dana, 2004). Her first novel, *A Woman,* was published in 1906.

In their study of homosexuality in modern Italy, Marzio Barbagli and Asher Colombo (2001) suggest that Aleramo's literature anticipates some contemporary Italian attitudes toward relationality, which can be interpreted as more interested in multiplicity than in stable family or couple formations.

Following this interpretation, one might be tempted to see Aleramo's writings (and her correspondence with her beloved Lina Poletti) as a declaration of a kind of love beyond heteronormativity. She did not regret her affection for Poletti at the same time that she had a male lover, Giovanni Cena. Aleramo regretted, however, a limitation she considered intrinsic to all female-female relations. In *Lettere d'Amore a Lina* (Love Letters to Lina), she differentiates the love she feels for Cena from the one she feels for Poletti, and characterizes female-female love as an intrinsic impossibility: "in fondo al nostro [amore] c'è la condanna atroce della sua sterilità" (at the bottom of our love there is the dreadful conviction of its sterility) (cited in Barbagli and Colombo, 2001, p. 201). I read in Aleramo's use of the term *sterilità* a reference to futility or despair rather than biological infertility. Aleramo's melancholic tone testifies to the condemnation that *Il Novecento*[8] imposed on homoerotic bodies, a condemnation sanctioned by the medical term *inversione* (Danna, 2004). Although it is usually accepted that Karoly Maria Benkert coined the term "homosexuality" around 1869 (see Saéz, 2004), until 1940 the word *inversione* was more common in Italy. It had replaced the use of the term *pederasty* and the model it implied—which could be traced back to the writings of Bernardino di Siena at the beginnings of *Il Quattrocento*. The more quotidian use in Italy of the term "inversion" after 1900 and the use of this word by some groups to represent themselves signaled, on the one hand, the increasing permeation of medical representations in everyday vocabulary. It meant a wider framework of interpretation for homoerotic desire, a timid first attempt to explore an identity that would not take shape until six decades later with the beginnings of the gay movement. Contrary to the pederasty model, which designated a practice of male subjects only, "inversion" was applied to the female and male genders equally. It modified the social asymmetry tacit in pederasty and was associated with more gender-endogamic relations (Cestaro, 2004; Dall'Orto, 2004a; Danna, 2004).

Aleramo elaborated on the notion of inversion in some passages of her writings to Lina, warning her of the risks of interpreting homoerotic love according to active-passive male psychology. Instead, she seems to suggest that female sexuality was irreducibly different from that of men, and thus remained critical of the word *inversione*: "Nel dono d'amore, la donna non ha fatto quel senso di *sottomissione* che tu, con psicologia maschile, supponi. . .È un'illusione quella che ti trae a *virilizzarti*. Tu sei donna. . ." (In the gift of love, the woman does not hold to submission as you, with masculine psychology, suppose. . .It is an illusion that makes you assume a virile position. You are a woman.) (cited in Barbagli and Colombo, 2001, p. 201; my translation). As suggested earlier in this book, the male active-passive dichotomy that Aleramo suggests had deeper roots in Italian culture than in other Western European countries, going back to slave-master relations in the Roman Empire (see Settembrini, 2001). The terms "inversion" and "pederasty" also coexisted for longer periods, and were notions not foreign to political propaganda. The rise of fascism, as will be discussed below, manipulated both of them in combination with racist slogans and military machismo.

Italian Feminism and Fascism

Early Italian feminism made women's voices audible. Although its struggle was sometimes grounded in a normative view of womanhood, it created the historical possibility for naming what had been unthinkable (this is precisely the way Aleramo's exhortation "You are a woman" should be read), formulated the first categories for thinking about gender oppression, and opened up spaces for political intervention. In addition, it problematized the dualistic rationality underlying patriarchy, a form of binary economy that excluded women from the public sphere and confined them to subordinate, marginal roles. Nevertheless, the Giolittian era and the failure to win suffrage in 1912 exhausted the emancipationist movement, which for the most part had faded away before the onset of fascism (see Cento Bull, 2001; Wood and Farrell, 2001).

This is not to suggest that fascism succeeded in erasing feminism, just as it did not completely dominate Italian culture. Indeed, Italians who resisted fascism invented a variety of subversive practices to contest its regulatory agenda (see Landy, 2000). While I am not concerned with an analysis of Italian fascism *per se* in this section,[9] I will briefly examine the interconnections among human rights, feminism, and representations of gender in Italy during the fascist period.

The rise of fascism originated in part in the crisis of liberalism and the increasing pains of modernity for Italy, symptomatically expressed by changing cultural conditions during the interwar era: "class conflicts, opposition to the liberal state, inflation, strikes, land occupations in the south, struggles for higher wages and reduced working hours, reaction against the country's traditional leadership, and increasing and aggressive nationalism" (Landy, 2000, p. 9). In 1921, during a period of intensified political confusion, Benito Mussolini was elected to Parliament as the head of a National Fascist Party. He led the march on Rome the following year, establishing himself as *Il Duce* (The Leader). The initial cohesion of socialists, early fascists, and some futurists was severed, signaling the consolidation of the dictatorial regime. Central to Mussolini's ideal of making Italy an oceanic empire was his obsession with the power of and experimentation with media (see Landy, 2000). Propaganda, Landy's work suggests, was an important method of control throughout the territory, and strategic manipulation of the media included *manifesti* (posters), radio broadcast services, and the compulsive repetition of slogans ("to believe, to obey, to combat"). After the march on Rome, the regime created private organizations under state control to "fascitize" civil society, to stimulate private enterprise, to reduce state spending, and to achieve tax and fiscal reform (Morgan, 1995). The tension between state control and the encouragement of privatization is one of the salient paradoxes of fascism, for at the same time that the regime attempted to build a consensus on the emblematic role of the state, it also stimulated private investment toward increased productivity and profit (Landy, 2000).

In many ways the regime wished to regulate Italian social life by generating nationwide "operations," creating institutions, and reforming cultural policies. For instance, the Balilla (Operazione Nazionale Balilla or National Operation Balilla) sought the indoctrination of fascist values in youth; the Gioventù Universitaria Fascista (Fascist University Youth) attempted to do the same with university students; the Operazione Nazionale Dopolavoro (National Operation After Work), counting 3.8 million members, standardized people's leisure-time activities; and the Operazione Nazionale per la Maternità ed Infanza (National Operation for Maternity and Infancy) advanced social policies by establishing "desirable" qualities for womanhood (Landy, 2000).

These numerous operations, intended to mobilize popular culture in general, aimed to discipline women's bodies[10] in ways that differed from those of other nations. For example, during World War II, U.S. women served in the military or were encouraged by propaganda to fill jobs that did not match their expected "natural" female abilities—from clerical work to heavy mechanical jobs requiring motor skills, etc. In contrast, during the same period in Italy the female body was imagined as the main instrument for achieving the fascist dream of a new Italian nation. Subject to the ideological interpellation of procreating, women were excluded from political life, and their "rights in the workplace, their contributions to culture and their service as volunteers were called into question by the official message that their permanent duty was to bear the nation's children" (de Grazia, 1992, p. 72). While prostitution and illegitimate sexuality were banned, homosexuality *per se* did not pose a challenge to the regime (Dall'Orto, 2004a). In fact, it was rendered virtually invisible. By assuming that there were no homosexuals in Italy, fascism erased a possible threat to the masculinity that was required to legitimate a new empire and populate the nation. While a *nuovo uomo* (new man) was prized in advertisements of homoerotic comrades-in-arms, a *nuova donna* (new woman) was cherished in mass spectacles celebrating maternity, reproduction, and the sanctity of the family space. For instance, a Mother's Day was instituted by the nation-state to reward fecundity (Landy, 2000).

While Mussolini thought that twelve was the ideal number of children for the Italian family in order to provide soldiers to fight Germans and Slavs, and while he imposed a tax on "unjustified celibacy" and ordered factories to discriminate against women in favor of family men, women in the resistance fought back and did not allow themselves to be completely constrained and oppressed by the promulgated values of child caring, domestic servitude, and Catholic religiousness (see Landy, 2000). Instead, there is evidence of practices subverting the fascist norm, observable in the surreptitious use of birth control, alternative family management, and in women establishing hidden alliances with the resistance, a practice that extended like rhizomes beneath the rituals of everyday life, exercising grassroots resistance to fascism in concrete daily settings (De Grazia, 1992; Landy, 2000).

Soon after fascism, a number of films explored the problem of resistance. One of them was Roberto Rossellini's *Roma Città Aperta* (Rome Open City, 1945), whose main theme is the grassroots struggle for liberation from the Nazi regime. This is a film that has been analyzed exhaustively several times before (see in particular Bondanella, 2003; Rocchio, 1999), and so I will not elaborate on it here. In relation to the problem of resistance, it is enough to point out, however, that the film honors the anti-totalitarian forces that combated fascism from below, in everyday life. Rosellini imagines a city, Rome, which is remade thanks to subterranean negotiations and alliances against the regime. Indeed, following Vincent Rocchio's (1999) analysis, Rome is represented in this film as a metonym for Italy, while resistance is the site where the nation, fragmented by the regime, attempted to construct social unity. The film narrative is closely tied to the role of geography and landscape, portraying Rome (and Italy) as a rhizomatic psychical apparatus that condenses opposing forces in tension with each other. After the war, with major film studios destroyed, Rosellini was forced to film the movie in the real streets of a Rome devastated by Nazism. This experience informed the further development of neorealism as a genre whose concern with the dignity of the oppressed is reflected in the use of non-professional actors, natural lighting, location shooting, and a determination to represent everyday life as it is (Bondanella, 2003; Landy, 2000; Rocchio, 1999).

Interesting in the context of a discussion of female resistance is the representation of three female characters: Pina (Anna Magnani), Lauretta (Carla Rovere), and Marina (Maria Michi). It is thanks to them that the destiny of all the other characters is tightly interwoven (Landy, 2000). Part of what has made this film legendary is (following Rocchio, 1999) its open exposure of anxiety and confusion that contravenes Hollywood narratives. Female characters are central in this respect insofar as they are "confusing and disruptive to the narrative rather than being a clarification of it" (Rocchio, 1999, p. 38). Perhaps what is most attractive about the female characters in this film is their symbolic relationship to Rome. While the geographical body of Rome represents the fragmented identity of fascist Italy, the psychological complexities of the female characters embody their effects—betrayal and envy (Marina), utopia and sacrifice (Pina), confusion and disruption (Lauretta), and so on (Landy, 2000; Rocchio, 1999). Indeed, the gestures of desperation in Anna Magnani's Pina connect with the equally distressed landscape of a Rome at war. Some critics have found this linking evocative of the way the female body was constructed in early Italian cinema. According to Augustus Pallotta (2002), *divismo* implies a close relationship between the diva's private self and her public image. In this light, Magnani's exuberant personality is most captivating. Magnani's "authenticity, that is, her being as a woman, flows from her being an actress, and both diva and woman are products of Magnani's genius for self-representation" (Pallotta, 2002, p. 114).

As Rossellini's film suggests, while women were subject to oppression or ideological subjugation during fascism, some of them were also resistant to the regime, often actively involved in opposing the propagandistic images of their roles within the nuclear family, the stereotypes of sanctity, and the narratives of virginal conception (see Danna, 1997, 2004; Landy, 2000). These narratives were deeply criticized by Antonio Gramsci in his analysis of the language of propaganda and Italian cinema. For Gramsci, Landy (1986) reminds us, hegemonic ideologies are reproduced in the practices perpetuated by social institutions and reproduced by the (then) nascent mass media. The status of socially subordinate groups, in particular women, is maintained by indirect control (as opposed to vertical or coercive), thanks to sexual politics. Gramsci asserts that

> the most important ethical-civil question tied to the sexual question is that of the formation of a new female personality: until women shall not only have reached a real independence equal to men but also have a way of conceiving of themselves and their role in sexual relations, the sexual question shall remain rich in morbidity and will necessitate caution in every legislative innovation. (Cited in Landy, 1986, p. 63)

As Landy (1986) explains, Gramsci situates women within similar parameters and social relations of domination as the ones oppressing workers and peasants, not only subordinated but restricted to the margins of culture. When the mass media enters to play a role in Italian culture, it appropriates these subordinated positions and represents them as abnormal creatures, Landy (1986) writes:

> Through the media and such spectacles as beauty contests, their images gain currency, a situation he [Gramsci] saw as deriving from the United States and having tremendous implications for Europe and for all classes of women. Gramsci anticipates not only the question of how women are positioned in verbal language but in cultural images. His comments on the important phenomenon of the Italian diva, as exemplified in such actresses of the teens as Lyda Borelli and Francesca Bertini, indicate his awareness that the diva phenomenon is closely tied to the culture's conceptions of sexual relations. He notes "the sexual element has found in the theatre its modern possibility of contact with the public, and it has raped their intelligence." (p. 63)

Italian queer theorist writer Daniela Danna (2004) contends that resistance to subordination was not uncommon in the literature of the period. Two distinguished examples that she cites are the 1926 Nobel Prize laureate Grazia Deledda, and Gianna Manzini's first novel, *Tempo Innamorato* (Time in Love), published in 1928 and awarded the Royal Academy of Italy prize in 1935. Deledda was a Sardinian writer concerned with the relationship between local morality and class issues. She depicted female Sardinian characters, from landowners to servants, confronted by complex moral problems. Manzini adopted Rome as a city to write about in her essays, contextualized within the early growth of the industrial city where her characters experience fright.

In addition, Danna (2004) argues that during the heyday of fascism, another text included positive images of lesbian love—Guido Stacchini's

Lesbiche (Lesbians)—inspired by the love verses of French poet Pierre Louys. Stacchini's work expresses his adoration of lesbians, who represent to him the very essence of love, according to Danna (2004). Occasional references to lesbian love also appeared in the erotic novels of Pittigrilli, and in Verona's 1930 parody of Manzoni's *I Promessi Sposi* (The Betrothed), which was burned by hordes of irate Manzonians in revenge. Finally, the same year, Radclyffe Hall's *The Well of Loneliness*, often considered the first lesbian novel, was translated into Italian (Danna, 2004).

Mussolini's regime fell in 1943, and with it went his dreams of misogynist grandeur. Soon afterward, as Italian women's rights re-entered political discussions, Italy's full liberation from fascism took place on April 25, 1945. Women's suffrage in Italy was written into law on February 1, 1945, thanks to many of the same activists who had struggled for liberation from fascism. In large part due to the bold interventions of these activists, Italian women voted for the first time on June, 2 1946, for a referendum to choose between a monarchy and a republic. A number of women were elected, and they took part in the drafting of the Italian Constitution (see Wood and Farrell, 2001; Passerini, 1996).

The Post-War Period

Paradoxically, with the collapse of the fascist state, some divisions within Italian culture were exacerbated. Vincent Rocchio (1999) suggests that the failure of fascism divided identity into three groups: opponents, ex-fascists, and accomplices. Further, the nation was divided politically between the Christian Democratic Party and a strong left. After 1945, however, Catholicism and communism became slowly but gradually less prominent as their national and international roles and ideologies diffused. Between 1945 and 1947, Italy was ruled by governments of national unity, with the participation of all anti-fascist parties. The First Republic was established, a constitution signed in 1947, and a new universal electoral suffrage introduced. In 1948, an election campaign concluded with the total victory of the Christian Democrats and the expulsion of the left from government (see Cento Bull, 2001; de Clementi, 2002; Passerini, 1996). Forty years of Christian Democrat rule began, and "Italian women continued to live as a minority group in a situation of serious inferiority, not unlike that reserved for them by the fascist regime that had just passed" (de Clementi, 2002, p. 333).

The most visible changes in Italian society after the war originated with the so-called "economic miracle" of the 1950s and 1960s (Cento Bull, 2001). This period was characterized by increasing exportation, the growth of consumerism, and the development of the mass media, specifically the centrality of television in a secularized society. The political use of television helped to modernize Italian subcultures, with its tendency to homogenize the North-Center-South divergences, making them appear integrated into the new image of a nation open to the world (Forgacs & Lumley, 1996). At the same time legal reform, the result of struggles carried out by feminists, modified the heterosexual conjugal family configuration. It should be pointed out that before the new decrees covering family rights were passed, some laws had already been incorporated under fascism. In this sense, the Lateran documents of 1929[11] sealed the mutual interests between Catholicism and the state (Wood and Farrell, 2001). The Catholic catechism was instrumental for Mussolini's dreams of Italy's grandeur, while the building of a *terra madre* (mother earth) was consistent with the church's promotion of the image of woman as wife and mother (see Landy, 2000). Historians make it clear that the female body was a metonym for the national body, a space of sanctity (the maintenance of the status quo), purity (through ethnic and religious cleansing and regional integration), and reproduction. Mussolini's dreams of population growth failed, however, in part due to the paradoxes of exalting motherhood on the one hand and exploiting women as cheap laborers on the other (see Landy, 2000).

Transitions

During the 1950s and 1960s, the Italian government's agenda was very much influenced by the pontificate of Pope Pius XII. Legislation regarding women's rights and family was narrow and reactionary. It affirmed the indissolubility of marriage and the state control of prostitution. At the same time, decrees indulged mafia criminals and punished abortion and adultery. Finally, some laws were clearly racist. For instance, the fascist code regarding abortion that was in force until the 1950s was grounded in arguments protecting the health and purity of the Italian race (see de Clementi, 2002).

Whereas the official governmental landscape was conservative, the cultural domain showed signs of change. Through the 1950s and until the 1968 revolts, feminists advocated breaking free from oppressive political divides that often frustrated women's aspirations and ambitions, and created instead marginalized groups that succeeded outside political orthodoxies (Wood & Farrell, 2001). They mobilized against domestic subjugation practiced both at home and in political quarters, celebrated the extension of communication and information resources, and were optimistic about the leaps in literacy for women,[12] which in the middle and upper classes meant attending university (Saraceno, 1991).

Women's achievements throughout this period were substantial. Unlike previous feminist movements, it was possible to organize on a large scale, attain a national plan for nurseries, family planning clinics, and the repeal of the legislation on rape—which had stated that a marriage of "reparation"[13] cancelled out the crime, thus preventing women from presenting their cases in courts. Reforms in labor rights included equal pay for equal work, paternity leave, and five months of maternity leave (Passerini, 1996).

Legislation reforming family rights was passed in 1975 (Law 151, Riforma del Diritto della Famiglia, or Family Rights Reform), and laws covering equal rights in the workplace were passed in 1977 (Law 903, Parità di Trattamento tra Uomini e Donne in Materia di Lavoro, or Equal Treatment between Men and Women Regarding Labor). In the context of the history of Italian feminist struggles, the reform of family law is very important, drawing directly as it does on the Italian Constitution of the First Republic (see Passerini, 1996). Article 3 of this constitution states:

> All citizens are invested with equal social dignity and are equal before the law, without distinction as to sex, race, language, religion, political opinions, and personal or social conditions. It is the duty of the Republic to remove all economic and social obstacles which, by actually limiting the freedom and equality of citizens, prevent the full development of the human being and the actual participation of all citizens in the political, economic and social structures of the country. (Cited in Passerini, 1996, p. 146)

In addition, drawing on constitutional articles 29, 37, 48, and 51, the new family law asserted the equality of partners within the family, the recognition of the wife's household labor, the right to equal payment in the workplace, women's electoral status and their full entitlement to take up public and elective office, the duty of holding property in common, and the equal contribution of partners to the maintenance of the family (Passerini, 1996). Finally, the natural family was recognized—by the assertion that family arrangements did not derive from legal matrimony (Passerini, 1996). Some commentators, however, have noted elements of inequality that remain in family law, abortion, and divorce. Fortino (1981; cited in Passerini, 1996) stresses that the new law forced the wife to take the husband's last name and required children to take the father's last name. In addition, the feminist group Rivolta Femminile (Feminine Revolt) was reluctant to support the abortion law because of its patriarchal philosophy: article 4 states that it is possible to terminate the pregnancy voluntarily during the first three months if the woman can prove that the pregnancy entails risks for her (Passerini, 1996).

During the 1960s and 1970s, Italian feminism engaged in forms of struggle that became more and more radical as they joined in the students' and workers' protests. In politics, the movement's main concerns were related to the presence or invisibility of women within the left. A most important spokesperson for women's politics and history was Franca Pieroni Bortolotti. According to Ergas (1982), Bortolotti criticized several communist leaders for their disregard for women's political strength and perseverance. However, she also rejected easy generalizations and did not accept the idea that the whole party was chauvinistic (Ergas, 1982). Bortoletti was also critical regarding transformations within the Italian family. She believed that in industrialized countries, liberation could turn to the psychological sphere because youth were independent, hence making the family obsolete in its role as economic unit. Within this transformation, Bortoletti hoped that sexual oppression would cease insofar as sexual repression would no longer be a way of subordinating women (Ergas, 1982).

Intellectually, the 1970s feminism was inspired by post-Freudian psychoanalysis and Franco-American feminism. The vanguard positions included the Milan group DEMAU (Anti-Authoritarian Demystification), which followed the writings of Herbert Marcuse; the Milan group Anabasi (Anabasis); and the already-mentioned Rivolta Femminile, founded by radical art historian Carla Lonzi (de Clementi, 2002). The title of a well-known book written by Lonzi, *Sputiamo su Hegel. La Donna Vaginale e la Donna Clitoridea* (We Spit on Hegel: Clitoral and Vaginal Women), illustrates the extent to which Italian feminism had become, by 1968, a site of radical opposition centered on the issue of sexual liberation (see de Clementi, 2002).

From de Clementi (2002) we learn that the 1960s and 1970s were marked by influential feminist works developed in conjunction with diverse academic and political platforms. This research therefore suggests that it is important to underline some differences that distinguished the work of Italian feminism from that of other countries. One of the critical qualities of Italian feminism to emerge in 1968 was its political appropriation of psychoanalysis and philosophy more for activist than for academic reasons. In particular, Lacan, Sartre, Foucault, and of course Marx and Gramsci were leading intellectual sources. Maria Serena Sapegno (2002) argues that it was mainly in France and Italy that psychoanalysis first met feminism, and it did so principally for political reasons. Consequently, when the North American tradition of "consciousness raising"[14] started to spread to Italy, it found a particular psychoanalytic and philosophical background that operated both as a form of resistance to and facilitator of psychoanalysis. The philosophical and political traditions of Italy facilitated a major reinterpretation of psycho-analysis into activism, a result of which was the *pratica dell'inconscio* (practice of the unconscious), a non-clinical use of Freudian categories to analyze the discourses about women's relations. As Sapegno (2002) notes, the articulation of psychoanalysis and politics was thereafter more influential, a situation different from other countries and rooted in diverse epistemologi-cal projects:

> In the Anglo-American world the rejection of psychoanalysis and the stress on indi-vidual rights set the feminist agenda in terms of political actions directed towards self-determination and strong individual and social identities. . .In continental Europe, however, where the philosophical tradition met up with the psychoanalyti-cal one, the road was open to a politics of the unconscious and to theories of the subject, the focus being on desire, in the text and in the overwhelming power of the symbolic. (2002, p. 111)

In Italy, that politics of the unconscious translated into direct interven-tion on the symbolic, including the legal sphere. By 1962, feminists had already reclaimed the equal authority of parents within the family by law. A new law, still in effect today, replaced the "paternal" authority by "parental" authority, and in 1963, the law gave parents equal power in certain family, business, and residence matters. Finally, in the same year, women were granted access to all public offices and the possibility of a full career in public administration (Passerini, 1996).

Changes in law were accompanied by new literary trends. Natalia Ginzburg's *Lessico Famigliare* (Family Lexicon) was awarded the Strega Prize, and Elsa Morante's essays *Lo Scialle Andalusso* (The Andalusian Shawl) were published as a book. These are texts of experimental writing, where the female self is at the center of the narrative (see Amoia, 1996). In addition, feminist intellectuals concentrated on the analysis of family formations as a vehicle of patriarchy through an invigorated reading of Marx and Gramsci, critiquing hegemonic ideologies that discriminated against women on the basis of their capacity for sexual reproduction. Within this framework, the family was the private sphere that mirrored the capitalist division of labor (see de Clementi, 2002).

In December 1970, after one hundred years of unsuccessful efforts, Parliament voted in favor of divorce. Nevertheless, Paul Ginsborg (2003) has emphasized that divorce law did not immediately change patterns of family cohesion in Italy. Indeed, some indicators suggest that formal transformations in the legal sphere translated only very slowly into effective separations and divorces. Twenty years after the referendum that ratified the divorce law, there were sixteen separations and eight divorces for every one hundred marriages in Italy, compared to thirty-five divorces in France and forty-four in Britain (Ginsborg, 2003).[15] Nevertheless, it should be taken into account that divorce laws and legal reforms favoring women's rights had been present in France and England for a much longer period of time than in Italy.[16]

It was in July 1970 that the movement Rivolta Femminile (Feminine Revolt) posted a manifesto along the streets of Rome and Milan proclaiming that women were not to be defined in relation to men. This action is sometimes regarded as the inauguration of a form of feminism that de Clementi (2002) calls Neo Feminism, a separatist movement emphasizing not equality but disparity or difference. Their members drew from middle class, university students, and intellectual circles. Sharing some of the preoccupations of their U.S., British, and French counterparts, these Italian feminists regarded domestic labor as reproducing the capitalist workforce physically (in domestic chores and maternal functions), culturally, and emotionally (through socialization). Most important, what distinguished Neo Feminism not only in Italy but in the world was its emphasis on questions of representation and gender, concerns that became more and more central in the 1970s and 1980s, following a linguistic shift that swept through continental Europe (Barker, 2004). Neo Feminism emphasized the separation between gender as a social construction and sex as a biological foundation as a means of unveiling the cultural and political discourses that legitimate discrimination, Barker's work suggests. This claim is consistent with Nicholson's (1995) notion of identity as a *coat-rack*: an object that supports cultural meanings. She argues that "one crucial advantage of such a position for feminists was that it enabled them to postulate both commonalities and differences among women" (cited in Barker, 2004, p. 240). In this view, gender analysis stresses that there is always a possibility of changing the social conditions that oppress women (Barker, 2004).

Adriana Cavarero (1999) argues that the gender paradigm normalized women under two laws, one juridical—and universalistic—that places women and men at the same level, and the other symbolic—and particularistic—that perceives the cultural discrepancies in gender construction between the sexes. Alongside the gender paradigm, a second analytical methodology emanated in the 1970s from Neo Feminism: an approach often termed "Feminism of Difference," because it opposed equality. This perspective suggested that sexual difference is inherent to the constitution of subjectivity. Indeed, sexual difference is considered for some feminist authors to be the foundation upon which all other differences in culture are structured. As Italian critic Carla Lonzi puts it: "[The difference] between men and women is the base difference of humanity" (1974, p. 20; my translation). Accordingly, the objective of feminism would be to unmask the modern fallacy of a neutral, universal (male) subject. If the neutrality of the modern subject is the intellectual instrument that legitimates the physical and legal subordination of women, then the female symbolic is virtually nonexistent: by structuring culture on male power, phallocentrism constitutes a symbolic order that is devoid of female representations. To put it in another way, modernity represents women through a male symbolic, which rejects the experiences, history, and materiality of women, depriving them of autonomous representation:

> The woman does not have a language of her own, but has to use that of the other. She does not represent herself in language, but has to welcome the representations that are the products of men's language. In this way the woman talks and thinks, talks to herself and thinks to herself, but not from herself. (Cavarero, 1987, p. 53; my translation)

The need to seek autonomous representation, apparent in this quote, articulates the political program of this train of feminist thought, which attempted to produce alternative symbolic models of gender interaction. It also introduced an important departure from Marxist equality feminism: the oppression of women does not result simply from socioeconomic determinants, nor can it be affected only by means of juridical struggles. More radically, cultural studies scholars argue, subordination is about structures of meaning and power played out at the level of the symbolic (Barker, 2004).

Sexual Difference

As stated above, Passerini (1996) argues that differentiation consolidated dialectically, in relation to the Italian feminist struggles for parity that, by the 1980s, had already deeply influenced gender relations and signifying practices. A sign of this influence was the creation of the Commissione Nazionale per la Realizzazione della Parità tra Uomo e Donna (National Commission for the Equality between Men and Women), which published *Raccomandazioni per un Uso non Sessista della Lingua Italiana* (Recommendations for a Non-Sexist Use of the Italian Language) (Passerini, 1996). During the 1970s and 1980s, a significant number of women's books were best-sellers, denoting perhaps a shift in the national taste in literature. New female narratives, biographies, and short stories raised female awareness and created original aesthetic sensibilities. Examples of these narrative works are Carla Cerati's *Un Matrimonio Perfetto* (A Perfect Marriage, 1975), Gabriella Ferri's *Un Quarto di Donna* (A Quarter of a Woman, 1976), Natalia Ginzburg's *La Famiglia Manzoni* (The Manzonis, 1983), and Dacia Maraini's *Donna in Guerra* (Woman in War, 1975) and *La Lunga Vita di Marianna Ucrìa* (The Long Life of *Marianna Ucrìa,* 1990) (see Amoia, 1996; Gatt-Rutter, 1996; Passerini, 1996).

In her study on twentieth-century Italian women writers, Alba Amoia (1996) characterizes the structural organization of feminism as well as the experience of writing it promoted as an inextricable liaison between the leftist cultural and political activism and the awareness of women's selves, resources, and visions. The feminist experience, however, has been vast and diversified, Amoia's work suggests. This diversification is partly explained as emerging from the regional, linguistic, artistic, and ethnic composition of the country. For this reason, Italian feminist writing permeates a multitude of genres and viewpoints (Amoia, 1996). Yet during the two last decades of the twentieth century it was possible to observe, among other themes, a focus on sexual and gender difference and their expression within social institutions. This was a time when "narrative fiction was reasserting itself as the dominant literary form, and as a medium through which new voices could make themselves heard" (Gatt-Rutter, 2003, p. 603). These writers argued that women writers' preoccupations extended to some male writers as well, who became allies of their cause. In recent decades, many writers have been concerned with the loss of sense and memory in contemporary postmodern societies. They have attempted to rediscover the origins of Italian culture and to contrast them with consumer culture: "The struggle both to give expression to a fictional past self and to understand. . .the interconnections between an individual and a historical past. . .is evident in the early fiction of a number of writers, all of them women" (Gatt-Rutter, 2003, p. 603). Accordingly, male writers have also embarked on such a journey to reinterpret (and challenge) the past. This is indicative of an awareness that, first, gender inequalities of the past have been overcome partially, and second, that these inequalities have a negative effect on society as a whole, not only on women.

In the following section I will elaborate on two short stories that illustrate two vectors of this concern for the past. The first one is Goffredo Parise's "Italia" (Italy); the second is Sandra Petrignani's "Donne in Piscina" (Women by the Pool). In my reading of these stories, a key protagonist is the Italian family, located either at the center of the narrative, as in the first case, or in its background, as in the second. In one case, the author highlights the monotony of family life, its emptiness of meaning, and the rigorous attachment to honor. In the other, the complications of contemporary love life are treated with irony and sarcasm, questioning the attainability of happiness with a stable partner, the uncertainties of growing old single, and the crisis of masculinity.

Two Short Stories

A writer and journalist from Vicenza, Goffredo Parise wrote about the alienation of humanity in modern life. Some authors (see Gnerre, 2000; Scalise, 1996) speculate about Parise's homoerotic fiction. His style is sometimes ironic or grotesque in his early works, which include *Il Prete Bello* (The Beautiful Priest, 1954), *Il Fidanzamento* (The Engagement, 1956), *L'Assoluto Naturale* (The Absolute Natural, 1967), and *Il Crematorio di Vienna* (The Crematorium of Vienna, 1969). Later he explored a more introspective approach, particularly in *Sillabario 1* (1972) and *Sillabario 2* (1982) (see Gatt-Rutter, 2003; Cavallini, 2002). The short tale "Italia" (Italy, originally written in 1982) comes from this period. Goffredo Parise (1999) describes with refined irony what he sees in it as a typical Italian couple at the turn of the twentieth century. Predictably, the couple marries, has children, and reproduces quite mechanically all of the traditions of their families of origin. Not even the eruption of the war challenges the monolithic solidity of the family. Further, Parise's story suggests that the family fixes gender roles in minute daily actions like preparing a meal, along with reifying them in wider contexts (see Roberts, 1999).

The story explores the lives of Giovanni and Maria from the moment they are united in marriage in a Romanesque[17] Catholic church until their deaths some sixty years later (see Roberts, 1999). As was the tradition, they had met as children and married young to the pleasure of their own families, who were acquainted with one another. Giovanni was seven years older than Maria, so they married with a difference of age signifying the paternal role of the husband, head of the family. The physical and psychological description of the couple seems to suggest that they are from southern Italy. For instance, Parise stresses that the couple were "visibly Italian: dark, with gleaming white teeth" (Parise, 1999, p. 17) and highlights the salty smell of their skin, a product of their proximity to the Mediterranean Sea. Psychologically, the tale conveys containment. Sexuality seems to be not only repressed, but highly ritualized and codified according to the community's expectations. Parise suggests a minimum of agency, however, for although the couple had sexual intercourse for the first time only after marrying, Giovanni and Maria had begun to "sin" as teenagers: "They would kiss at length on spring evenings by little springs in a tufa quarry, hidden amongst tufts of dripping maidenhair fern which smelt of damp and soil" (Parise, 1999, p. 19).

Giovanni and Maria were deeply in love and remained faithful to each other throughout their lives. This does not only mean that they never cheated on each other, but, most important, they preserved the honor of their marriage. This is a central notion in the story, which in its reinterpretation of the past praises past traditions. Parise criticizes those traditions for their implicit backwardness and oppression (see Roberts, 1999).

Clarifying the meaning of honor in Italy, David Kertzer and Richard Saller (1991) suggest that the value of honor that comes from southern Italy extended to several Mediterranean family cultures. However, they argue that

the concept of family honor is itself complex, incorporating such facets as sex, status, and domination, which have received varying emphases in different times and places. Whatever the variation, a striking conclusion. . .is the resilience of the value placed on honor in Italy throughout the centuries, especially the notion that a family's honor is tied to the virginity and sexual fidelity of its daughters and wives. (p. 17)

In the preceding sections I have discussed changes in Italian law regarding marriage, gender relations, and labor, the result of over a century of struggle on the part of women. Strikingly, since adultery was the greatest threat to family honor, until 1981 the law granted protection to those who murdered adulterous offenders.[18] Parise often encodes honor into metaphors of kindness and sexual intimacy (Cavallini, 2002). He also suggests that honor is intrinsic to the couples' southernism when he writes of enjoyable skin smells of bread and the seductive, salty tastes of the southern Mediterranean Sea in the mouths of the lovers. It appears here that honor is a quasi particularistic value: "This deeply *engrained mentality* [of the South] assured them that *honor* would not allow anyone to show them anything other than respect, and for this reason they both adored sleeping together at night in the same bed" (Parise, 1999, p. 19; emphases added).

Giovanni and Maria had only two children, perhaps quite a disappointment for their relatives, who regarded numerous offspring as a treasure promising a better future. The parents named their children after their grandparents. They raised the children, a boy and a girl, with care and effort. The years passed slowly as they worked to sustain the family. In a changing world, the family built a wall that distanced them from others in the community, whom they regarded with suspicion and distrust (Parise, 1999).

The story's name, "Italia," stands for the country's containment—its frontiers divide a secure inside from a frightening outside, as is suggested by the conversations about the war that the male character has with a friend (see Roberts, 1999). However, this is a narrative of one family only. In this case, that one family seems to represent all the country, "Italia," as a national unity. In comparing the family with the country, the title serves to allude to the family as an enclosure difficult to penetrate. In addition, the family would seem the ultimate metaphor for talking about regional cultural values—particularly honor: "The fact that they were so deeply rooted in their own region meant that nothing could change their way of seeing things. The other regions of Italy were rather like foreign states, but they gradually began to understand that. . .they were all. . .wrapped up in their own form of honor" (Parise, 1999, p. 21). Perhaps Parise's assessment of values (and his indirect reference to "foreign states") represents the dramatic changes undergone by Italy after the war. This claim is supported by literary critic Gian-Paolo

Biasin (2001), who sees Parise and other writers concerned with societal transformations:

> After the Liberation and the reconstruction, Italy quickly became an industrialized country with all the characteristic phenomena of a modern, affluent society: urbanization, mass media, rapid transport, consumerism, alienation, pollution, and then women and youth movements. . .All these phenomena powerfully contributed to a radical reshaping of the traditional family and societal structures and values, and all were represented in the films. . .as well as in the narrative works of the period. (p. 167)

The importance of the preservation of values appears several times in the story, particularly in the upbringing of children. Readers are told that Maria and Giovanni never argued; they would spend their days in silence, learning to love each other in different ways or teaching their children the values of family trust. Indeed, Parise strategically interrupts their monotony only once, and does so through an ambivalent reference to either the Great War or Mussolini's regime. What matters here is to show how an outside disjuncture may test the impenetrability of the Italian family, but not challenge it. The tale closes as a French friend, worried about the political future of Italy, asks for Giovanni's opinion. He circumspectly says that "all remains for ever the same in Italy." This line can be read as "all remains for ever the same within the Italian family." This is certainly an arguable reading of Parise's story, a look at the suffocating permanence of tradition and regionalism. Indeed, regionalism is a central theme in Parise's work. In his preoccupation with morality, he "distilled *exempla* of moral or psychological behavior, organized under the heading of an affective quality ('Friendship,' 'Goodness') or generic indication ('Cinema,' 'Family')" (Gatt-Rutter, 2003, p. 593).

In contrast, "Donne in Piscina" (Women by the Pool, originally published in 1984), by Sandra Petrignani (1999), is a short, sarcastic narrative that centers on events experienced by four women as they relax on a summer day and enjoy swimming and small talk. An art journalist who has written about the condition of women writers, Petrignani belongs to the last generation of writers affected directly by 1970s feminism (see Gatt-Rutter, 2003). In this story she focuses on the themes that animate the conversations among women relaxing at a poolside. Their reactions to a man approaching them raise questions of gender, sexuality, and their feelings about middle age. All are independent women in search of relationships that do not reproduce old-fashioned models (see Roberts, 1999).

In comparison with Parise's story, Petrignani's narrative does not easily offer the reader indexes of cultural specificity. Instead, she seems to erase from her narrative any mark that could link the characters and their vicissitudes with particular social circumstances beyond the crisis of the feminine condition in postmodernity (see Roberts, 1999). She emphasizes the anodyne tone of conversational topics that range from body image, to tips for dating in women's magazines, to stereotypes about male sexual behavior: "In some ways thirty-nine years are not so many, but for somebody doing exercise they are what they are, inscribed in the softness of the flesh. She says this to her friends by the pool. . .'That's just what men like,' says Gabriella, the expert, 'these signs of mature femininity. I feel more attractive now that I did when I was twenty'" (Petrignani, 1999, p. 97).

The pool is a figurative laboratory, a microcosm where Gabriella, Valeria, Laura, and Paola look at themselves in the mirror defined by the rippling of the water. The subjects they touch on may seem at first unimportant, but indeed they carry significance for the protagonists; the women project the female dilemma onto the depth of the pool: their gazes resting upon each other's bodies, all trying to figure out a meaning for their lives, and hypothesizing what it is that makes a woman desirable. Each of them is trying to discover an attribute that might constitute them as objects of male desire. A young, muscular man swims back and forth, every now and then holding on to the edge of the pool. He is trapped in the image of a perfect body. He does not look at them, causing them some degree of frustration. This frustration is not foreign to their psychologies. In a way, it seems that they have become accustomed to it. One of them then remembers a song that says "a permanent sense of gravity is what I'm looking for, my ideas in things and people no longer a revolving door. What I need is. . ." The words stop there, a blank that suggests that there is no *one* signifier of desire.

A toad makes its way to the edge of the grass and comes next to Paola's feet. She finds it disgusting. It is so ugly, adds Valeria. However, the ugly toad suddenly evokes childhood memories: "When she was a child the title of one of her favorite fairy stories was *King Toad*" (Petrignani, 1999, p. 101). This reference to a fairy tale within the story serves in the narrative to explore archaic and popular fantasies behind the gender divide and to fictionalize the differences between the sexes. In this case, it is a patriarchal fiction that strengthens the subordination of women to paternal authority. The tale narrates the tragedy of a man trapped in the repellent body of a toad.

He is first betrayed and abandoned by a princess after she had given him her word to eat and sleep by his side as compensation for his retrieval of her golden ball from the waters where it had fallen. The first act of subordination also implies the degradation of the sexual object in the act of an exchange where the retrieval of an object is equal in value to possessing the female body: he demands sexual intercourse with the princess in exchange for retrieving the ball. Later, she is summoned by her father, the king, who mandates that she be faithful to her word. This is a second form of subordination. Here Petrignani's allusion to the fairy tale seems to be recoding the question of honor—honor to one's word. Petrignani might be noting that a person's relationship to his/her own speech has little to do with the representations of virility and masculinity implied in the notion of honor. In the fairy tale of the "King Toad," the princess's destiny is decided exclusively between the enchanted toad and the princess's father—the king orders her to take the toad to her bedroom after listening to the toad's version of the story. Her word does not count; she has no say in sexual matters.

Folk specialist Alessandro Falassi (1980) published the first complete Italian version of the tale as he obtained it from original sources it Tuscany. His structural anthropological study suggests that the tale is among the oldest and most influential in Italy, passed orally from older generations of grandmothers to younger generations of women. Its function, as that of many other folk tales, is to clearly assure the values of heterosexual marriage:

> This fairy tale too ends in marriage: the loss of the magic object makes it necessary, in trying to get it back, to nourish and take the frog to bed because he has the golden ball. The girl has to overcome her aversion to the frog, a phallic symbol repulsive at first but rewarding at last. A similar process happened in the sexual maturation of the young women to whom the story was familiar. . .In folktales, families always know the youngsters' plans, as they should, according to the social norms, in real life. (Falassi, 1980, p. 41)

The ball falling into the waters in the fairy tale duplicates the scene at the pool in the tale: also in the tale there are waters, a female character (or characters), and a male swimmer. Although the muscular male character is more attractive than the toad, he catches the women's attention just as much as the toad does in the story. Finally, the inclusion of the toad at the end of the tale duplicates the early conversation about meeting the right man. Indeed, these women are at a crossroads of the dictates of a postmodern society and their desire to meet a partner. They might despise the idea of having to conform to a fairy tale narrative, but they are equally aware that such a fantasy is part of the historical definitions they need to challenge every day.

Petrignani's recoding of honor as a theme—probably the only specific cultural reference—is different from Parise's. She investigates the way women appropriate a culturally specific value, how they transform it, and how they conserve it (see Roberts, 1999; Roman, 2003). Here, the pool, a site for relaxation, socialization, and erotic negotiations, replaces the household unit. Petrignani uses a fairy tale to demonstrate the minute inculcation of subordination and gender inequalities in oral stories that are told from one generation to another. She is not only critical of these stories, but ironic. Indeed, as opposed to the fairy tale, there is no happy ending in "Donne in Piscina." A male friend of Gabriella's—Fabrizio—comes close to Valeria. "He has the lazy, almost effeminate walk of some men who are very confident of their own virility." For a moment, it looks as if a romantic encounter may take place between Fabrizio and Valeria, but then something both ironic and hideous occurs. Fabrizio sits on and brutally squashes the toad, which explodes in the air, its fragmented body parts continuing to pulsate as they hit the ground. For Valeria, the enchantment of the fairy tale is interrupted by a sudden arrival of the real.[19] She returns to the shadows singing "a permanent sense of gravity is what I'm looking for. . . .What I need is. . . ." A tale like Petrignani's questions the extent to which women achieve liberation, for it explores the persistence of fantasies about falling in love and finding the "right man," the man of one's dreams, the enchanting prince. This is a recurrent preoccupation in Petrignani's fictional work, especially in her erotic narrative, which "explores desire and love, body and suffering—in other words, an imaginary 'cannibalism' based on sexual desire—in the confession of former lovers" (Roman, 2003, p. 122). In this case, however, Petrignani's story emphasizes the problematic nature of relationships across the gender divide through a look at the uneasiness of the postmodern condition, the fragmentation of beliefs about romance, love, and marriage— all themes I explore in more detail in chapter 5.

La Lotta Continua

Both Parise's and Petrignani's pieces were first published in the early 1980s, at the pinnacle of shifts in gender relations in Italy. Central to this shift was the partial emancipation of Italian women from the domestic sphere, coexistent with their equally increased presence in the labor market. As Passerini's (1996) essay suggests, the 1970s were marked by changes in law regarding marriage and birth control, including the legalization of divorce (the 1974 referendum) and abortion (the 1977 referendum). This conjuncture prepared the grounds for a process that eventually distanced women from norms governing maternity, including increased participation of women in the work market (in the Center-North part of the country) and increasing use of contraception. Let me expand on this briefly with an interpretive passage.

I first read Petrignani's story in 2002, encouraged by Caterina, a lady whom I met at an Italian reading group in Champaign, Illinois. Caterina wanted me to read the story because she felt it represents the quirks of fate that have befallen the women in her generation. When I asked her how so, she shared with me a very personal anecdote that left an everlasting impression on me and, in the long run, encouraged me to write this chapter.

When she met Duman back in the 1980s, Caterina was living on the outskirts of Bologna. There she carried out research for the university. After some months, she started seeing Duman more frequently, because there was a leak in her apartment that he helped her fix. Although he had a university degree, he was working in the maintenance department of the building that Caterina rented. Duman had come from the Middle East to start a small business with a friend. Caterina and Duman dated for some months, and then he moved into her apartment, where they lived together for a year. Six months later, they decided to marry. Duman obtained his Italian citizenship and, after long bureaucratic lines and tricky university exams, he was also able to validate his diploma and start working as a professional in Italy. In the meantime, they had two sons, Paolo and Giuseppe, now young adults.

Because Caterina and Duman had met years before marrying, the process of obtaining citizenship and a work license was a long one; it involved discrimination, economic crises, alienation from the family of origin, and the creation of their family of choice. During the waiting period, Caterina's elective family included Duman and their sons, as well as their friends in common, and Duman's *extracomunitari* (immigrants to Italy who do not come from within the European Union) allies. In addition, it included Duman's sister, who had moved before him to Italy and had already been granted citizenship. Although these people did not live together, they spent several hours a day together and shared responsibilities, including the care of the kids and, sometimes, grocery expenses.

What still hurts Caterina today, more than the painful adjustments that had to be made while waiting for her ex-husband's citizenship, is the rejection by her family of origin and some of those she considered her closest friends. They would not accept her loving a Middle Easterner—or *extra-comunitari* for that matter. They would gossip around, discrediting the marriage; they would say he married her for the passport. Other times, however, a close female friend would ask her how good he was in bed, expecting her to feed her fantasies about silky Turkish nights of endless sex. In some aspects, these representations are reminiscent of Edward Said's (1979) notion of Orientalism, in that they express a latent set of beliefs describing a Middle Eastern person as diffident and passive; he is an outlaw, and at the same time the object of exotic sexual fantasies.

Caterina knows that I plan a future in Italy with my partner. As I write these lines, I wonder to what extent she shared her experience with me out of sympathy. Was she trying to warn me that the process of creating an elective family in a foreign country was more painful than some romanticized versions described in books and films? Was she simply trying to connect and tell me that straights can also make families of choice that differ from the normative heterosexist family?

Caterina's experience illustrates one of the points I have discussed in this chapter: that the struggle of Italian women to transform the private, domestic sphere has repercussions in the public and political arenas. In this case, Caterina made a choice to distance herself from those she had considered her family; she chose to create a new family network in which to live and raise her children. She also chose to love someone and to assume the responsibility attached to that love. These are decisions that have political implications: they challenge patriarchal assumptions about the proper roles that women are supposed to play within the traditional family structure.

Although generally unacknowledged, it was the personal involvement of women and the feminist activism that paved the way for the current struggles of the queer movement in Italy. In fact, not appreciating this antecedent would make it quite difficult to recognize the specificity of the current Italian GLBTQ movement's demand for civil unions. Women fought (and still fight) a battle against the cultural and, more important, the legal status quo. It is a battle that granted them independence from the domestic sphere, the laws on divorce and abortion, the fight for parity at work, and so on. Building on this centenarian experience, the queer movement struggles today for cultural and legal recognition of, among other issues, same-sex unions, adoption, and procreation technologies.

Preconceptions about gender roles continue to be present in Italian society, and thus the liberation of women is an unfinished and continuous process. Among other pressing issues, salaries are not infrequently unequal between men and women; women continue to bear the weight of domestic chores; social policies regarding maternity are few and impractical; and men tend to avoid domestic chores and child care (Balbo, 1978; Barbagli, 1984; Ginsborg, 2003; Saraceno, 1991). In addition, women need continually to renegotiate their spaces. Currently, even though partial emancipation was achieved with much pain, Italian women must engage in the conflict of, on the one hand, being emancipated to work, and on the other, being pressured by deep-rooted Italian standards dictating what society expects from them. Working women find themselves exhausted by their double presence in their homes and in their jobs. Some might therefore agree with de Clementi (2002) that "as far as professional visibility and the giving of responsibility goes, almost nothing has changed" (p. 338).

Despite de Clementi's justified criticism, it seems fair to say that women's voices, activism, and interventions have made identifiable changes in Italian society. The importance of a century of feminist struggle to attain the divorce law and enact family reform in Italy cannot be underestimated. As Passerini (1996) suggests, this has been a struggle concerning parity *and* difference, with repercussions that exceed the mere formal sphere of law and statistics. While many laws have been introduced, the struggle for gender equality and for the recognition of sexual difference is far from ended. As the secrecies of power, violence, and inequality have been removed from the household unit, what Foucault would call the "reverse discourses" of GLBTQs reclaimed the lessons from feminism, built their own organizations, and made their voices audible for the first time in Italy. This chapter has set the foundation for contextualizing the value of the current plea for civil unions in Italy. This is a request into the technical domain of law, but whose significance transcends the rights of a limited number of individuals as much as it transcends their sexual preference. As with the reforms introduced thanks to the success of feminism, this is a plea that challenges the very same bases of the Italian culture, and which opens a new page in the history of the country, as I will discuss in the following chapters.

ℭ Chapter 3 ℬ

Gay and Lesbian Activism, from Homophiles to Arcigay

In chapter 2, I examined Italian feminism as an antecedent to the struggle of GLBTQs to argue that it is impractical to value the complexity of the queer movement in Italy without acknowledging the crucial changes in law and society introduced through the efforts of feminists. The pivotal role women have played for more than a century has resulted in concrete social reforms, including legislation on divorce, abortion, and equal paternal responsibility.

In this chapter, I will deepen this line of inquiry by examining the constitution of the gay movement in Italy up to the formation of a national gay organization, called Arcigay, and the political coalitions that emanated from its early activity. While doing so, I will discuss theoretical notions that were prominent for Italian queer authors, including Mario Mieli, who discussed them in the course of their political commitment.

From Feminism to Gay Activism

The interconnections between Italian feminism and the GLBTQ movement were discussed by Italian women writers in the context of an ongoing dialogue with queer theorists during the late 1990s. In an interview with Judith Butler (1997b) about contemporary European women's studies, Italian writer Rosi Braidotti suggests that the notion of gender entered into crisis in Europe when its theoretical power proved only partially sufficient to explain politics after 1989. Borrowing from Liliana Borghi, Braidotti discusses the inadequacy of the notion of gender, which she calls a cookie cutter: "It can take just about any shape you want" (p. 40). She explains that the gender paradigm rooted in the Anglo-American tradition collided in 1990 with the French and Italian emphasis on sexual difference, due to the increasing reflexive awareness of culturally specific forms of feminism.[1] As was discussed in the previous chapter, the specificity that Braidotti refers to originates from tensions between the recognition of sexual difference and the need to achieve gender parity. The sexual difference paradigm—somehow represented in Italian feminism by Braidotti herself—asserts that sexual-difference asymmetries are irreducible and irreversible, and that it is this irreducibility (and not the pursuit of gender equality) that can create the foundations for original feminist politics. Similar to Leo Bersani's (1995) critique of the anti-essentialist view on identity, Braidotti suggests that feminism should not disembody sexual difference through the valorization of a postmodern subject. The curriculum of contemporary European women's studies, she concludes, is silent in its tendency to defer confrontation with the more immediate symbolic order. Ultimately, Braidotti complains that contemporary feminist struggles in Italy are unspecific, or merely theoretical, and she aims to renovate the feminist vocation to challenge the juridical and cultural arena from grassroots levels.

Braidotti's claims apply to certain issues that are intrinsic to the status of queers in Italy, issues that are discussed in detail in this chapter. I agree with her stress on the cultural specificity of the interplay among gender, identity, and politics. The strategies currently adopted by GLBTQ organizations in Italy, for instance, have oftentimes evolved from gay male political agendas that failed to include a critical consideration of the notion of gender. In many cases, the category of gender has remained unquestioned, and gay activism has failed to notice the mechanisms of social construction of sex and the cultural constraints that delineate male/female binaries as a natural datum. As was stated before—borrowing from Argentine writers Rapisardi and Delfino—considering that gender is natural overlooks the existence of a system of meaning that positions individuals in a preconceived political map with deferential advantages, and leaves unresolved the issues of gender parity and sexual difference. This is a view that disables the power of queer politics, for, as Riki Wilchins (2004) argues, gender as a gay issue has vanished from civil discourse. It is simply "not mentioned in polite com-pany" (p. 17).

I will engage in a discussion of some of these issues in this chapter. Fol-lowing the outline of the previous chapter, I will examine here the constitu-tion of gay and lesbian activism, from the appearance of the first homophile organizations to the gay and lesbian liberation movements of the end of the twentieth century. I will then take up in later chapters the matter of the types of queer activism that have emerged more recently in Italy.

From the outset, it should be emphasized that, when discussing the foundational basis of queer politics in Italy, it is not useful to isolate this phenomenon from the work of other forms of organized struggle against dominant power. Drawing too rigidly defined boundaries around all the diverse organizations that came into being early in the twentieth century might therefore prevent us from pondering the ways that politics centering on sexuality was linked to more general leftist political resistance movements in Italy. Nevertheless, I agree with Annamarie Jagose's (1996) model that a differentiation between early homophile organizations and a later gay and lesbian liberation movement can be heuristically useful in the case of Italy. Among other advantages, a model like hers stresses the gradual passage from non-cohesive to more consistent forms of political struggle. As will become clear in the course of my analysis, however, I use the term *homophile* to refer to early (usually not cohesive or politically organized) interventions against the discrimination of *homosexuals*. I believe that this meaning is somewhat different from Jagose's (1996) use of the term, which I understand she uses to identify early homosexual organizations, mainly in the United States. Nevertheless, I agree that the term *homophile* is useful in that it conveys the idea of sympathy toward *homosexuals*, hence suggesting that the meaning of any one term depends on that of other signifiers being circulated and used at a particular historical time in a particular social context.

Doctors, Lawyers, and Homophiles

Although there is enough historical evidence supporting the theory that same-sex desire has been part of all human cultures, the conceptualization of homosexuality as a condition or *species* classification, as Foucault would have it, surfaced in the late nineteenth century (Jagose, 1996; Saéz, 2004). Even newer is the term *gay movement*, whose early antecedents can be found in Western Europe at the end of the nineteenth century. A number of philanthropists, doctors, and aristocrats founded organizations sponsoring educational and political programs to foster the acceptance of homosexuality. These homophile organizations, as Jagose (1996) notes, were humanitarian groups aiming to decriminalize homosexuality. Because these early organizations were formed in times when homosexuality was sanctioned as a form of being rather than a variety of erotic acts, they are emblematic of what French sociologist Georges Lapassade (1967) called the interplay of *l'instituant et l'institué*.[2] In other words, they are not only a response *instituted* by the precise historical moment when a homosexual identity was embodied, but also constitute a reflexive movement that embodies that identity in specific subjects, regulatory practices, roles, definitions, and spaces. In this case, classification itself makes or *institutes* a homosexual identity by asserting its concrete existence in the articulation of medical or philanthropic discourses. Considered in such light, homophile organizations are a symptom of history.

The second half of the nineteenth century witnessed the first homophile organizations and writings, inspired by the works of Karl Heinrich Ulrichs and Karl Maria Kertbeny in German-speaking countries, as well as the founding of the first institutes for research in this area (see Jagose, 1996; Saéz, 2004). The term *homosexuality* was coined in 1869 by Kertbeny as a lexical hybrid at a time when Ulrichs and Carl Westphal talked about an inherited or inverted sexual sensibility symptomatic of a neuropath constitution (Danna, 2004; Jagose, 1996; Saéz, 2004).

While I have not found evidence supporting the idea that organic homophile organizations were ever formally created in Italy, some homophile ideas germinated, imported by or used in the writing and case analysis of doctors and *giuristi*. As Daniela Danna (2004) documents, Arrigo Tamassia's article "Sull'Inversione Sessuale" (On Sexual Inversion) presented the fourteenth confirmed clinical case of inversion, and Guglielmo Cantarano's *Contribuzione alla Casuistica della Inversione dell'Instinto Sessuale* (Contributions to the Casuistic of Sexual Instinct Inversion) discussed a case of a female patient with transsexual characteristics. In a rather essentialist tone, Cantanaro asserts that "the man who never feels drawn to the enchanting beauty of women is not a man; the woman who feels no desire to be wrapped in two strong, manly arms is not a woman" (cited in Danna, 2004, p. 119). Accordingly, Cantanaro believed that lesbian love was a monstrous parody of real love, for a female-female relationship represented "the strangest, most depraved, and fortunately rarest type of relationship that two people can have" (cited in Danna, 2004, p. 130).

Research like Cantarano's was possibly the first scientific attempt to teach Italians how and what to think about homosexuality. While doctors might have been believed to be sympathetic to homosexuality, the Italian treatises inspired by their medical philosophy were far from kind. In their combination of legal and anthropological notions, they meticulously classified the homosexual body and its "aberrant" behavior. Further, Danna (2004) indicates that research penned by Italian jurists and forensic surgeons scrutinized the body of the degenerate. In 1857, while legal doctor Ambroise Tardieu individuated two signs that, when presented together, evidently distinguished homosexuals (a funnel-type anus and canine-like penis), Cesare Lombroso, the great Italian criminal anthropologist, assumed in *La Donna Delinquente* (The Delinquent Woman) that homosexuality was always accompanied by epilepsy, delinquency, and stupidity (Danna, 2004). Lombroso also supervised the Italian translation of Richard Freiherr von Krafft-Ebbing's *Psichopatia Sexualis* in 1889. Adhering to the principles of this masterwork of psychiatry, Lombroso attributed the causes of homosexuality to hereditary constitution, degenerate surroundings, and excessive libido. He focused on the cases of women in asylums and penitentiaries who, under the influence of inborn lascivious inverts, found occasion to feel not only apathy and disgust for men but to invert their natural sexual tendencies (Danna, 2004).

Abnormal sexual behavior was scrutinized at the same time that racial characteristics and psychological aptitudes were invented, measured, catalogued, and documented. A complete scientific method developed in Western Europe beginning in the nineteenth century, aimed at creating a language for classifying everything that was residual of and disposable for early industrial capitalism: homosexuals, criminals, abnormals, and degenerated individuals. Classifying Otherness was the earliest scientific way to police the industrial city.

Oddly enough, at a time when, in Vienna, Sigmund Freud and Josef Breuer's first cases of hysteria concentrated on the psychological etiology of neuroses—hence challenging essentialist and one-sided perspectives—German neurologist Magnus Hirschfeld linked homosexuality and heredity, placing homosexuality within a classifying map of biological conditions (Danna, 2004). In doing so, he ironically wished to decriminalize homosexuality, authors agree. In a renowned epistle signed in 1897 and addressed to the Scientific Humanitarian Committee he had founded, Hirschfeld persuaded its members to advocate the abolition of the legendary anti-sodomy "paragraph 175" of the German penal code that had became part of national law twenty-six years before.[3] The letter, endorsed by Hermann Hesse, Thomas Mann, Albert Einstein, and Emile Zola, is a document that bears witness not only to Hirschfeld's ideas, but to the discursive constructs linking homosexuality and nature at the end of the century. In it, Hirschfeld talks about a "third sex," a congenital, intermediate condition that combined masculinity and femininity (Danna, 2004; Jagose, 1996, Rossi Barilli, 1999). Another homophile organization, the Community of the Special, supported Hirschfeld's campaign but opposed his representation of inversion as "degrading and beggarly. . .[and] pleading for sympathy" (Jagose, 1996, p. 23). Hirschfeld responded by editing the *Yearbook for the Sexual Intermediates*, which published research data and information about homosexual men and women (Danna, 2004).

Danna (2004) and Rossi Barilli (1999) are helpful here in understanding that homophile discourses were assimilated into the Italian imagination in at least two ways. First, they were incorporated into literary works such as the 1889 novel by Alfredo Oriani, *Al di là* (Beyond), and Enrico Butti's 1892 *L'Automata* (The Robot), which included lesbian characters. Second, homophile ideas were received within activist circles, an example of which is the 1896 edition of Edward Carpenter's *Love Coming of Age,* translated into Italian as *L'Amore Diventa Maggiorenne* by Florentine socialist activists advocating sexual freedom (Rossi Barilli, 1999). Writing on libertarian ideas, Rossi Barilli tells us that Carpenter, a socialist utopian and defender of homosexual love, was of the opinion that same-sex love was to be considered independently of the norms that govern the formal organization of society and its institutions; homosexual desire could be thought of, Rossi Barilli points out, as an ideal representation for a society brought into being on non-capitalist principles. (Some of these ideas would reappear in the 1970s in the works of Mario Mieli.) Finally, there was a homophile orientation in the activist work of Aldo Mieli,[4] who is usually referred to as *il primo militante omosessuale dell' Italia* (the first homosexual Italian activist) (Rossi Barilli, 1999).

Rossi Barilli calls Aldo Mieli the first full-time activist for homosexual rights in Italy. Aldo Mieli was born into a wealthy family in Tuscany; he was first interested in science, and so he studied chemistry at the University of Pisa. Later he became a university professor in Rome, an activity that he pursued at the same time that his political ideals grew. He joined the Socialist Party and openly advocated for the rights of homosexuals. Being forced to abandon his militancy for his sexual orientation, Aldo Mieli continued to participate in political discussions and, in 1916, started a literary career. He authored *Il Libro dell'Amore* (The Book of Love) and became familiar with the work of Hirschfeld, whose First International Congress for Sexual Reform he attended in 1921 (Consoli, 2000; Rossi Barilli, 1999). As a result, by the 1920s, a germinal idea of homosexual rights was fostered within literary and educational circles.

Only a very small number of people participated in these circles, however. According to Rossi Barilli (1999), the only Italian to attend the 1921 congress was Aldo Mieli. He came to adopt many of Hirschfeld's ideas and eventually edited the *Rassegna di Studi Sessuali, Demografia ed Eugenetica* (Review of Sexual Studies, Demography, and Eugenics), the official journal of the Società Italiana per lo Studio delle Questioni Sessuali (Italian Society for the Study of Sexual Matters). In addition, he disseminated the ideas of the Lega Italiana Contro il Pericolo Venereo (Italian League against Venereal Risk) and the Società Italiana di Genetica ed Eugenetica (Italian Society of Genetics and Eugenics) (Consoli, 2000). With the rise of fascism, Aldo Mieli ended the publication of the periodical and was forced to move to France in 1928. In 1939, fearing the German invasion, he left France and emigrated to Argentina with his lover, where he continued to write until his death in 1950. Although he admired Hirschfeld, Aldo Mieli did not share the idea of a "third sex"; rather, he thought that homosexuality was an inborn quality attributable to hormonal imbalances (Rossi Barilli, 1999).

Aldo Mieli, homophile writers, and socialist activists helped question the theory of a degenerative origin of homosexuality. Thanks to their interventions, the idea of the psychological nature of homosexuality displaced the emphasis on organic causes. To be sure, this effort was a redirection from the realm of nature to the realm of emotions and ideas, a shift that was taking place at the same time in several other research centers. What soon drew the attention of doctors was the association of homosexuality with normal psychology, more than its relation to abnormality. Crucial among these intellectual efforts was Freud's and Jung's stress that certain psychical conditions, such as homosexuality or psychosis, were not diseases in the same way as biological illness, but that there were unconscious motivations and complexes guiding their psychical organization, and that these motivations included sense and meaning. In particular, regarding sexuality, it is well known that Freud emphasized that all human beings were constitutionally (that is, culturally and psychologically determined, not biologically or naturally) bisexual. He insisted that all individuals make a homosexual object choice that remains so in their unconscious (Dean, 2003; Dean & Lane, 2001).

Following Petrella (1998), it could be argued that the promulgation of psychoanalytic ideas in Italy was met with resistance by organized psychiatry under the influence of Lombroso and Kraepelin, who monopolized medical opinion in matters of mental illness. Freud's anti-humanism, this author clarifies, was further eclipsed by the philosophical idealism of Benedetto Croce and by the fascist principles of Giovanni Gentile. The theoretical and clinical proposals of Freud were considered to be anomalous, hardly scientific, or far too compromising for scientific psychology and biology. In addition, the Catholic Church rejected and opposed what was termed the Freudian pansexual-materialism. Nevertheless, an incipient Italian psychoanalytical movement did begin to develop in the 1920s as a response to the tragedies of the Great War. Marco Levi Bianchini, the director of the psychiatric hospital of Teramo, founded the Italian Psychoanalytical Society in 1925. Freud approved of this society and affirmed its aim to deepen and spread the theoretical study and clinical practice of psychoanalysis (Petrella, 1998). Even so, the dominance of the paradigms of positivism, idealism, and Catholicism delayed the translation of Freudian works into Italian and, most important, the development of a critical understanding of the Freudian thesis about sexuality and desire (see Petrella, 1998). As discussed later in this chapter, such decisive critical understanding of psychoanalysis was developed much later, during the political commotion following 1968 and largely because of Mario Mieli.

Although their influence was not as direct in Italy as it was in other countries, it could be argued, following Jagose's (1996) model, that homophiles were the earliest predecessors of the gay and lesbian liberation movements. It would be naïve to assert, however, that these predecessors were always sympathetic with homosexuality. It would be unfair to state that medicine was the only form of discourse presenting the homosexual as a species, although this was undoubtedly one part of the problem. Another was the complex interplay of religious, academic, literary, juridical, and activist forces that between 1890 and 1920 were in dispute with one another in trying to decide on the destiny of the newly born Italian nation (Danna, 2004). The homosexual body, the female body, and the male body all offered different metaphors for the nation. In the next sections, I will discuss some of these metaphors and their use in fascism.

Repression and Invisibility under Fascism

While there has been recent interest in reviewing fascism from a cultural studies perspective, at the time I started this research, cultural studies works on fascism and homosexuality in Italy were scarce considering the impact and effects of fascism upon subjectivity. The most authoritative sources in Italian cultural studies (among others, Allen and Russo, 1997; Baranski and West, 2003; Forgacs and Lumley, 1996; Stajano, 1996) address questions of gender and the centrality of the family within fascism, but they do not always address the question of homosexuality directly or the relationships between homosexuality and racism under Mussolini's regime. The most important research on oral testimonies of homosexual men persecuted during the fascist era is that of Giovanni Dall'Orto (1994, 1999, 2005). More recently, Gianni Rossi Barilli (1999) has examined the relationships among homosexuality, fascism, and the emergence of the Italian homosexual movement. In addition, Gary Cestaro's (2004) collection of essays on same-sex desire in Italian literature and film includes chapters like Daniela Danna's, which scrutinizes lesbian literature during fascism, and like Derek Duncan's, which examines the theme of racism and its implications for homosexuality during the regime. While I base my writing on these existing sources, and while many of them are in English, I believe that it is important to stress the very limited re-sources and energy that most Italian university centers direct toward these issues in literature, as well as the paucity of undergraduate courses and graduate programs in this area, in part due to institutional censorship and homophobia.

In his ethnographic research, Dall'Orto (1986) is concerned with the dearth of studies on fascism and homosexuality, criticizing "serious" historians and thanking filmmakers for approaching a subject that academics did not dare to broach themselves:

> Two years ago, while concluding my essay on the homosexual condition under Fas-cism. . .I regretted the absence of any study on the repression of homosexuality dur-ing the twenty years of the regime [il Ventennio]. . .Only novelists and film directors dared to confront this argument, for example Piero Chiara in *Il Balordo*, or Ettore Scola in the unforgettable *Una Giornata Particolare*. Besides, the initiative of gay historians, which many times made up for the reticence of the so-called "se-rious" historians, was held back because of the difficulties and costs of research of this kind. (1999, p. 1; my translation)

Part of the challenge in conducting research on homosexuality and fascism, the passage suggests, is that the researcher needs to take up the task of making visible an allegedly non-existent subject. Dall'Orto teaches that homosexuality *was not* a punishable act under fascism and that homosexuality was strategically concealed. Laws did not decree the penalization of homosexuality in Italy, thus extending a veil of invisibility on homosexuality. Homosexuality was part of the scandals threatening the domestic sphere or was an indulgence to be redeemed in the confessional, but, most often, it simply was *not*. Yet, as William Van Watson (2002) indicates, Mussolini's Italy was intensely homosocial; the regime's promotion of male bonding was necessary to counter its inner homoerotics, to the extent that "males succumbed to Fascist machismo posturings and women, depending on their class, were rewarded as gestational devices" (p. 175).

Rossi Barilli (1999) notes that Mussolini's dictatorship did not introduce any restrictive law regarding homosexuality, although an early draft of the 1920s Rocco Code called for detention from six months to three years for *atti di libidine su persona dello stesso sesso* (libidinal acts between people of the same sex) as well as up to five years for the recurrence of the act, or sexual involvement with minors and/or prostitution. The draft was criticized for introducing a rupture with the general policies of the regime, and the articles penalizing homosexually were finally removed (see Giartosio, 2004; Rossi Barilli, 1999).

Rossi Barilli (1999) also suggests that Alfredo Rocco, the author of the code, was of the idea that the *turpio vizio* (shameful vice) did not exist in Italy to the "alarming" degree of requiring legal intervention. Indeed, Dogliani (1999) suggests that homosexuality was considered so marginal to the fascist cult of virility that it could be dealt with just by granting police officers the despotic power of arresting or deporting homosexuals. Although penalties were applied unevenly inside the Italian territory, and even in the period after 1938–the year of the introduction of the race laws that, following the Nazi model, characterized homosexuals as a perverted race—when laws were rigorously enforced, there is enough documentation to prove that no fewer than ninety cases of severe human rights violations were unleashed on homosexuals in the short period from 1936 to 1939 (Rossi Barilli, 1999).

Although Nazi laws served as a model for the code, Dogliani (1999) points out that if Italian authorities had had the intention of persecuting homosexuals following political mechanisms similar to the ones used in

Germany, fascists would have had to face a conundrum, for it would have been necessary first to acknowledge the existence of what had been kept invisible for political convenience. However, once homosexuality came into existence, Dogliani suggests that fascists would have had to repress and hide it from view again.

Dall'Orto (1994) suggests that in allowing the Catholic Church to manage and shape lay opinion in matters of private morality, fascism reinforced the strategy of the liberal state founded in 1870. This strategy implied making homosexuality—and sexual life in general—the realm of the unsaid, of whispers and euphemisms, a world that *is* but does not *exist*. Rossi Barilli (1999) concludes that fascist ideology was not contingently but intrinsically homophobic:

> The attitude of negation was accentuated during fascism, in part because machismo was a most important dogma, incarnated in the *Duce* himself and synthesized in his popular "three 'm's (Mussolini, male, man [man as in *marito*: husband]) and in part because the regime brought to perfection the petit-bourgeois tendency to remove from existence anything that was inconvenient. (p. 20; my translation)

Arguably, homosexuality was made invisible through the act of police repression, which kept homosexuals under strict surveillance. The relative lack of fascist concern in regard to homosexuality during the late 1930s, when homosexuality became a political crime (Duncan, 2004), seems more an ideological tactic than simple denial. As an *Italo-Argentino* doing research on queer Italy, I cannot help finding these pieces of information to be terrifying. They remind me of the *desaparecidos* during the last *golpe de estado*. The military government that killed and forced into exile thousands of my people pretended that they had never existed. The meaning that Argentine *militars* like Videla gave to the word *desaparecido* is somehow similar to the way homosexuals were represented in the psychopathic mind of fascists. I hear them saying: they are not here now, and they were never there, they just do not exist for us. They do not deserve a proper symbolic inscription.

In the case of Italy, nevertheless, Dario Petrosino (1996) suggests that while legislators opted for making homosexuality invisible, the press of the period showed an ominous interest in discussing it, although it was usually presented as a disease endemic to other groups—Muslims or Jews, for example. In addition, there is some indication that repression within fascism was substantial (Duncan, 2004). Paradoxically, the invisibility of homosexuality—that is, the fact that homosexuality was a taboo subject about which nothing should be said—supported long-standing beliefs of Italy as a sexual paradise, one where to fulfill fantasies about the *turpio vizio* (evil vice) (see Rossi Barilli, 1999).

In a 1983 radio survey for Radio Popolare di Milano (Milan Independent Radio), Paolo Hutter interviewed survivors of the regime that declared that homosexuals would not be persecuted if they remained silent about their affairs and did not bother the police, Rossi Barilli reports. Oral testimonials recorded by Dall'Orto, like that of Berbardino Del Boca, imply that "sex tourism" was common in Italy during fascism "because sex was free and nobody said anything" (cited in Rossi Barilli, 1999, p. 22; my translation). It was just a matter of knowing how to deal with police officers, as the interviewee acknowledged.

Although the making of *il turpio vizio* into a nonexistent entity was consistent with the fascist glorification of homoerotic bonding and with its obsession with male muscles, strength, and determination, one should also bear in mind, writers suggest, that a large number of representations constructing the homoerotics of fascism happened *a posteriori,* and are therefore retroactive significations (see Sedgwick, 1994).[5] To put it as Duncan (2004) does, in these representations homosexually is foreign to Italy and endemic to foreigners:

> The inescapability of homosexual characters in novels set during the regime by such major antifascist writers of the 1940s and 1950s as Pavese, Bassani, Moravia, Morante and Pratolini belies the commonly held belief that until very recently homosexuality in Italy was unmentionable. Films made in the 1960s and 1970s, that intensified and made ever more graphic the link between Fascism and deviant sexuality, extend this cultural narrative. (2004, p. 187)

The connection between fascism and homosexuality is not to be understood mechanically, even if this regime, as other military organizations, appears to have been founded on homoerotic attachments. Fascism recreated the male body as a cult that exalted male bonding, apparent in its obsession with paternity, sports, and physical perfection. An example of the fascist fascination with manliness is the construction of the sports complex Foro Mussolini (Forum Mussolini) and the Stadio dei Marmi (Marble Stadium). These grandiose architectural works create metaphors for the national "body." In the Stadio dei Marmi, more than fifty statutes of young male athletes are either totally or half naked, revealing their genital potency, which is offered to public sight in a gesture that reveals the *Trieb*'s mechanism of fixation, a form of "pulsional" attachment to an object. Particularly intense is the gaze of the statue of Catania, his eyes wide open, lacking pupils but showing a defiant expression and exuberant genitalia. This is optical, voyeuristic enjoyment at its best, an enticement to the eye to keep looking. These male bodies stand in triumphant poses around the top of the terrace, as if they were saying to the eye: do you want something to see (do you want something to be made visible), then see and enjoy this!

Sedgwick (1994) warns against a too-rapid interpretation of fascism's iconography as expressively homosexual, though. She clarifies that if homosexuality has been encoded as deviance, it might be because these representations are mechanisms for rendering fascist perversity intelligible:

> Fascism is distinctive in this century not for the intensity of its homoerotic charge, but rather for the virulence of the homophobic prohibition by which that charge, once crystallized as an object of knowledge, is then denied *to* knowledge and hence most manipulably mobilized. In a knowledge regime that pushes toward the homosexual heightening of homosocial bonds, it is the twinning with that push of an equally powerful homophobia, and most of all the enforcement of cognitive impermeability between the two, that will represent the access of Fascism. (1994, pp. 50-51)

Homoeroticism and homophobia, Sedgwick (1994) makes us note, are not contradictory. In fact, it is such schizophrenic attachment to homosexuality that best characterizes the close libidinal connection of the male bonds within the military and within the church.

The fall of fascism did not automatically translate into improved conditions for homosexuals in Italy. Without a doubt, the political preponderance of the Christian Democratic Party in the post-war period facilitated the Catholic Church's implementation of a program for cultural reconstruction based on utterly conservative cultural policies (see Allum, 2003).

Pasolini and Post-War Italy

In the period from the end of World War II to 1968, new international political hierarchies positioned "first world" countries—mainly England and the United States—as economic and cultural world leaders. Within the Italian peninsula, the Christian Democrats secured their power in Parliament, and a new social configuration emanated in the country, partly because of a boom in technological industrialization, and partly because of shifting social values that were reflected in new stylistic approaches in literature, film, and in embryonic social movements (Forgacs, 1997). It is in this context that we can best appreciate the importance of Pier Paolo Pasolini's work.

Pasolini was born on March 5, 1922, just at the outset of fascism. Until his death[6] in 1975, this most distinguished writer and film director built a controversial persona, gaining the love and also the hate of Italians, who were usually divided by his declarations and nonconformist attitudes (see Moliterno, 2003). He elaborated on various literature styles and was also the author of rebellious articles for the press: among other topics, Pasolini was fascinated with Italian society, sexuality, the family, language, religion, and Marxism. His first essays were published when he was a teenager and already a militant within communist groups from Bologna. According to Gatt-Rutter (2003), the first poetic works of Pasolini used dialect. Pasolini used the *Friulano*[7] as a means of complicating standard Italian, a form of literary rebellion he would continue to work on and perfect over the years, until converting his words into weapons of political struggle: "Pasolini used dialect as a means of escaping from the prefabricated discourse of hermeti-cism into an even more private world of sweet, sinful innocence" (Gatt-Rutter, 2003, p. 556). Pasolini's *œuvre* was a deep and personal research into a variety of topics and characters that seem to reflect the impasses and paradoxes that new generations confronted in Italy. For instance, the situa-tion for homosexuals was at once charged and ambivalent at this time, for the post-war period presented the important advantage of being a transition toward more representation and visibility than did the prior, more obscuran-tist decades. Nevertheless, the reality for sexual minorities continued to be tormented and tragic.

After being drafted into World War II, and while imprisoned by the Germans, Pasolini joined the Communist Party, from which he was expelled (see Moliterno, 2003). Van Watson (2002) clarifies the repulsiveness of homosexuality in Italian communism, which he compares to fascist intoler-ance: "Just as Marxism has traditionally ignored the body as site of libido rather than labor, so also communism has historically been as intolerant, if less punitive, of homosexuality as fascism, and this was particularly true in Italy" (p. 187).

Rossi Barilli (1999) points out that the Communist Party expelled Paso-lini in 1949 after being condemned for committing an *atto impuro*[8] (impure act) with young men. (There seems to have been an involvement on the part of the church in presenting the case to the court.) Pasolini was then sentenced to prison and lost his university teaching position (Rossi Barilli, 1999). This event might have pleased some Christian Democratic Party and Communist Party leaders, who had been awaiting a private scandal so as to expose Pasolini's sexual life publicly. The episode is interesting, for it clarifies the hegemonic position of the Catholic Church within Italy, as well as a surprising alliance between the church, the Communist Party, and the Democratic Party on the basis of queer panic—entities that are otherwise represented as opposed to each other (see Rossi Barilli, 1999; for details on the murder of Pasolini, see Siciliano, 1982).

Pasolini's imprisonment took place at a time of changing attitudes toward sexuality, both domestically and internationally. A year after Pasolini was judged, a new periodical called *Scienza e Sessualità* (Science and Sexuality) appeared in Italy for the purpose of discussing the subject of sexual freedom in the world (Consoli, 2000). An antecedent to this periodical was the magazine *Problemi Sessuali* (Sexual Problems), which regularly published articles signed by Gino Olivari, who advocated the human rights of homosexuals as much as he believed in the scientific cure of homosexuality (Rossi Barilli, 1999).

Scienza e Sessualità encountered general opposition in the cultural establishment and was retired several times from circulation under charges of obscenity, Rossi Barilli (1999) insinuates. The scientific commitment of the publication—as the representative in Italy of the International Committee for Sexual Equality—prevented censorship, but the editors were subject to scrutiny several times. Frequently, the periodical challenged local authorities by publishing articles and letters to the editor that discussed homosexuality in Italy (see Rossi Barilli, 1999). Letters to the editor signed by self-described homosexual men would make public declarations about homo-erotic sexual life and romance, an extraordinary event at this time in Italy. Public interventions of this kind constituted acts of rebellion against what Rossi Barilli (1999) calls the idiot perversity of a backward morality. That homosexual men engaged in public discussion is illustrative of what Foucault (1976/1984) terms "reverse discourse": self-identified *omosessuali*, *checche*, *froci*, *femminielle*, and *invertiti* (all different words to refer to queers) appropriated hostile categorizations as platforms for a positive naming of their identity.

As conflict-ridden and contentious as the 1950s were, there existed in Italy a number of venues for queers to express themselves and connect with each other, including magazines like *Arcadie* (a French, homosexual-oriented magazine with a section devoted to news about homosexuality in Italy); periodicals like *Scienza e Sessualità;* essays written by salient authors like Alberto Moravia, Elsa Morante, and Giorgio Bassani;[9] public personages like Giò Stajano; and scientific institutions like the International Committee for Sexual Equality (Rossi Barilli, 1999).

In February 1956, Nikita S. Khrushchev denounced Stalin for human rights violations at the Twentieth Congress of the Communist Party. This news from the Soviet Union caused much friction between communist partisans and the scholastic left, making many sympathizers withdraw their support for the Italian Communist Party, and so a period of critical relationships between literature and politics began (see Dombrosky, 2003). What is more, the rapid expansion of the Italian economy in the boom years of 1958–1963 was accompanied by increasing educational levels, better wages in some regions of the country, and more equal gender relationships (Saraceno, 1991). New levels of prosperity redefined everyday cultural life according to the dictates of consumerism. There were new opportunities to achieve a school degree, as well as programs encouraging other, more informal, educational opportunities, which flourished together with record industrial and commercial activity (see Wood & Farrell, 2001).

Before the new decade, Pasolini had explored a writing style that was self-reflective and deeply critical of Italian mainstream culture, Gatt-Rutter (1999) observes. With *Le Ceneri di Gramsci* (Ashes of Gramsci), Pasolini wrote about the ideas of this political philosopher and criticized "Italy's inability to live up to Gramsci's historic vision of proletariat revolution" (Gatt-Rutter, 1996, p. 557). Pasolini's first novel, *Ragazzi di Vita* (The Ragazzi) appeared in 1955 and resulted in charges of obscenity.

In Pasolini's film *Comizi d'Amore* (Love Meetings, 1964), the intricacies of sex and power are explored. This is perhaps the earliest Italian (auto) ethnographic documentary to investigate the relationships among family life, sexuality, and the nation. I mention that this piece can be considered (auto) ethnographic in the sense that the topics covered seem to reflect some of the complicated angles of Pasolini's persona. For this reason, I want to highlight the relations among knowledge, sexuality, and power that are intrinsic to

Comizi d'Amore (following primarily Landy, 2000), and to suggest a reading of the film that can be useful for current queer politics.

Comizi d'Amore. This film was released in the early 1960s, after Pasolini had already authored important films that built him a controversial persona and reputation as a filmmaker in Italy. Pasolini was unique in his constant preoccupation with prostitution, criminality, and poverty. Despite possible readings of his films as portraying the underworld of Rome, it must be emphasized that Pasolini was obsessed with demonstrating the dangers of mercantile societies, and he considered the degradation of social life as social phenomena intrinsic to the logic of capitalism, not as personal or isolated experiences (see Bondanella, 2003). Both *Accattone*'s and *Mamma Roma*'s exploration of the slums of Rome and the psychological lives of their inhabitants need to be interpreted as the work of a passionate intellectual whose research was both objective and subjective insofar as he conceived of himself and his dilemmas as an integral part of the object of his inquiry.

Awarded with honors at the Venice Film Festival and praised at the Montreal and Karlovy Vary Film Festivals, *Accattone* and *Mamma Roma* were to generate much scandal in Italy, probably because they contravene and criticize the morals that conservatives wanted to promote in the country. The script of *Comizi d'Amore* unveils the hypocrisy of the educated middle class, questions the meaning of progressiveness, and, finally, critiques the alleged ingenuity of the working class (see Landy, 2000).

To film *Comizi d'Amore*, Marcia Landy (2000) suggests, Pasolini became familiar with the techniques used in cinéma vérité. Throughout the film, Pasolini interviews individuals from different parts of Italy, including Naples, Palermo, Cefalù, Rome, Fiumicino, Milan, Florence, Viareggio, Bologna, Venice, Catanzaro, and Crotone. The interviews are intended to represent the different social strata of the nation. In addition, Pasolini dialogues with writer Alberto Moravia and psychiatrist Cesare Musatti, and talks with female intellectuals like Camilla Cederna, journalists like Oriana Fallaci, actresses like Antonella Lualdi, personalities like Graziella Granata and Antonella Luadi, singers like Peppino di Capri, and soccer players from the Squadra di Calcio del Bologna (the Bologna Soccer Team).

In the documentary, Pasolini is interested in situating knowledge as a result of culturally specific social practices, Landy (2000) suggests, "adhering to its more reflexive orientation rather than adopting an objective perspective" (p. 223). In addition, by questioning the hegemony of certain social institutions, Pasolini is loyal to Gramsci's notion of reality. For Pasolini, Gramsci's philosophy is essential; it supports his belief in the revolutionary potency of the Italian peasantry and working class (Bondanella, 2003; see also Landy, 2000). This vision emanates from Pasolini's reading of Gramscian Marxism. According to Peter Bondanella (2003), the filmmaker praised the working class because "a specific part of this class, the subproletariat, has retained a preindustrial, mythical, and religious consciousness, a sense of mystery and awe in the face of physical reality which Pasolini defines as a prehistorical, pre-Christian, and prebourgeois phenomenon" (p. 180).

Landy (2000) suggests that in *Comizi d'Amore*, Pasolini equates the worldview of the subproletariat with the production of knowledge and power. According to this reading, in the film's interviews the viewer is confronted continually with the presence of Pasolini by his repetitive insistence on certain questions that relate to society, sexuality, the meaning of matrimony, etc. Ironically, by directing the interviewees toward particular answers, he appears to confront the public with topics he was persecuted for. The movie can be read as a fictional auto-ethnographic piece that serves to locate Pasolini as a cultural icon within the social changes triggered by the increase in consumption in the Italy of the industrial boom. In 1964, this was a film that talked about Italian modern society, the Italy of social ascendance when *operari* could afford a new house built by strong companies like FIAT, for example, an Italy whose people had renewed hopes for the future of the whole nation (as a more integrated society), and about ideals of progress and modernization. At the same time, this film is Pasolini's auto-ethnography, a site where each of the individuals he interviews performs: they are a metaphor for his own complex and multifaceted life and work.

Performance should not be understood here as artificial, but as a calculated representation of the self to affect social reality. As has been pointed out, "the value of *Comizi d'Amore* is to be found in the documentary representation of men and women, young and old wearing *masks*" (Viano, cited in Landy, 2000; my emphasis). The interviewees can be understood as being involved in a filmic process in which they write narratives critical of their culture by performing with their bodies, voices, gestures, postures, and the like (see Landy, 2000). In particular, as Landy suggests, respondents from the upper class react to Pasolini's questions with clichés and superficial answers, while lower-class respondents are more spontaneous and creative. Neither group, however, gives a factual representation of the country and its traditions, as it is clear that all social responses are internalized in the context of social milieu, learned, reproduced, and performed. In this light, *Comizi d'Amore* questions not only the cinematic production of truth, but the social construction of knowledge (Landy, 2000).

According to Landy (2000), Pasolini's inquiry was aimed at offering a critique of the then-recently passed Legge Merlini (Merlini Laws), which penalized prostitution and sexual encounters in brothels. This included sex houses that might have been used for occasional sex between men or with male hustlers. In addition, the documentary's title plays with the word *meeting*, extracted from the language and tradition of the Roman Empire: the word *Comizi* designates a form of meeting practiced in ancient Rome where magistrates would decide important issues affecting the whole community. The film is useful in making accessible to a large audience a document that can be interpreted as an analysis of the relations among law, society, discipline, and change (Landy, 2000). As the documentary unfolds, Pasolini is active in eliciting answers from the participants, including young and old individuals who are confronted with issues about culture, eroticism, and sexual life, and are asked to identify whether the modernization of Italian society translates into profound changes for their lives and customs. Further, in his research about what scientists have to say regarding some of these issues, in asking the opinion of public and well-known academics, one sees a Pasolini who is ironic and who anticipates poststructural critiques of discourse and performance. His appeal to the expert voices can be interpreted as the unveiling of another social performance. What fascinates Pasolini is the stereotypical response that people give when confronted with issues like sexuality and relationships, an attitude that is revealing of the double standards of a society that is, hypothetically, progressing toward the acceptance of difference. His own life and the reaction to his work, however, suggested to Pasolini that in matters of morality, Italians were far from permissive (see De Melis, 1995; Landy, 2000; Schérer, 2005).

Michel Foucault (1977/1994) wrote one of the earliest critiques of the film, in which he reflected about the nature of social progress and tolerance in Europe. For the French philosopher, Pasolini's film critiqued the age of tolerance (Schérer, 2005). In his examination, Foucault sympathizes with the Frankfurt School in stressing that social tolerance can be more dangerous than radical opposition, because capitalist progress assimilates everybody into a matrix of consumption that is humiliating and oppressive, and which has erased the possibility of dissent (Schérer, 2005).

All the class groups interviewed by Pasolini have something in common: the perpetuation of secrecy, the "constraints of living in a cultural situation where one can neither speak nor act on what one knows" (Landy, 2000, p. 224). An important impression that is drawn from the film, this feminist writer argues, is that of a widely spread ignorance on sexuality, a deep backwardness and fear of the average Italian of confronting the subject of sexuality (see Moliterno, 2003). Having said this, however, I would suggest that the viewer of this particular documentary can identify with the interviewees in their construction of a satirical and fantasized Italy. In this reflexive process, the film evidences that there is not one, but multiple conceptions of Italy.

John Dickie (1996) exploits the metaphor of *imagined Italies* in an extraordinary essay on the relationship between identity and nation in Italy. He argues that we are made by the language of nationhood as much as we make it. When it comes to the nation, that language articulates different Italies. One would say that one of these imagined Italies is rooted in the idea that the peninsula is a fertile Mediterranean soil that produces rustic wines and home-made olive oil, and which is corrupted by mafia and deficient governments.

A second imagined Italy can be characterized as that land of wealth, design, and industry (e.g., Benetton and Ferrari), efficiently governed by the neoliberal politics of Berlusconi—*Bush's best European friend*. What is most striking about these always-changing archetypes is that they appear to have a density of their own that influences our understanding of Italy: "The very ambiguity of the terminology of nationhood allows "Italy" to be constructed in a variety of fantasy scenarios, narratives, imperatives and arguments that help to give this notion its intellectual and emotional hold over us" (Dickie, 2001, p. 31).

There is yet a third imagined Italy, that of *Catholic*, moralizing Italy. Although the church as a social apparatus is not the main aim of Pasolini's documentary, *Comizi d'Amore* is useful in indirectly shedding light on fears and representations instilled by religion. The film also refers to the responsibility of the political class and the educational system for holding back the nation (Landy, 2000). At the end of the film we see a man and a woman in a marriage ceremony. This is a sardonic image that refers to the ideological values that maintain the status quo and that divide the nation into class or North-Center-South segments, each with its traditions and rituals, but all oriented to the maintenance of romantic notions of love and marriage. I cannot help reading the documentary as a provocation to understand that in the Italy of Pasolini, homosexuality is identified as a threat to society's reproduction (procreation) and the ultimate form of deviance of which Italy should be cured. Pasolini's documentary concludes that though Italian society has entered a period entitled Modernism, particularly in the North, archaic attitudes remain toward sexuality: "Pasolini's film offers no solutions, though it suggests that thinking differently is imperative to altering power relations in society" (Landy 2000, p. 226).

Although interested in analyzing the role of the state and Catholicism in shaping the ideas that perpetuate dominant ideologies, authors like Landy agree that Pasolini's *Comizi d'Amore* is more concerned with the production of and challenge to hegemony. Landy has suggested that, drawing on Gramsci's notion of knowledge as commonsensical, Pasolini investigates how uncritical views of the world can be mobilized so as to create ascendant ideologies (Landy, 2000). Landy's reading is useful in reminding the reader that ideology, in Gramscian theory, is not an exact and official version of history mechanically imposed by the state, but a form of knowledge that crafts subjectivity from within. In this vein, the interviewees' responses represent a worldview that corresponds to the way ideology and knowledge-production processes can position individuals in fixed cartographies of class, race, gender, and even social geography. In this way, the film aims to show the continual flux of power, discourse, and knowledge that offers us a way of positioning ourselves within specific social relations from where we continuously remake our world and ourselves (see Landy, 2000).

As the interviewees in *Comizi d'Amore* demonstrate, language is deeply illustrative of internalized meanings aligned with the nation, family, and sexuality, through everyday practices that produce knowledge and shape consciousness, Landy (2000) would point out. As Foucault (1977/1994) noted concerning the documentary, the "predominant feeling in the film is the apprehension of a new era of tolerance in Italy, which in turn creates tension between people" (cited in Michalczyk, 1986, p. 93). Ultimately, all social practices are fictional, for they have been internalized through the repetition of rituals and customs since the earliest stages of our lives. What the film brings into question, however, is the extent to which these internalizations need to be followed to perfection, or the extent to which they can be transgressed, modified, or altered. According to these interpretive models, Pasolini's film teaches, ultimately, that if social practices have been internalized or repeated, they can also be challenged to a certain degree, provided that social actors are aware of their roles and of the ideologies they have incorporated. This would be a process that would dismantle assumptions about nature and that would, therefore, unveil the social bases of knowledge. Consequently, this film is useful for questioning the basis of current queer politics grounded in similar beliefs of progress and tolerance that Pasolini criticized. Arguments for the recognition of social and human rights for GLBTQs based on notions such as liberalism, tolerance, and individualism can be dangerously naïve if they assume that society is a map of pre-established identities (see Lehr, 1999; Rapisardi, 2003a). It is important that, together with the struggle for these rights, queers remain vigilant and critical of the assimilating power of the state. Equally important, the documentary teaches us to be critical about the mechanisms of heterosexism. Heterosexist supremacy does not simply impose itself mechanically from afar. However, in the next section, I will look at a particular period of time when such an understanding took its place at the center of the Italian GLBTQ movements, namely, the decade of the 1970s.

Years of Freedom, Identity, and Division

In different Western countries, the events surrounding the uprisings and revolts during and following 1968 stand for a revolutionary momentum centered on the activities of students, workers, artists, and minority groups, as well as a rebellious drive to subvert the traditional structures that reproduced the capitalist class system. The effects of countercultural movements included the involvement of leftist gays and lesbians. As Rossi Barilli (1999) reminds us, some of the gay movements of this time took the name of *Front*, echoing the Vietnam War resistance. In England it was the GLF (Gay Liberation Front); in France the FHAR (Front Homosexuel d'Action Révolutionnaire or Homosexual Front of Revolutionary Action); in Belgium the MHAR (Mouvement Homosexuel d'Action Révolutionnaire or Homosexual Movement of Revolutionary Action); and in Italy it was the FUORI! (Fronte Unitario Omossesuale Rivoluzionario Italiano or Italian Unified Homosexual Revolutionary Front). The political and cultural contexts of each of the countries where radical liberationist movements emerged were not identical,

and their constituencies differed according to the diverse social circumstances they encountered.[10]

Some authors argue that these movements had in common similar liberationist ideals. "Gay Liberation," argues Jagose, "did not imagine a future in
which everyone would be homosexual. What it claimed instead was that
homosexuality has the potential to liberate forms of sexuality unstructured by
the constraints of sex and gender" (Jagose, 1996, p. 40). Freedom to explore
sexuality beyond structures of oppression translated into a struggle to
challenge the family, the factory, and the church. In Italy, FUORI! aspired to
create a revolutionary subject, declaring a war opposing all expressions of
the heterosexist, classed society (Rossi Barilli, 1999).

It should be emphasized that, influential as it was, FUORI! never constituted an all-encompassing Italian organization. In other words, it was not
until the creation of Arcigay that a national base for political struggle
appeared in Italy. The work of FUORI!, however, was exemplary in what
today would be called queer politics: despite many contradictions (notably its
tendency to alienate feminist and lesbian concerns), the liberationist movement anticipated a theoretical framework for notions like radical difference,
desire, and gender performance. One foundational wing of the movement
explored the politics of the transsexual, while another dealt with the implications of sexuality in capitalism, and a third proposed radical sexual practices
for radical leftist politics (Rossi Barilli, 1999). Very soon, however, FUORI!
experienced the first of several internal fractures when, in 1972, a more
conservative faction from the Milan branch founded the Associazione
Italiana per il Riconoscimento dei Diritti degli Omofili (Italian Association
for the Recognition of Homophile Rights), a group inspired by a homophilic
yet more conservative philosophy.

The same year—just months before the American Psychiatric Association removed homosexuality from its list of mental diseases—a conference
on sexual deviance sponsored by the Centro Italiano di Sessuologia (Italian
Center of Sexology) and partly financed by Catholic groups, took place in
San Remo. The events that surrounded the conference during the first week
of April 1972 became popularly known as the Italian Stonewall (Consoli,
2000).

Italian historians of queerness indicate that the first signs of a revolutionary consciousness appeared during the political campaigns for the upcoming
elections, which were to be won by the Conservative Party, the head of

which was Giulio Andreotti (see Rossi Barilli, 1999). The party had presented a bill to criminalize homosexuality (see Consoli, 2000) that was based
on the Francoist model used in Spain. As the conference progressed, a
number of experts presented different alternatives for psychiatric treatment.
Just after British psychiatrist Philip Feldman announced a new form of
electroshock therapy for the cure of homosexuals, a group of forty demonstrators (from FHAR, FUORI!, MHAR, and the International Homosexual
Revolutionary) broke into the conference room with posters and flyers,
shouting "Normal" and singing "Psychiatrists, we have come to cure you!"
(Rossi Barilli, 1999, p. 56; my translation). The organizers summoned the
police, who confiscated all materials and imprisoned demonstrators after
beating them, a terrible incident that was caught by all the television cameras
present (Consoli, 2000; Rossi Barilli, 1999). When the congress resumed,
protestors interrupted again, and this time took control of the microphone.
The first one to talk was Angelo Pezzana, who re-named the conference
Congresso di Sessuofobia (Congress of Sex-phobia); he was followed by
feminists and militant gays and lesbians (Rossi Barilli, 1999). Next, Rossi
Barilli tells us that *Arcadie* published a comprehensive review of the events
in an extensive article, and the president of the Partito Radicale (Radical
Party)—a liberal, non-Marxist group formed in May 1968—called the
representatives of FUORI! to lend his support. After the events of April 1972,
and thanks to the political support of the Partito Radicale, branches of
FUORI! were gradually established in the major cities of Italy. In October of
the same year, homosexuals and feminists organized the first congress
against patriarchal Italy (Arcigay, 2005; Consoli, 2000; Rossi Barilli, 1999).
    During the 1970s, FUORI! remained more closely attuned to the needs
of gay men than to those of lesbians; in addition, although heterosexual
women participated in some gay male groups, they advocated a politics of
difference that distanced themselves from lesbians (see Danna, 1997;
Passerini, 1996). During a meeting held in Milan on October 15, 1972, the
main concern of the attendees was how to create strategies of participation
that would enable lesbians, homosexuals, and feminists to resist heterosexism. There was ample disagreement among the participants, and a FUORI!
reporter described the event as a gloomy extravaganza (Rossi Barilli, 1999).
Anna Siciliano (cited in Rossi Barilli, 1999) explained that women did not
have breathing space within the association, in part because the lesbian
groups assimilated their issues into those of male gay groups. Plans were

made to create a women's branch of FUORI!, which materialized years later. To be sure, internal fissures like the one of October 15 were a symptom of a deeper crisis within FUORI! that related to the language of political struggle, representation of difference, and a general political dismay. Only four years after the events of 1968, the political panorama of Italy and Western Europe had changed enough to reassess not only the motivations, but also the tactics of a group that started with the explicit objective of creating a revolutionary subject (see Rossi Barilli, 1999).

It is interesting to consider that there were some similarities between the Italian homosexual movement of the1970s and feminism: both movements organized their structures as collectives; both were interested in redoing the self as well as remaking society; both believed that politics begins with the personal. Further, some of their most important representatives embarked on a critique of psychoanalysis, the analysis of gender and sexual difference, and the critique of the family and the church (Passerini, 1996). Echoing some feminist voices, Rossi Barilli reports that the representatives of FUORI! adopted the maxim of *l'autocoscienza* (self-consciousness) and supported the election of new theoretical leaders. It is at this point that FUORI! began to incorporate strategies developed by the United States's gay liberation movement. Self-consciousness meant the process of "coming out"—a phrase that ever since has remained in its original English in Italy—and how to elicit the right kind of support from friends to make the process less stressful. In articles appearing between 1972 and 1974 in the magazines and flyers edited by FUORI!, there are tips to help gay men to come out, with an emphasis on the importance of recognizing one's own homosexuality first to oneself, and only then to others (see Rossi Barilli, 1999).

The revolutionary ideals of FUORI! started to change as the group in-corporated elements from the United States' GLBTQ politics. A pop psy-chology ethos imported from North America governed the political program of FUORI!: "being gay" eventually became more important than "producing a revolutionary subject." The claiming of identity followed a systematic three-step program resembling the wellness workshops organized by the Esalen Institute of Gestalt Therapy in California: first, recognize yourself as gay; second, come out publicly; third, take pride in who you are.[11] This humanistic line of self-inquiry gave rise to a new form of political activism, less oriented toward the factory and more interested in the celebration of the "individual," more oriented toward the constituency of a new "gay" identity and less interested in the previous project of universal liberation.

Mario Mieli and the Politics of the Transsexual

Following Dombroski (2001), the Communist Party gradually softened the revolutionary principles originally formulated in the 1920s. During the 1970s, Dombroski (2001) suggests, instead of defending the idea of a subversive proletariat, the party started working within the parliamentary system to forge alliances with other political parties. The initiative—known as the "historic compromise"—was considered a fundamental step toward preserving democracy from a possible rightist coup, following the students' and workers' protests that had occurred in some South American countries (Dombroski, 2001). After Enrico Berlinguer was elected party secretary in 1972, Dombroski (2001) shows, the Communist Party progressively adopted some of the more conservative codes it had opposed in the past. During this period, FUORI! representatives chose to negotiate with the Radical Party, making some candidates abandon the tactics of transgression. Rossi Barilli (1999) documents how, as a consequence, the movement fragmented, resulting in a secessionist congress that exacerbated the struggle between defenders of the compromise and defenders of the politics of transsexualism represented by Mario Mieli under the dictum: "El pueblo [sic] unito è meglio travestito"[12] (a difficult rhyme to translate but that might be put as "One people united!, one people cross-dressed!" or "The people united, is better if cross-dressed") (Rossi Barilli, 1999, p. 81; my translation).

On November 2, 1975, Pasolini was assassinated in Ostia, a city near Rome. Giusepe (Pino) Pelosi was suspected to be the primary perpetrator of the homicide. He was a working-class teenager who confessed to the crimes (Rossi Barilli, 1999) and admitted having been picked up, probably to have sex with Pasolini. In response to the events, Angelo Pezzana talked in public about homophobia and the circumstances that surrounded Pasolini's death. At this time it was suggested that it was no secret that political and religious groups contributed to the spread of homophobia in Italy. Pezzana's presentation was useful in reminding the audience that crimes against homosexuals were not infrequent in Italy, although they were hypocritically neglected (see Pezzana, 1996; Rossi Barilli, 1999). Rossi Barilli's research suggests that Pezzana's words, as a memorable speech given by an activist in Italy, were important because they confronted the public with the two-faced morality of the Italian media, which had sentenced to silence innumerable cases of violence and homicide perpetrated against homosexuals in Italy. The assassination of Pasolini could not remain unnoticed, partly because of his controversial personality in 1970s Italy. But even in this case the police investigation did not completely clarify all the critical issues and implications of the crime (see Moliterno, 2003; Siciliano, 1982).

The death of Pasolini had many repercussions in the Italian gay community. Apart from exhortations against political compromise, street demonstrations, experiments in theater, and explorations of the "homosexual" self in literature began to address the social construction of heterosexuality as a regime of privilege. Among these initiatives, as Rossi Barilli (1999) points out, it was the experimental theater of the Collettivi Omosessuali Milanesi (Homosexual Collective of Milan), which produced the celebrated *La Traviata Norma, Ovvero: Vaffanculo. . .Ebene sì!*, (The Dishonest Rule: Fuck Off. . .All Right!), a comedic parody of heterosexuality, that actively engaged the audience in deconstructing the minuscule gestures that make up heteronormative customs. Performance pieces like *Pissi Pissi Bau Bau*[13] took place regularly at a house occupied by the Collettivi Omosessuali Padani (Homosexual Collective of Padani). Rossi Barilli's work also suggests how groups of activists would reproduce and confront the sexual codes of heterosexuality. In 1977, the Centro di Documentazioni Morigi (Morigi Center of Documentation) was founded, offering library and archival services to subscribers. Initiatives multiplied. For instance, some of the actors from *La Traviata* formed the group Immondella e gli Elusivi (Immondella and the Elusives), and with the help of Mario Miele performed *Questo Spettacolo non s'ha da Fare: Andate all'Inferno* (This Show Can't Go On: Go to Hell) in 1977 (Rossi Barilli, 1999; see also Consoli, 2000).

That same year, amid terrorist attacks and demonstrations against the left-right compromise, probably the first and most significant Italian queer theory piece was published: Mario Mieli's *Elementi di Critica Omossesuali* (Homosexuality and Liberation). Mario Mieli was born into a prosperous Milanese family, and there he became politically active in the student uprisings of the 1960s. In 1971 he moved to London and participated in the Gay Liberation Front. He also studied moral philosophy in Milan and became a founding member of FUORI! However, when FUORI! weakened its political aims under the historical compromise, Mario Mieli left the group to continue his activist work at the Collettivi Omosessuali Milanesi (Homosexual Collective of Milan). Here, he joined a radical theater company and edited his work, published by Einaudi in 1977 (see Rossi Barilli, 1999).

Mario Mieli writes about sexuality as a political force to be contextualized within the Italian atmosphere of the 1970s. In this vein, his ideas about homosexuality include a more general theoretical and social aspiration. Dean and Lane (2001) suggest that Mieli relies on a hydraulic hypothesis: the social repression of Eros is internalized by the ego's repulsion of forbidden ideas. Thus, liberated from social constraints, the original, undifferentiated Eros can regain its transsexual character, which transcends the gender divide and goes beyond object-subject divisions. Illuminating the Reichian-Marcusian vein in Mario Mieli certainly serves to warn the reader not to assume a too deterministic understanding of the workings of power. Yet, it should also be taken into consideration that Mieli is less interested in discussing the specificities of the Oedipus triangulation and more concerned with the interplay of erotic intimacies and the historically oppressing social domain. As other writers have indicated, read in the present context of a more liberating social milieu, a too-deterministic historiography of the persecution of homosexuals over the centuries might sound impractical, but in the cultural context of Italy in 1977, it was meaningful, politically and theoretically (see Rossi Barilli, 1999; Fernbach, 1980; Weeks, 1978). As Giovanni Dall'Orto (2004a) writes:

> Even at the risk of overdramatizing a bit, in 1977 it was essential to uncover and denounce the suffering of homosexuals through centuries. It was necessary to show how homosexuals were an oppressed minority that needed to fight for social equality. (p. 83)

Mario Mieli is unique in his theorizing of what we could consider today the symbolic law. Mieli differentiates the paternal or symbolic law from the rules and norms that govern any particular society. Moreover, Mario Mieli's critique of sexuality rests on a close reading of Freud that would later be emulated by other queer theorists: human desire is polymorphous and perverse (that is, it does not follow the socially designated path). In fact, Mario Mieli's work seems to be echoed in Tim Dean's statement that "all sexuality is queer sexuality" (2000, p. 92). Similarly, Marco Pustianaz (2004) writes that:

> By establishing a paradigm of perpetual transformation, Mieli's theory of transsexuality strives to erase the psychic patterning of the real, which is to say the dichot-

omy of man/woman. Mieli emphasizes that for him desire is transsexual both in relation to objects and within the subject. This means that the transitivity of desire can only lead to liberation once the subject actualizes within him/herself the fullest intersubjectivity. (p. 210)

Mario Mieli further explains that by confronting the capitalist family structure—or God Capital—for repressing Eros, a classless society might be attained by liberating the energy within a desire that is socially contained (see Dean and Lane, 2001; Fernbach, 1980; Moon, 1993; Pustianaz, 2004; Weeks, 1978).

Heterosexism can be regarded as a system of representations and norms that make the body, that is, the desiring being, *suffer*. This suffering emanates, in part, from harsh divisions, including class divisions and divisions of gender and labor within controlled family relations and the educational system. This apparatus acts as a monster for Mario Mieli. He calls it the "automatic monster" and suggests that it performs repression against the original polymorphous desire (the desire is originally transsexual, chaotic); it is an encompassing power that shapes social relationships and all bodies of desire, including the homosexual's. By discussing the effects of repression upon all subjectivities, Mieli's is an explanation that attempts to characterize human desire beyond the confines of sexual orientation.[14] In doing so, Mieli challenged the homosexual/ heterosexual divide by thinking about the social and psychical dynamics present in all individuals. Political and sexual liberation comes about with the destruction of dividing categories and the consequent advent of nonidentity. Mieli proposes that true awareness of the inextricable connection between politics and sexuality would break down the barriers between ego and non-ego, self and other, body and mind, word and action (see Altman, 1982; Dean and Lane, 2001; Fernbach, 1980; Weeks, 1978).

Instead of casually celebrating an early chapter from the history of Italian gay activism, I would like to suggest that the 1970s experimentation and concomitant faith in the revolutionary potential of homosexual subjectivity—as is visible in works like Mario Mieli's—relied on a double universal conception of the subject as political and psychical. Indeed, from a Lacanian perspective, the political subject coincides with the subject of the unconscious. Its continually unfolding ontological status resists class, ethnic, or gendered closures: the subject of the unconscious is the subject of a lack that interrupts any symbolic stabilization. Lacan teaches that this lack or hole in the structure can be imagined as radical difference, an intolerable impersonal presence, a functioning "it" (see Dean, 1987; Fink, 1995). In other words, what is intolerable is the confrontation with the Other as incomplete (the castration of the Other). Possibly, the gay leftist movements of the 1970s in Italy failed to recognize that their revolutionary project was traversed by the same lack they successfully denounced in the capitalist regime. Or, probably, they had a glimpse of this constitutive lack during the disintegration of FUORI!

In either case, by the end of the 1970s, it was quite clear that some segments of Italian gay activism had given up the radical politics of the 1970s in favor of an identitarian framework imported from the United States (see Merlini, 1977; Rossi Barilli, 1999). As will be shown later, assimilation of the U.S. gay experience had ambivalent consequences. Among others, it faded the revolutionary potential of the early Italian homosexual movement. A comparison of the Italian gay framework with others allowed the advancement of a critique of the civil, social, and human rights in Italy as perhaps never before in the history of the movement.

Some of these political concerns are anticipated in Mario Mieli's work. His awareness that a gay project might heal the rift intrinsic to the subject of the unconscious—that any "gay" identity is the result of imaginary identifications—is expressed in some excerpts from *Homosexuality and Liberation* that seem to elaborate on the logics of the Lacanian imaginary. The following excerpt is worth citing in its entirety:

> The crystallizing of desire onto acquired images tends to lead, and at times in an unambiguous way, to ruling out all other images that are different from these. Only certain images of man and woman are sought (whether heterosexual or homosexual), and we pursue physical types that we have associated with these images: Young or old, blond or dark, with or without beard, bourgeois or proletarian, male or female, etc., tending to selectively rule out one of the two terms. The fixation of behavior to family models, moreover, determines the type of relationship with the partner. . . Yet, if these filters and diaphragms, these mechanisms, are in part common to both heterosexuals and gays, it is also true that, on the basis of the flaw that our behavior, as a transgression of the Norm, represents for the present society, we homosexuals are in a position to put them in question, by discovering in our own lives a deep gap between the rules transgressed and the norms still accepted, and by the contradiction this creates in the system of prevailing values. (Mieli, 1980, pp. 224-225)

In this passage, Mario Mieli illustrates the Lacanian *I* of *The Mirror Stage*, an agency of misrecognition formed in a dialectical process that implies alienation and identification with imaginary totalities, alluded to here as the "crystallizing of desire onto acquired images." The ego is the result of the sedimentation of ideal images that compose a fixed object that the child learns to identify with during an experience that does not happen in isolation (Fink, 1995). Next, Mieli seems to situate this dialectic as intrinsically connected with the social experience of depending on a primordial Other, and which usually involves family dynamics: "Only certain images of man and woman are sought. . .and we pursue physical types that we have associated with these images. . .The fixation of behavior to family models, moreover, determines the type of relationship with the partner" (1980, pp. 224-225). Accordingly, the images in the mirror are not floating images, but deeply invested reflections that are bathed in gendered and sexualized signifiers, phrases and power-sentences pronounced by a significant Other. In this case, I take it that Mario Mieli is referring in his own terms to the symbolic order, which mediates the internalization of images. Similarly, in 1949, Lacan stated that the jubilant assumption of the specular image by the *infans* seems to "manifest in an exemplary situation the symbolic matrix in which the *I* is precipitated in a primordial form, prior to being objectified in the dialectic of identification with the other" (Lacan, 1949/2002, p. 4).

In discussing the crystallization of identities that might produce stereotypical *gayness*, Mario Mieli takes into account that psychical time is not chronological time. Although the first images that form the ego organize the imaginary register of the infant at a very early stage in life, the ego continues to be influenced by and subject to identifications throughout its existence. Alienation, Mieli argues, has an equal impact on men and women. Images are not assimilated in a straightforward manner, but instead are mediated by the personal history of each subject in a temporality that psychoanalysis describes as retroactive, in which later experiences re-signify previous ones.

Finally, it is in the last lines of the quoted passage that Mario Mieli attempts a differentiation between homosexual and heterosexual subjectivity, which I read as a difference in the position that a speaking subject can assume—but not necessarily freely choose—respecting the cultural norm "on the basis of the flaw that our behavior, as a transgression of the Norm, represents for the present society. . ." Ultimately, Mario Mieli could be read as an author that highlights the singular potential power of homosexuality and, simultaneously, as an author that makes evident that all human beings are equally traversed by a constitutive lack. Being a human subject means confronting the castration of the Other, which in this case is equal to dealing with the castration on oneself and of the symbolic domain in which we develop our politics. Hence, he concludes that we are "in a position to put them [the norms] in question, by discovering in our own lives a deep gap between the rules transgressed and the norms still accepted, and by the contradiction this creates in the system of prevailing values." Unfortunately, Mieli took his life after his second book, the autobiographical novel *Il Risveglio dei Faraoni* (The Awakening of the Pharaohs) was censored (Pustianaz, 2004).[15]

The suicide of Mario Mieli took place at a time when the Italian gay movement was changing its tactics and aims. Eventually, this led to the foundation of a national coalition named Arcigay. This change of direction in gay politics was necessary in part due to the urgent need to achieve results rather than engage in mere speculation. Accordingly, the gay movement has been successful in achieving increased political representation of gay activists in Parliament by presenting anti-discrimination proposals in the Senate and advancing a model for the legalization of civil unions (see Arcigay, 2005). In part, however, the gay movement seems to have somewhat de-emphasized the revolutionary courage and practices that inspired the activism of writers like Mario Mieli, and this point will be made in the following chapters. But before I do so, it is important to pay attention to the web of discourse and circumstance surrounding the turning point in Italian gay politics and the creation of Arcigay.

The Twilight of Hope

Pope John XXIII's catechism and his Second Vatican Council profoundly changed the course of history in the Catholic Church. Using the language of reconciliation and mercy, it renewed ecclesiastic doctrines and called everybody to love rather than to condemn, and to embrace the world issues of poverty, liberation, and peace (Allum, 2003). The more innovative aspects of the council did not have a chance to take hold, as Pope Paul VI, successor to John XXIII, soon after made a conservative speech reminding the members of the church of the importance of doctrinal continuity (Allum, 2003). The Catholic catechism of the time, and in particular encyclicals like *Su Alcune Questioni di Etica Sessuale* (On Some Questions Regarding Ethics on Sexuality), teaches the devout that to be ethical one should sometimes split one's identity. Not doctrinally far from previous Catholic persecutions, this ethics condemns abortion, premarital sex, masturbation, and the use of contraceptives. In addition, however, there was a new perspective regarding homosexuality: the homosexual is not a sinner *per se*, but a person who can attain salvation provided that he/she abstains from practicing deviant sex. The individual who recognizes him/herself as homosexual is not to be condemned, but he/she should not perform or practice any "sinful" (sexual) behavior. In other words, it is the homosexual act that constitutes a sin, rather than the condition of homosexuality *per se*. On this split representation of homosexuality rests the moral dilemma for the homosexual, who is now constrained to search his soul, confess to a priest, and determine the right path to take. Thomas Lacquer (1990) has described this reflexivity as being determined by the disciplining of the body and its desires.

Homosexuals in Italy have always felt discriminated against by the church. Clearly, the strong influence of the Catholic institution promotes behaviors and rules that not only label sexual life but that severely oppress non-heterosexual individuals in particular. Strong opposition to the church from the gay movement was always a thorny subject, not only because church authorities tend to make difficult any open or democratic dialogue with activists, but also because there are groups of homosexuals who identify themselves as Catholic and want to observe the catechism's ethics. This has created some problems within the gay movement. In 1986, for example, while gay organizations held a national conference entitled Omosessuali e Stato (Homosexuals and the State), the church released the document *Sulla Cura Pastorale delle Persone Omosessuali* (On the Pastoral Attitude Regarding Homosexual Persons). Again, this one condemns homosexuality, but is also particularly punitive toward the Catholic who repeats the sin (*repetita iuvant*) and explicitly states that same-sex intercourse cannot be approved of under any circumstances. *Sulla Cura Pastorale delle Persone Omosessuali* also exhorts the church to withdraw any sort of support for homosexual groups or activities, including their philanthropic or Catholic affiliates (Rossi Barrili, 1999). More recently, the gay community has participated in more aggressive mobilizations against discriminatory reli-gious discourses and practices, including the already-discussed Gay Pride Parade during the celebration of the Jubilee conducted in Rome. It is also worth mentioning that Arcigay organized activities to protest the Catholic Church's policies at the end of the 1980s and 1990s and has formally intervened to eliminate religious bias in education. In recent years, thanks to the growth of the Internet and access to it in Italian homes, Arcigay's website has followed closely the speeches of Ratzinger and has addressed the issue of homosexuality and religion on an almost weekly basis (see Arcigay, 2005).

Before the 1980s began, however, FUORI! was highly disorganized, and its representatives confronted the need to establish the conditions under which the group could continue and become unified. Internal fragmentation, lack of funding, and disagreements on legal reform made this a most urgent agenda that could be avoided no longer. Leaving the issue of internal differences aside, FUORI!'s activists tried one more time to achieve the integration of the different regional "homosexual collectives" and to search for an all-encompassing and nationally cohesive political movement (see Rossi Barilli, 1999). This meant adopting a pragmatic orientation that recognized that what was absolutely necessary was to create unity so that the voice of sexual minorities could be heard and so that political participation by gays and lesbians within the Parliament could lead to concrete results. Nevertheless, this pragmatic orientation had the unfortunate effect of distancing FUORI! from its original radical potency. Gradual abandonment of radical leftist politics and efforts to negotiate with parliamentary allies were consistent with the introduction of new political strategies that were usually imported from abroad, oriented to emulate the "pride" strategies of the U.S. and Northern European gay "communities." Consequently, energy was directed toward bringing together gays and lesbians from all around the country to strengthen practical interventions into culture. This strategy probably provoked a critique of Mario Mieli's work, somehow clear in Sismondi's allusion to Mario Mieli's work when he says: "Between the danger of a shallow pragmatism and that other one, of an escape into abstraction or mysticism, I clearly prefer the former one" (cited in Rossi Barilli, 1999, p. 102; my translation).

It was time to get down to business and to ground activists' efforts in observable and concrete practices, strategies, and demands. The extraordinary efforts of writers like Mario Mieli faded, and more suddenly than expected FUORI! activists were less inclined to spend time discussing theory and more interested in seeing real changes (Rossi Barilli, 1999). To be clear, this orientation was useful insofar as it planned to create a network of services and support for lesbians and gays, but it seems in practice to be incongruous with earlier revolutionary ideals. It appeared that revolution and everyday life could not blend; it was either one or the other, and in view of the evident lack of support for gays and lesbians, the movement opted for concentrating efforts on building a set of services with cultural programs, health-care centers, entertainment venues, and information offices. For instance, in June 1978, the first homosexual film week took place in Turin: Da Sodoma a Hollywood (From Sodom to Hollywood), the forerunner of the still internationally renowned Gay Film Festival held yearly in the same city. Also in 1978, the first public television program devoted to gay issues appeared on an improved RAI (the National Radio Broadcast system). It is worth mentioning some other initiatives that flourished at the time, according to Rossi Barilli (1999): the periodical Lambda and its successor Babilonia, which eventually gave birth to bookstores specializing in gay issues; the cultural center Sandro Penna, the cultural collective "Narciso" in Rome, and the Mario Mieli cultural center, founded right after the death of the author in 1983 (Rossi Barilli, 1999). Some of these institutions still exist and actively participate in Italian cultural life; others have changed names or have merged into other organizations.

Undeniably, the new strategies for achieving equal opportunities for sexual minorities and for creating networks of support for the gay community were decisive; nevertheless it is important not to overlook the political context in which this pragmatics appeared. Specifically, this context is reflected in some films of the time. The growing symptoms of an up-to-the-minute consumer culture were, for example, satirically elaborated upon in Nanni Moretti's film Palombella Rossa (1989) about the serious situation of the Communist Party in Italy. The leading character, Michele Apicella (Nanni Moretti), is an activist at pains to help the Communist Party find a new political identity. His anxiety is seen against the backdrop of the Italy of the late 1980s and early 1990s, immediately after the fall of the Berlin Wall. This is a character who suffers from witnessing the twilight of his most fundamental leftist principles and who is depressed at seeing Italy's politics become more and more influenced by the United States. The film is almost completely centered on the character's performance during a water polo contest. Right before the competition, Michele crashes his car in an accident that affects his capacity to remember. Moretti transforms the metaphor of the sports competition into a competition with his own self, a quest to remember who he really is. This is, of course, an exhortation that appears in several of Moretti's films, a gesture that advises Italians to recapture their integrity and principles. Moretti's film criticizes the consumer ethos that is devastating the

Italian middle class through several succinct intertextual references to Italian culture, both before and after the fall of the Berlin Wall. For example, he criticizes the mass media in a scene where participants in the contest stop to watch a television broadcast of *Doctor Zhivago* (1965) (see Testa, 2002). Unfortunately, all the efforts made by Moretti's character in and outside the swimming pool—an allegorical allusion to Parliament—cannot defeat the opposite team, and he leaves the pool to discover, in a postmodern fashion, the unbearable lightness of human existence. The film illustrates Carlo Testa's (2002) suggestion that the Communist Party's identity crisis at the end of the 1980s was "a consequence of the Italian Communists' failure to draw explicit lessons from an ominously circular past" (p. 134).

It is interesting to note that Moretti's filmic investigation pays attention to microscopic shifts in language, which are reflected in the characters' use of words imported from the world of business conducted in English, articulating a metonymic association with the industrial and labor changes of the period, synthesized in the uprisings of the Fiat workers in Turin. David Hine (1997) understands this period as the triumph of economics over politics. The end of the Cold War and the exposure of political corruption on a massive scale affected the results of votes as well; individuals would start to abandon ideological loyalties and orient their political aspirations according to candidates' personalities and charisma (see Cento Bull, 2001; Eve, 1996).

Anna Cento Bull (2001) believes that the end of the Cold War exposed the sub-national, territorial character of Italy's political cultures. Profound tensions among these cultures were reinforced when a new regionalist and secessionist political party, the Lega del Nord (Northern League), presented a plan to divide Italy into two different nations, reasoning that the South represented everything that Italy's founding fathers despised. The league wanted to construct a new territorial consensus based on representations that resembled the unification period, although with diametrically opposed political implications: the task of state-building was understood by the league not as unification, but as a battle to rid Italy of the alleged presence of racially inferior segments of the population. The few times Lega representatives talked about homosexuality, they described it as a crime against the natural family, and in conflict with fascist values about procreation. Accordingly, Lega's political platform relied on building dualistic representations between the North and the South: people versus politicians; regionalization versus centralization; strategic talk versus jargon; northern whiteness versus southern diversity (African, Sicilian); workers versus welfare leeches; change versus corruption; homosexual sodomy versus family normalcy (see Cento Bull, 2001; Dickie, 1996). John Dickie (1996) summarized the representations encoded in the League's crusade and what they meant in relation to Italian political cultures of the early 1990s:

> The South against which the North is defined in Lega discourse provides a power-fully charged emblem of threats which are seen to come from outside Lega territory. Rising crime and drugs are thought through the issue of the Mafia. The dysfunctions of the state can be seen as the result of Southern clientelism and benefit dependency which contrasts to 'typically' Northern self-reliance. Economic slowdown can be attributed to the way the South supposedly acts as a 'lead ball' tied to the feet of the North. (p. 30)

At the start of 1990, Italy was a puzzle composed of very irregular political pieces. In the context of a nation wounded by internal corruption, many Italians were rendered speechless by the renewed alliance between Christian Democrats and Socialists, and dismayed to witness that a party like Lega Nord threatened to divide the nation along racist and economic lines. Confusion and distress influenced Italians' electoral behavior, and in the 1992 elections some preferred *votare scheda bianca* (abstention). Others, including a large proportion of the upper class and the young generation, or those probably frustrated by left and socialist parties' repeatedly inconsistent political performance, chose new political actors, like television magnate Silvio Berlusconi. In 1994, Berlusconi organized a political movement following the business principle of company merger. Its name: Forza Italia. It was a coalition of forces protecting in part the Lega and the Movimento Sociale Italiano. Berlusconi's government was not stable, and he had to resign shortly after under suspicion of corruption and bribery (see Ginsborg, 2003). Although a leftist alliance replaced Berlusconi's government for a short period of time, the political culture of Italy had already shifted drasti-cally toward neoliberalism. This trend, some Italians hoped, would be challenged in 2006, with the election of Romano Prodi as head of Parliament.

ೞ   **Part Three**   ಐ
Politics of Queer Italy

ℭℬ Chapter 4 ℬ⌘
From Fragmentation to Unification

Chapter 3 elucidated the social and cultural conditions surrounding the making and eclipse of the radical first Italian GLBTQ movement, FUORI!. The radical philosophy that inspired the activism of this movement was best represented in the work of Mario Mieli, Pier Paolo Pasolini's films, and the passion of leftist activists advocating the subversion of oppressive social institutions such as the nuclear family and the Catholic Church. After the 1980s, however, a different type of activism emerged in Italy, forging an understanding of queerness that blends peculiarities of the Italian subjectivity and the North American activist experience. The principles of political groups such as Arcigay were oftentimes less radical than those of FUORI!, but usually more effective or pragmatic in achieving visibility and social reform. Some activists abandoned the left to join liberal political groups; the principles of the political agenda often took into account the expertise of American identity politics. Since 1989, the issue of legal partnerships or civil unions and their related rights has been central to the program of virtually all the GLBTQ organizations in Italy. These changes, triggered by the modernization of Italy, its inclusion within the EU, and the relative softening of religious traditions, were not unrelated to a more general cultural shift affecting definitions of intimacy, family, and civil society that emerged after the fall of the Berlin Wall (see Weeks et al., 2001). Consequently, without minimizing the importance of civil unions for GLBTQs, the contexts that I am exploring here redirect attention to the wider sociopolitical and cultural circumstances surrounding the plea for PACS, and are instructive of dynamics very much intrinsic to Italian GLBTQ politics in general.

From Dissident to Normal

With the end of the Cold War and the fall of the Berlin Wall, two entirely different worldviews came into contact with each other, signifying a complete reconfiguration of geopolitical forces. As capitalism extended to Eastern Europe, more totalitarian ideologies that had lent sense to some communities entered into crisis. For Italians, it appeared that this process would entail a break with two central ideological institutions that guided the organization of culture: Catholicism and communism (Cento Bull, 2001). The more integrated participation of Italy within the EU was expected to transform the internal social geography of Italy as well. However, by the end of the 1980s, changes in regional asymmetries were still scarce. The political unification of the country had taken place more than one hundred years before, and yet the expansion of capitalism that introduced changes in communication technologies, transportation, inner migrations, and customs did not guarantee inclusive geographical or social integration (Cento Bull, 2001). It is outside the scope of this chapter to discuss to what extent Italy is unique in its lack of a single cultural identity. What I am interested in, however, is observing the interrelation of larger structures and processes and the gay political movement in Italy that emerged during the 1980s. As in chapters 2 and 3, I am here interested in observing interconnections between the GLBTQ movement and a number of sociopolitical contexts, including juridical and religious institutions. Examining the social processes under which the GLBTQ movement has evolved necessitates a consideration of the forces under which it developed from unification to diversification, while paying attention to the means of representation in which these changes and these relationships of forces have unfolded. For instance, the period from the beginning of the 1980s to the first parliamentary victory of Silvio Berlusconi in 1994 coincided with the founding of Arcigay as a national organization and the founding of Arcilesbica as a non-separatist yet autonomous lesbian group (see Gramolini, 2000). Circumstances causing rifts within the gay and lesbian movement in Italy during this period included the break with communism as a radical set of principles guiding the activism of different homosexual groups, and the struggle against state corruption known as the "Clean Hands" investigation, which was an exhaustive denunciation of organized enticements and bribes in which political parties and public companies had been participating.

According to Cento Bull (2001) and Forgacs (1997), the amalgamation of Italian regions has always been problematic, due to economic as well as historical divergences. These divergences were epitomized, during the 1990s, by the formation of the secessionist Lega, the success of the Communist Democratic Party of the left, and of the Fascist Alleanza Nazionale in the South, stressing persisting geographical, cultural, and political divisions. In directing electoral behavior, these factions turned to mobilizing feelings of duty to deep-rooted ideologies and affiliations. Forgacs (1997) shows that while there has been a high degree of cultural variation along Italian territorial divides, there has also been a growing cultural interdependence among rural areas, cities, and even other European centers. In the last twenty years, Italian cultural policies have been oriented toward achieving increasing international and domestic integration in accord with the EU's interest. Nevertheless, Anna Cento Bull (2001) suggests that economic and social modernizations are not uniform processes, and so Italy does not constitute an exception among other Western democracies with strong regional divergences. Subnational boundaries can be strengthened, rather than cancelled, when there is a strong emphasis on the building of a unified nation by means of cultural processes reinforcing imaginary identifications. These boundaries can coexist and draw new cultural cartographies that acquire racial, ethnic, ideological, and spatial salience. The identity of Italians has been strongly associated with an attachment to these affiliations that derives from historical and territorial traditions upon which communities have organized their lifestyles. These identities, which vary so much from region to region, have usually been more effective than the state in providing Italians with shelter and unity (see Ginsborg, 2003). In this sense, we can understand that Italian identity receives a double inscription into the symbolic. One inscription comes from affiliations and attachments to the nation as a whole or unified space, while the other derives from regional and more local affiliations. Italian citizens are, however, quite interested in state politics, and they usually discuss and take sides on daily affairs, although they generally distrust their parliamentary representatives (Ginsborg, 2003; see also Cento Bull, 2001; Dickie, 1996, 2001; Forgacs, 1997).

Political corruption has been a significant obstacle in Italian politics for several years, to the extent that some authors have questioned the democratic basis of the state. For example, Patrick McCarthy (1997) claims that the time has come for Italians to produce a wholly new state:

The gamble of the last three years [1994-1996] has been that the protesting social groups—the urban middle classes of Northern Italy, the small and medium-sized entrepreneurs of Lombardy, the anti-Mafia movements in Sicily, and so on—will not be able to realize their goals merely by gaining a greater share of power in a clientelistic state. Nor will they be bought off by the new version of clan government offered by Berlusconi. Rather they will have to create a state, which is neither overbearing nor absent because it is no longer overworked, in which the market functions and public goods are not sold to the highest bidder but are distributed in a manner that is recognizably fairer and more efficient. In short these and other groups will break out of the trap. . . and citizenship will cease to be elusive. (p. 241)

McCarthy's argument resonates with GLBTQ politics in that he supposes that it is the task of dissident groups to produce critical practices conducive to altering the very foundations of the liberal Italian state. Arguably, however, the homosexual movement's revolutionary agenda, which was really invested in transforming the state apparatuses during the 1970s, was not really successful in its aim. This is not an extraordinary case, for many other countries where GLBTQ politics were equally strong or even stronger also failed in overturning heterosexism. What might be regarded as different in the case of Italy, however, is that GLBTQ groups have had relatively less success in achieving or securing basic civil and social rights for sexual minorities in comparison with other Western European countries, particularly in the last decade of the twentieth century. To understand the low degree of success of the radical GLBTQ politics in Italy during the 1980s, it is important to ponder not only the internal disagreement and agenda-switch in GLBTQ politics, but to contextualize these phenomena in the atmosphere of a country deeply influenced by religion and different conservative administrations that have helped to depict homosexuality as radical and evil. The vehicle for manipulating Italians was the concept of the nuclear family, to which homosexuals, illegal immigrants, communists, and feminists represented important threats. Since the institution of family, and not the state, often works for Italians as a model in building solidarity and commitment, conservative parties have exploited a rhetoric centered on the family (see Ginsborg, 2003; Cecchi Paone, 2004). The alleged collapse of the Italian family has been repeatedly announced as a way of intimidating the Catholic devout or the conservative of mind. The family appears as a Master signifier that takes up different forms, from state corruption (depicted as *familiarism*) to violence and *domestic* crisis, not to mention a therapeutic ethos to address the cause of homosexuality (absent *fathers*, excessive *motherly* love) (see

Ginsborg, 2003; Cecchi Paone, 2004). Not surprisingly, then, during the 1980s and most notably during the 1990s, the remaking of the family became—slowly but incontestably—the passion of Italian gay and lesbian politics.

"Some might think of homosexuality as subversive, but this is not true," declared the prominent Italian philosopher Gianni Vattimo in an interview with the newspaper *Corriere della Sera*:

> Everything is shockingly *the same*. There are the problems of the couple, the rent to pay, the lack of communication, the trash to take out. Also between two people of the same sex a family can be formed, with all the problems that a family has. One day [e allora] faithfulness, another day [e allora] the cheating; one day [e allora] I want to see this TV channel and you that other one; another day [e allora] jealousy. The only difference is that no children are conceived. (Cited in Rossi Barilli, 1999, p. 128; my translation, emphasis added)

This statement, made on October 25, 1980, illustrates a shift within the Italian gay movement. It signals the search for *sameness* (normal, well-adjusted, or assimilated into the norm) rather than difference (counter-normative, queer, or radical). Indeed, taking advantage of conservative rhetoric, GLBTQ activists tried to reappropriate the metaphor of the family by strategically inverting the discourse of the right. Here, the family is not a regressive social institution, but it provides a new foundation for the rethinking of gay sexuality. Following Vaid and Lehr, it can be argued that the politics of sameness has brought much visibility to the quest for equality for gays and lesbians and has strengthened the coalition among GLBTQ groups and between GLBTQs and their allies (Lehr, 1999; Vaid, 1995). Nevertheless, particularly in the case of Italy, if we want to sustain the singularity of queer experience, subjectivity, and activism, it is crucial that we remain critical of a politics that tends to institute resemblance with heterosexual languages, norms, and symbols, these authors suggest. (See also Kitzinger and Wilkinson, 2004.)

Visibility or Desexualization

While I am critical of normalcy, it must be pointed out that Gianni Vattimo's political alliance with the Italian gay community is constructive and well known. His and other scholars' international reputations have contributed to bringing visibility to a population otherwise very much ostracized. The nexus of a scholar with the GLBTQ political movement is central here, for queerness transcends sexual orientation to imply a strategic coalition of political resources and forces against governance and discipline. Such a coalition suggests the inseparability of the personal, the communal, and the political. Nevertheless, while comparisons between gayness and heterosexuality might be strategically important, they can be dangerous in that they might have the potentially negative effect of regulating queerness and gender by comparing all sexuality to heterosexual sexuality. This desexualization of queerness favors "lifestyles" that are potable: normative society cannot digest racial, ethnic, or sexual impurities—everything that counts as difference, unless difference itself can be marketed as profitable merchandise.

Torn between visibility and ostracism, queers in Italy face a paradox: When we want to sustain forms of intimacy that are different from the traditional nuclear heterosexual family, should we act "normal," camouflaging the existence of forms of relationality that are, nevertheless, concrete and realizable in their own terms? Should we act as if we were presenting to society a model for relationality that is completely subversive and original? Or should we just equate ourselves with being "in the middle"? And are these the only alternatives we can imagine? No matter what we say or do, it just seems to me that we are constrained by the Others who inhabit ourselves and that we will never fit in. Most important, should we even care that we do not fit in? When we act queer, we're eradicated or policed, whereas when we act "normal," we're regarded as a cheap replica of the heterosexual "original." We are left with the choice of either muting our relationships or accepting the experts' advice about how to act "normal." If we act normal, we're subject to state control. If we reclaim the right to find alternative forms of intimacy, our voices are silenced or ignored. Even today, it is not uncommon to find similar potentially normalizing views that suggest that "the [Italian] gay man of today can propose and function with coherence in his choice of coming out; with pride and assertiveness, but without futile clamor, he has the possibility of engaging in a satisfying, stable relationship" (Iaculo, 2002, p. 10; my translation). More and more, the current form of queer panic expresses a schizophrenic imperative, one that commands queers to be assertive and take pride on the one hand, while on the other, conceals the fear that queer pride threatens the norm and hence needs to be kept in private. Consider, for example, the most recent form of derisive queer panic: when in 2006 a large number of GLTBs voted for the left, they did so expecting that the PACS project would finally take on a concrete reality, and that it would be discussed as one of the most urgent issues to be treated in Parliament. While I have expressed the opinion that this project needs critical consideration, it is clear that Italians should not be deprived of a document that recognizes the rights of same-sex couples or heterosexual couples who do not want to get married. Projects like this have been successfully put into practice in a large number of Western European countries. It was expected that the new administration would pass a law like this one in a timely manner. However, as of this writing, this has not happened. When in the summer of 2006 representatives of the newly elected government met in Rimini to discuss this and other items on the government's agenda, the GLBTQ population was shocked to discover that, in fact, this most important project to us is not one of the administration's most pressing issues.

A Technocratic Society

According to cultural historian David Forgacs (1997), one of the most profound changes in Italian culture following the economic boom of the 1960s was the development of an overreaching communication infrastructure, as illustrated by the pervasive role the media came to play in the everyday life of Italians. Regional differences were steadily integrated into the unified nation as a result of a web-like network of transport and telephone cabling that enabled better communication among the twenty regions of the *bel paese*. During the 1960s, Italian industry expanded at an annual rate of 8 percent, and exports almost doubled (see Cento Bull, 2001). These authors suggest that the marked increase in living standards throughout the 1960s and 1970s resulted in rising waves of consumerism by the *ceti medio* (middle class). In contrast, health care, education, and job opportunities were highly inconsistent throughout the peninsula, a situation that would not improve noticeably in the following decades. These were times of marked regional differentiation. According to Arnaldo Bagnasco (cited in Cento Bull, 2001), three emergent regional sectors replaced previous economic divisions: the Northwest, with large industrial plants and service sectors; the Northeast and Center, with smaller industries and primary social networks; and the South, economically and socially underdeveloped (Cento Bull, 2001). To soothe emergent regional asymmetries, the government passed a long-awaited law on regional government (Law 382 of 1975) which offers more independence and autonomy to some provincial authorities, hence slightly decentralizing the influence of the Italian state.

As Forgacs (1997) explains, *il miracolo economico* of Italy was effected through an unremitting process of amalgamation and secularization, in which the mass media played a chief role. This can be illustrated, Forgacs points out, by the increased use of national television and radio channels as a means of bringing information about the nation to Italians of all regions. By the early 1980s, the average Italian spent twenty hours a week watching television ("the first truly ubiquitous cultural form in Italy," according to Forgacs [1997, p. 318]) and ten hours a week listening to radio. Italians were also avid readers of newspapers like *La Repubblica* or *Corriere della Sera*. While dialects continue to be spoken all over the country, the mass media and the educational system have contributed to making Italian the standard language used in everyday transactions and conversations in most urban centers, affecting in part the more local identities and traditions of individuals living in smaller cities (see Forgacs, 1997). Not surprisingly, a favorite topic of mass-media coverage of the period was the threatened status of the traditional family, and homosexuals were once again in the eye of the storm. Rossi Barilli (1999) reports that newspapers interviewed gay activists on their plans to present a bill for gay marriage, and even if activists thought of the issue as a provocation more than a vehicle for political action, journalists hurried to report on same-sex marriage as a modern degeneration intrinsic to urban life.

Under the new leadership, FUORI! was less inclined to adopt radical politics and preferred a strategy stressing familiarity and mainstream behavior—a far cry from the subversive transsexual of Mario Mieli. Some left factions were completely opposed to the strategy of normalizing queer life and repudiated the idea that queer intimacies could resemble the normal family. There was much discontent in presenting queerness as equivalent to standard life. Reactions to the new political orientation of FUORI! included demonstrations and performances, including several parodies in the form of marches, manifestos, and magazines. The idea behind parodying normal life was that of exaggerating the romanticism of family life and the *normal* path that individuals should follow: dating, kissing, and getting married in a church; having two or more children and a pet; and so on. Despite the original cultural interventions, little materialized out of the homosexual revolution theorized by Mario Mieli. In June 1980, around the same time that Vattimo's declaration was printed in *Corriere della Sera*, Roman and Bolognese activists declared the death of the Italian gay movement (Rossi

Barilli, 1999). As Francesco Merlini (1977) had anticipated three years before, whatever remained of the original movement was noteworthy only as a linguistic remembrance.

Illustrative of the values that emerged with the new foundations of the GLBTQ movement is an essay written in the 1990s by the former president of Arcigay, Franco Grillini, which looks back at the 1980s and evaluates the changes in the way the GLBTQ movement functioned. This essay is part of a book entitled *Stonewall*, an indication of how much the movement of the 1980s was influenced by the American GLBTQ movement. Even more surprising is the subtitle to the book—*Quando la rivoluzione é gay* (When the Revolution Is Gay)—especially given the fact that the book criticizes the idea of revolution in the following terms:

> The movement shifted from a culture of "provocation" in the 1970s to the pragmatics of the 1980s, when the objective was not ideological anymore (the revolutionary anti-capitalist transformation, the destruction of the bourgeois family, the pansexualism of Mario Mieli), but above all it pursued a practical objective, that is, "how to modify the life conditions of millions of Italian gays for the better." (Grillini, 1990, p. 115; my translation)

In the few histories of the Italian gay movement that are available, it is not uncommon to see similar references to the *pragmatics* of the 1980s. What is surprising, however, is the characterization of these pragmatics as purely humanitarian and not ideological. In fact, this rhetoric appeals to imaginary common ground, veiling one's political interest—a strategy that corresponds to the most ideological moment, or what Stuart Hall (1983) designates the *of course moment*: a moment when the political subject is devoured by ideology. In a subsequent passage, Grillini expands on the need for more pragmatics:

> In Italy, in order to operate within an extremely difficult situation, we needed a lot of fantasy and political inventiveness. Indeed, here in our country, it was and is not practical to have a lobbyist line of politics, nor a politics of the big communities, nor the politics of the big demonstrations out in the squares. The only possibility that we had was that of making alliances with other movements, of presenting our objectives as objectives of general interest, of making politics inside of other political parties by using the ability of a few gay political leaders to reach the power which was socially denied to us. (Grillini, 1990, p. 116; my translation)

Grillini's commentary is interesting in that it suggests that the queer movement in Italy can be characterized by two dialectical phases—the second one denying the first one, or going astray in the revolution of society. As with all ideological erasures, the second moment, or what Hall (1983) calls the *of course moment*, negates the first radical moment by annihilating a part of history and its agents. While I agree with Grillini that a lot of creativity is needed to operate in a country with deep-rooted traditions about family life such as Italy, it is also important to offer a reasonable appreciation of the contexts in which those creative processes occur, so as not to divorce queer politics from culture and society. This is to suggest, therefore, that the crisis of FUORI! indeed coincided with the country's metamorphosis under domestic and international pressures. To be sure, during the 1980s, the queer movement's radical impetus softened as much as many other leftist groups' politics did. Political discussions centered on the importance of achieving economic growth and positioning Italy as one of the most salient of the EU nations. Technocratic priorities were to be considered more important than the makeover of society; it was not as important to make party loyalties survive as it was to transform the nature of these affiliations in order to embrace individualism, materialism, and consumerism (see Cento Bull, 2001; Parker, 1996).

While the disintegration of FUORI! did not mean the complete eclipse of radical leftist politics, it forced a change in principles of action guiding gay activists, including the pursuit of practical solutions for concrete problems. I have sufficiently underscored the fact that gay politics during the 1980s was indissolubly connected with the more general deadlock of left ideologies, which at the same time was the result of national and international reconfigurations affecting Europe. It is clear that political parties and independent social movements of all kinds, including FUORI!, could not easily avoid being affected by these circumstances. According to sources I consulted, there were a number of issues that affected the change of politics and the demise of FUORI!, among which stood the need to foster the creation of a national organization that would unite all regional gay and lesbian factions, and the AIDS pandemic (see Gramolini, 2000; Rossi Barilli, 1999). The queer community's demand that a new, organized center operate at a national level to struggle for the rights of gays and lesbians was finally realized after a most tragic event took place: the suicide of two young Sicilian gay lovers who had been ostracized by their community.

On Nameless Intimacies

On a cold day in November 1980, Italian gays awoke to some most upsetting news. They opened the newspaper and read about the suicide of two young Sicilian men. They would discover, by reading between the lines, that these young men were indeed lovers, and that they had taken their own lives rather than face the impossibility of continuing their relationship. They had long been ostracized by their own families and were a target for gossip and laughter in their small city, Giarre (Rossi Barilli, 1999; Suicidio su commissione, 2005). One of them was fifteen years old, the other one twenty-five. Farmers found their bodies in a state of decomposition, fifteen days after the suicide. According to reporters (see Suicidio su commissione, 2005), a twelve-year-old boy, a nephew of one of the victims, declared he had killed them at their insistence in order to stop their suffering. The child fired a family gun seven times, killing both of them. A letter, written by both lovers, rested next to the cold bodies. In the letter, they assumed full responsibility for the act and explained the reasons for it. The newspaper *Il Manifesto* titled the story: "Due cadaveri abbracciati trovati in un agrumeto di Giarre. Due 'giovani' scappati da casa perché perseguitati dalle dicerie" (Two cadavers embracing each other found in a citrus orchard in Giarre. Two "boys" escaped home, persecuted by rumors). *Il Messaggero* wrote: "Giarre: Il dramma del pregiudizio. Il bambino che ha ucciso lo zio e l'amico 'diverso' ha taciuto per quindici giorni" (Giarre: The drama of prejudice. The child who killed the uncle and his "different" friend was silent for fifteen days). In addition, in *Corriere della Sera*, Adriano Baglivo reported that both male friends had "made an impossible relationship come to an end" (see Suicidio su commissione, 2005).

There are several aspects of this case that are particularly intriguing: the apparent overwhelming alienation the lovers were victim to, the young age of one of the lovers and the nephew, and the prejudiced construction of the case as chronicled by the media. What stands out, however, is that all of these issues entail the efficacy of language. In other words, they are illustrative of the symbolic linkage between the subject, desire, and the community—alluded to in the quotations from newspapers.

When heterosexism takes the form of hate speech, it becomes a weapon of destruction, a bloodsucking form of violence that insidiously penetrates the mind, body, and soul of its victim and that makes individuals inflict and suffer pain. When subjectivity is over and over subject to blame and hate, the subject of full speech becomes opaque; it can barely articulate words. While suicide can be regarded as a non-motivated act in the sense that nobody can directly force somebody to take his/her life, sometimes social circumstances can be so devastating that the subject is reduced to a mere body that suffers, as Juan Jorge Michel Fariña would say. Wordless. The newspaper term "impossible relationship" implies a form of intimacy prescribed by the community not to be (or, in the language of chapter 1, prescribed to inhabit a space of pure negativity), an intimacy kept from its ontological existence.[1] The media reports emphasized that villagers felt no sympathy whatsoever for the lovers and wanted to bear no responsibility for their deaths. The villagers seemed shameful about their community having made the cover of newspapers with the word homosexual, a word nobody in this community would dare to speak (see Suicidio su commissione, 2005).

This impossible relationship represents a love for which there is no proper name. Media reports described this relationship as one between "boys" (hence withdrawing subjective responsibility by making it appear as an innocent or insignificant act); or between "special friends" (hence erasing sexuality); between a "minor and an ex-convict" (criminalization); or between "homosexuals" (medicalization) (see Suicidio su commissione, 2005). The older partner had been sentenced to jail for engaging in sexual relations with minors and for stealing. He therefore fitted the profile of the pedophile, the criminal of the sinful aberration, the new species described by Foucault in *History of Sexuality*. Ostracized by the community, made docile first through schooling and disciplinary reform later,[2] alienated by their kith and kin,[3] and made into unwilling examples of stupor and shame in newspapers for a day: these are the abject subjects of an impossible relationship.

An impossible relationship is a possible relationship that has been outlawed, one for which there is no proper name, a relationship in which the lovers are deprived of naming their bond or prevented from locating it within their speech. Indeed, the operation of naming that I am writing about refers to the act of becoming/recognizing the subject of the enunciation and should therefore not be mistaken for the activity of speaking, for in fact, as Lacan (1953) reminds us, most of the time we use empty words in our speech. The newspaper *Il Manifesto* stated: "In paese tutti sapevano del rapporto tra i due ragazzi, era anzi uno degli argomenti preferiti dei pettegolezzi da caffè" (In the village they knew of the relationship between the two boys; it was indeed one of the favorite topics of small talk at coffee time [Suicidio su commissione, 2005]). This small talk or empty speech is the discourse of rivalry, characteristic of imaginary relations, sustained in the illusion of a coherent ego.

The partners in this impossible relationship were positioned within their community as those who should not name their love. Going back to my discussion of the term negativity in chapter 1, I want to examine here what it means to occupy a position of negativity that is legitimated by the absolute power of others, a position that entails the annihilation of desire.

On the handwritten letter of good-bye found next to the lovers' bodies, Antonino Galatola and Giorgio Agatino wrote of their love without a name: "Our life has been intrinsically linked to the other's sayings. We can't live like this" (see Rossi Barilli, 1999; Suicidio su commissione, 2005, n/p; my translation). To live within a space of intimacy whose ontological status is purely dependent on the sayings of others means that the lovers do not say "We can't go on like this" or "We don't like it this way." They say, instead, "We cannot live like this." To my understanding, they are saying: "this life is not *human* life anymore."

There are at least two meanings of life at play in these statements. Following Lacanian theory, the life that interests me in this case refers to something other than the register of human experience or (imaginary) intersubjectivity. Indeed, as I have shown above, this life was acknowledged: they had a life for the others, they occupied a place within the community's imaginary, and the others spoke for them. What was lacking instead was proper symbolic recognition of their relationship or community legitimacy. Before the lives of these lovers were taken away by the suicide, they were already dead symbolically, and they were linked to each other by this death as well. It is the relationship to death on the one hand, and the extraordinary burden of the others of the community on the other, that makes this a real case study for exploring the Lacanian theses in *Seminar VII*.

Considering that one of the fundamental teachings of this seminar is that subjective responsibility is inseparable from the relationship that the subject establishes with the law, it might be useful to inquire about the functioning of the law in general and in this case in particular. The symbolic law is the arbiter of cultural mediation, translated as it is into social norms. Although particular norms cannot express the vastness of the symbolic, they can reflect it (see Fariña, 1999). It is important to remember as well that law—expressed at the level of language—structures the psychical life of the human subject.

There is therefore a logical articulation—although not a linear determination—between the order of norms (culture) and the structure of psychical life (subjectivity). Both are contingent, historical, or singular articulations of the symbolic law, as seen in the norms, for example, of the others of Giarre.

The relation between the subject and law is a relation of possibility, not of determination, for the subject (of the unconscious) appears in the interstices (symptoms, dreams, jokes, or between two signifiers), where desire fails to be completely articulated. Indeed, since all human interchanges and interactions are based on language structures and their derivates, the identity of law is symbolic, which is the same as saying that the only law is the law of the Signifier. Lacan (1960/2002) suggests, therefore, that the subject appears as a contingent element.

The case I am considering demands that a distinction be made between the order of norms or social customs and the order of law. For this reason, what follows here is a brief discussion on both orders as they appear conceptualized in Lacanian psychoanalysis. The symbolic law functions through interdiction (Lacan, 1953/2002), which is illustrative of the order of sexuality as recognized by Lévi-Strauss: in all cultures, at least one sexual object bears forbidden status. Such interdiction should not be mistaken for the norms written into codes. In each culture, something of the symbolic is inscribed in norms, but norms and codes can never completely codify the symbolic. Here it is useful to look toward etymology for further clarification. The Latin word for the act of inscription, *inscribire,* points to the effect of writing the law, which subjects nature to language. In this sense, law implies a sort of violence: it separates and orders while creating culture *ex nihilo*. However, Fariña's research[4] (1999) teaches that, for the very same reason that law means an activity of structure and order—that is, for the violence that its function implies—its effects can't be anticipated, and may be chaotic. In other words, the effects of the inscription of the law cannot be predictable before the act of the inscription itself, because they are a matter of conjecture, or a happening *a posteriori*, and count differently for each subject. One aspect of the inscription of the law is therefore always erratic and transitory, and, more important, it opens subjectivity—individual and social—to the encounter of the symbolic. In this sense, law and the symbolic cannot be separated; they are, as Italian philosopher Giorgio Agamben (1993) puts it, a *forma-di-vita* inextricably political:

All actions and forms of human living are prescribed not by any specific biological vocation, nor assigned to any necessity, but, in spite of being ordinary, repetitive, and socially prescribed, they consistently conserve the potential of being a possibility, that is, they always put into play the living itself. Because of this—namely, since it is a being of potency that can make and not make, succeed, or fail, lose or find itself—man [sic] is the only being in which living always implies being happy, whose life is irrevocably and painfully assigned to happiness. But this constitutes immediately the *forma-di-vita* as a *political living*. (Agamben, 1993, p. 108; my translation, emphasis added)

This statement is crucial for understanding that subjectivity is intertwined with the political, understood here as a form of primary social bond. Following this model, human subjectivity is not *pre*scribed, but *in*scribed into the symbolic. This act of inscription opens subjectivity to the potency of the political as a force in the way that Agamben's text suggests. The symbolic law is not guaranteed, but its inscription needs to be continually built upon. In other words, the law of the symbolic can operate only as refracted in particular forms (Fariña, 1999) in the norms of culture. Law does not operate in a void, but instead on the material supports offered by cultural codes. However, because particulars (norms) can never encode the universal completely, the refraction of the symbolic in codes is always erratic and incomplete. There is no system that encodes the symbolic completely, a reason why the symbolic always represents a surplus regarding the particulars (Ignacio Lewkowicz in Fariña, 1999). Law, then, is not something given from the beginning to endure unchanged forever, but instead is something that is *always being* inscribed and necessarily recoded.

In chapter 6, I will go back to the issue of death and sexuality while examining the filmic work of Özptek. Nevertheless, I would like to make a final comment here. The fact that the lovers take their lives but leave a letter next to their bodies is crucial for understanding the ethical dimension of the act. As in Antigone's act, these lovers compensate for the psychotic symbolic order in which they lived. Just a letter: a mark of the signifier offering a symbolic burial for the bodies. The letter in this case stands for the funeral rituals and guarantees that they will forever continue to be part of the human symbolic order, even if they had been forced to silence.

The Giarre case illustrates the danger for subjectivity of collapsing (confusing) the order of law (symbolic) and the order of norms (imaginary). The particular morality of a community was taken by its members to represent the supreme good, or imperative, crazy law to which *all* should comply. An "impossible" relationship was inconceivable under the dominance of the imperative law. This collapse therefore not only had tragic consequences for the two individuals Antonino Galatola and Giorgio Agatino, but also prevented the symbolic universe of a particular community to be recoded, or enlarged, by conceiving of *difference*. The imperative law is a law of sameness: what cannot be conceived under its rule does not exist, is silent, or is impossible. Had the community been open to thinking of its own difference (to think that it is intrinsic of any community to produce its own difference reflexively), another history could have been written.

The political consequences of the suicide of Antonino Galatola and Giorgio Agatino served to precipitate the founding of Arcigay, the national GLBTQ movement in Italy. This was an emergence fully comparable to an ethical gesture. It contrasted with, and resisted, the apathies and silence of the community of Giarre. Indeed, the first Arcigay association started in Palermo on December 9, 1980, two months after the tragic deaths of the two young lovers. Other Arcigay associations were subsequently established in various Italian cities (see Arcigay, 2005; Consoli, 2000; Rossi Barilli, 1999).

The End of the Decade

As in other parts of the world, the AIDS pandemic in Italy changed queer politics and precipitated the creation of the national group Arcigay. In affirming the need to assure effective dissemination of information through pamphlets and flyers, and in multiplying the number of small health centers or educational programs with the ministry of education and the health department to prevent the spreading of the disease (see Rossi Barilli, 1999), the Italian reaction to the pandemic differed little from that of other European countries. Each nation infused particular cultural values into these tactics, however. Larry Gross (1995) explains that in the United States

> the willingness of the gay movement to respect the privacy of political closets was increasingly strained in the late 1980s as the reactionary backlash against the gains of the 1970s was fueled with AIDS-induced association of gay sexuality and deadly disease. . .Just as the Third Reich forever changed the history of European Jews, revealing the fragility of the ground on which Jewish assimilation was built, the AIDS epidemic fundamentally affected the fate of gay people and dramatically reminded us of the deep-seated homophobia of American culture. (p. 33)

The sources I consulted indicate that the pandemic affected Italy later than the United States, and so, between the end of 1983 and the beginning of

1984, there was intense activity in gay groups, which tried to learn as much as possible about the disease and the means of infection. They also tried to keep the population informed and to counteract the morbid ways in which coverage of the "gay" disease was presented in the mass media. As in other countries, AIDS was first seen as an illness that targeted homosexuals and that was the result of promiscuity and perversity. The first known cases in Italy were reported in large cities with intense tourism—Rome and Milan. Newspapers covered the first cases as "gay cancer," or "gay plague" (Rossi Barilli, 1999).

Because of the relatively late arrival of the disease in Italy, gay groups had access to international media and medical information and tried to prepare the GLBTQ population before the pandemic. Rossi Barilli (1999) explains that the Mario Mieli cultural center and Arcigay worked in concert with the Instituto Superiore di Sanità (Advanced Institute of Health) and the Italian Ministry of Health to organize prevention and awareness campaigns against AIDS and other sexually transmitted diseases.

The origins of Arcigay are therefore contemporaneous with the AIDS pandemic, for the group strived to *degay*[5] AIDS (to make it more main-stream), following the strategies adopted in the United States (see Vaid, 1995), by retreating from the liberationist tactics of earlier decades and by ascribing the criticism to heterosexism. Opportunely, the AIDS pandemic translated into new programs oriented toward educating the GLBTQ and straight population and promoting the formation of national alliances across gay groups, an aim in which the organizers of Arcigay invested plenty of energy during the first years of the organization. Nevertheless, it should be pointed out that a strong difference between the Italian and North American experience regarding AIDS is that in Italy, as in other economically strong Western European countries, presumptions about AIDS and HIV are often tied not only to representations about homosexuality, but also to racial stereotypes and racial profiling. The role of educational campaigns is fundamental here. Nevertheless, immigrant groups coming to Italy from North African countries have been most affected by prejudice.

Although Arcigay had been founded in 1985 as the first Italian national network struggling for the human and civil rights of sexual minorities, it was only on June 20, 1986, that it held its first conference uniting most small groups. The event was called Omosessuali e Stato (Homosexuals and the State) and took place in the Sala del Cenacolo in the Parliament building

(Consoli, 2000). The work of Arcigay within parliamentary lines has been successful. The group has been functioning as a unifier for many regional centers and has achieved representation in Parliament. For instance, the third Arcigay congress, held in 1987, was attended by several members of Parliament (Arcigay, 2005). It was after this congress that Arcigay representatives started to press Parliament to pass a first proposal for legally registered partnerships and formulated the initial proposals to address discrimination based on sexual orientation. Every year, more and more individuals ask for an Arcigay membership—currently there are some 150,000 Arcigay members (see Arcigay, 2005). Writing as a person who has participated in the evolution of Italian gay politics, Rossi Barilli (1999) estimates that in actuality a much less significant number of members are currently actively involved in politics, and he laments that the majority of members enroll in the organization only to get discounts in gay bars and clubs or, one would say, to be "cool."

Consoli (2000), Gramolini (2000), and Rossi Barilli (1999) suggest that the beginnings of Arcigay were not easy, however; the ideal of achieving national coordination of all gay associations did not go unchallenged. In particular, some lesbian groups were critical about the male, phallocentric orientation of the group, and criticized the fact that the leaders of the organization were primarily men. In addition, not all factions agreed with the idea that Arcigay needed parliamentary participation, a movement that some regarded as assimilationist and regressive. Some feminists and lesbians, for example, believed that such politics belied the phallocentric inclinations of Arcigay's governance (see Gramolini, 2000). As an interesting way of resisting, some lesbians did not wait to be secondarily included within the programmatic lines of Arcigay, but started regular meetings on their own terms, right after long-term tensions between lesbian and gay groups exploded in 1989. This bloc of activists aimed to revitalize the spectrum of queer politics and to break free from a political arena represented as a male-only territory. The meetings led to the creation of Arcilesbica, introduced in Bologna in February 1990 and consolidated in 1996 (see Arcigay, 2005; Gramolini 2000). Eventually, the decision to create a national association was not politically appealing to all chapters and, as a result, activists in Turin, Firenze, Sassari, Verona, Catania, and Padova decided to act with autonomy (Arcigay, 2005).

Arcilesbica

As I suggested in chapter 2, there are several reasons why the political activism of women in Italy demands special consideration. One that stands out among them is the incessant search for a self-governing means of political activity and representation, independent of the ways in which FUORI! or Arcigay used to represent male gay sexuality. Nevertheless, the new quest for an autonomous lesbian symbolic was not only a response to the male dominance within the gay movement—both in number and in ideology—but also a reply to other groups, including the Italian feminist movement (see de Clementi, 2002). Because there have been theoretical and activist discrepancies between lesbian and feminist groups, the search for a common framework has not been easy, and discussion has led to intense debates about the intersections of these groups and their relations with (male) gay activism (see de Clementi, 2002). As in other parts of the world, the intersections between feminist and lesbian politics and the intersections between these politics and the gay movement in Italy imply considerations about different subjectivities and dissimilar political power, as well as intense discussions about what constitutes a female symbolic (Braidotti and Griffin, 2002). While there was tension between different coalitions of feminists, they could compromise and, by 1996, arrive at an agreement on how to move forward. The negotiations were important in offering a quick and practical response to the asymmetrical situation of women in Italy, and in drafting the constitution of Arcilesbica—a federal branch of Arcigay (see Gramolini, 2000).

The evolution of the lesbian movement in Italy is not separate from the erosion of the foundations of feminism, which can be conceptualized in terms of the instability of sex and gender. Judith Butler refers to this erosion as "a certain sense of trouble, as if the indeterminacy of gender might eventually culminate in the failure of feminism" (1990, p. vii). Because initial waves of feminism in the world were invested in the representation of "women," they relied upon the existence of a universal subject toward which it was possible to direct theoretical or political energies (Barker, 2004). Thus, the representation of women implied a notion of agency that was ultimately fixed. During the last two decades of the twentieth century, as is well known, feminist authors constructed frameworks from which to contest the assumption of a unique experience of women, and therefore criticized the notion of a uniform political representation of all women (see Barker, 2004). This criticism took the form of a paradigm concerned with the social construction of sex and gender, as was outlined in chapter 2.

Maria Cristina Gramolini's (2000) essay on the origins of Arcilesbica suggests that to judge the negotiations leading to the formation of Arcilesbica, it is important to remember that during the 1970s, the two most frequent venues for lesbians for getting involved in politics were either the mostly male gay FUORI! or the rather anti-lesbian feminist movement, a situation that complicated and delayed the consolidation of a pure lesbian organization. The word "pure" is useful here because the initial attempts to form such political affiliations were referred to as *separatism*—Gramolini explains—a word that came to characterize the Italian lesbian struggle to achieve differential political recognition. Indeed, it was only in the mid-1980s that some lesbian groups (Identità Lesbica [Lesbian Identity] first and Collegamento fra Lesbiche Italiane [Coalition of Italian Lesbians] later) started giving form to this differential form of political representation usually called *lesbofeminism* (Gramolini, 2000).

Lesbofeminism, Gramolini's essay suggests, defined more than an activist enterprise. It was above all a new type of identity and representation of the self with a clear philosophical purpose that emerged from years of being overshadowed by male subjectivity and symbolics. As such it was of particular importance for groups of women with fewer resources, either material or symbolic, who perceived that their status was structurally neglected in two ways: first as women, and second as lesbians (see Gramolini, 2000). More important, lesbofeminism intended to demonstrate the specificities of a subjectivity that cannot be considered equal to that of heterosexual women and/or male gays, but that includes problematics and pleasures that are unique in their own way. For these reasons, lesbofeminism was conceived of as intrinsically separatist, a political quality that would prove influential and remain crucial for lesbian politics (Gramolini, 2000).

In *Arcilesbica Perché* (Arcilesbica Because), Gramolini (2000) mordantly states that the lesbofeminist mobilization did not prosper because, more than being separatist, lesbians were *separated*. She suggests that no matter how much the lesbofeminists struggled, the kind of visibility necessary to attain a minimum degree of political recognition was never granted or achieved. The regrettable result, she shows, was that, by 1990, most lesbians preferred to adhere to the principles of the gay movement rather than to be completely alienated from the public sphere. That same year, therefore, discussions started within Arcigay about the possibility of creating an independent, women-only branch of the movement. By 1994, however, the question of lesbian political representation within Arcigay had worsened, and lesbian groups across Italy pushed Arcigay's agenda further (see Arcigay, 2005; Gramolini, 2000; Rossi Barilli, 1999).

The creation of Arcilesbica was finally facilitated by discussions around the Strasbourg Resolution, passed to secure equal rights to homosexual persons in the European Union. Roth (1993) reports that the purpose of the resolution was to establish that a sexual act between individuals of the same sex should not be forbidden under the European Convention of Human Rights. The Strasbourg Resolution was far from well received in Italy. According to Daniela Danna (1999), media campaigns were decisive in constructing a negative representation of homosexuality in Italy immediately following the resolution, and they opposed the unification of gay and lesbian factions under the umbrella of Arcigay. As had happened before, Danna (1999) explains, media coverage attempted to manipulate Italian conservative morals, this time using the case of a child from Savona, in northern Italy, who was living with two stepmothers. She further documents that, in an opinion poll commissioned by the agency Panorama for the Cirm Institute at the pinnacle of the mass media debate, 77 percent of the Italian population was decisively against the adoption of a child by a same-sex couple (Danna, 1999). The National Committee of Bioethics issued a document on new reproductive technologies stating that homosexual individuals did not match the selection standard for the use of fertilization technologies. The document argued that "such criterion suggests that, in general, the better [sic] condition in which a child can be born is being conceived and raised from one couple of adults of different sex: a married couple, or at least stably tied by community of life and love" (cited in Danna, 1999, p. 4). Similar documents issued during the 1990s troubled lesbian (and gay) groups. In her report, Danna suggests that particularly controversial was the 1998 law on fertilization, which excluded homosexual and single persons from the right to use reproductive technology. This took place, one might add, at a time when there were ads placed in news magazines by wealthy heterosexual couples looking for donors with blue eyes and an elevated IQ. Not only a homophobic, but also a mercantile ethics separated those who could afford the use of these technologies from those who were discriminated against based on their sexual orientation.[6]

Parody animated the approach of lesbian groups in the 1980s regarding the use (or rather, selective proscription) of reproductive technologies. A memorable example is a 1998 Arcilesbica awareness campaign that included a mock kit for self-insemination. At the center of an image for the "kit," there were two (perhaps lesbian) pregnant women and behind them, in the top right corner, a (perhaps gay) pregnant man. In a defiant pose, they smile condescendingly. They also hoist protesting flags with the iconic elements of the kit: spermatozoids, a syringe, and gloves. On the bottom right, a conservative (perhaps Social Democrat) Member of Parliament is hiding in embarrassment behind a doctor from the National Committee of Bioethics. Finally, a heterosexual couple standing on the right completes the image. The man looks down in anger, arms crossed, almost as if parodying the constraints of a straightjacket. The image can be interpreted in two ways. First, it codifies the sentiment raised and expressed by the actual protest of the lesbian groups. Second, it can be read as a reverse discourse. In this case, the image asks any reader how heterosexual people would feel if gays and lesbians were the only ones with access to reproductive technologies. In this sense, the image mimics the social construction of gendered positions and the body as the privileged product of contested power relations, as evident in the portrayal of the pregnant man.

When different lesbian groups finally came to the agreement that a national coalition be created, it was called Arcilesbica and consolidated as part of Arcigay. The final resolution that formalized the institution was signed two years later, though (see Arcigay, 2005; Gramolini, 2000; Rossi Barilli, 1999). It is worth citing the following paragraph of one founding document in its entirety:

> Arcilesbica is born in times when the exigency to start working in a politically autonomous space is absolutely inescapable. Such space needs to be visibly lesbian, far away from the constraints of the usually neutral gay politics (and we know that neutral means male), but at the same time far away from the separatist way of thinking that we consider now to have been left behind long ago. The urgency that has moved us is that of constructing an organization that will become an instrument to intervene within the political and social life of Italy, to neutralize any form of discrimination, to oppose even diffuse forms of prejudice, to attain justice. This will be an instrument rooted in our national territory to involve all lesbians—from the North and from the South—as well as to encourage the dialogue with local and central institutions. Therefore, the foundation of our choice is the affirmation of the principle of autodetermination, and the will to represent lesbianism in our contemporary society. (Cited in Gramolini, 2000, p. 117; my translation)

Surely, I agree with Gramolini that the creation of Arcilesbica represented the most significant achievement of the homosexual community in
Italy during the period from 1980 to 1996. It was a political victory with
consequences not only for lesbians, but also for all of the gay movement, and
it was a material, symbolic victory in which the power extended beyond the
private sphere of the political movement as well. More than anything,
Arcilesbica has implied the concrete materialization of years of struggle of
lesbians in Italy. This is a gigantic step in a country where the visibility of
this group is minimal. The effect of founding Arcilesbica is, for this reason,
far-reaching. In inscribing Arcilesbica as a social institution, there is a
symbolic gain for all Italians, not only for lesbians. It affects the working of
the symbolic as a whole insofar as a social institution guarantees the inscription of this subjectivity within culture, but in doing so there is a surplus that
modifies the whole social domain. Creating a social institution like Arcilesbica enlarges, literally, the limits of the cultural symbolic, and opens up
space for future reforms and for the symbolic inscription of other groups who
continue to be similarly discriminated against. Arcilesbica affected the whole
gay movement in reversing stereotypes and practices that tend to reify sexual
and gender differences. The affecting of the symbolic I am referring to
implies not only creating a way of speaking and doing that enables new
representations, but also the effective materialization of resources available
to guarantee the existence of Otherness. This is clear in the debates about
transgender subjectivities, which came to the forefront of the Arcigay agenda
only after the creation of Arcilesbica. Indeed, before Arcilesbica, both gay
men and lesbians had adopted an ambiguous position regarding the political
visibility of sexual difference (as well as class and race difference) in Italy,
an ambiguity that subtly admitted the existence of lesbians at the same time
that it kept them at the margins of what was considered to be politically
correct. The public and private struggle involved in the creation of Arcilesbica illustrates that internalized homophobia is a powerful force that operates
from within, and not only from afar. Even if not purposely, the gay movement had partly contributed to the silencing of sexual difference, sometimes
reproducing the patriarchal and heterosexual structure of society that it was
supposed to defy. Finally, Arcilesbica reminds us that the self is always
political, and the private sometimes coincides with the public. As Gramolini
(2000) puts it, "the heterosexual fate of women can only be resisted if one

speaks out as a lesbian. It is fundamental to raise lesbianism to the political level, to take it outside the purely private sphere" (p. 119; my translation).

A New Beginning

While the United Nations' Universal Declaration of Human Rights (Articles 2, 7, 12, 16, 22, and 30) is fervent about the recognition of the universal human right to create a family, and while it speaks against discrimination, the situation for GLBTQs in Italy and other countries continues to demonstrate that the way each country interprets and puts into practice these codes differs greatly from what the international agreements express. This is, one more time, an example of a gap between the symbolic law and the norms that only partially reflect it. For instance, in the United States, same-sex partnerships are not legally recognized in all fifty states. And in many cases, recognition does not even embrace legitimate civil unions, but merely offers contracts that bind two individuals and that grant them some very limited rights (see Jacques, 2004). In addition, civil unions in the United States differ drastically from those in European countries, particularly from those of Denmark, France, Greenland, Iceland, the Netherlands, Norway, and Sweden. For instance, the French PACS is a legal national contract, while civil unions or registered partnerships in the United States are sometimes valid only within the boundaries of a city.

The French contract is quite exemplary. It creates obligations, protections, and rights that can be compared (in some aspects) to those that heterosexual marriage grants in many countries. In contrast, civil unions in the United States do not offer the partners the benefits that are offered by a marriage license. As Jacques (2004) puts it, "couples in a civil union have no access to the federal laws like the Family and Medical Leave Act, to equal immigration rights, to continued health care coverage. Under federal law, same-sex couples are strangers" (p. 1). In the United States, the situation of same-sex couples and the rights that would derive from passing a law on civil unions have raised the most intense debates. For example, many members of the GLBTQ community of the United States were shocked to discover on February 24, 2004, that George W. Bush had announced his support for a constitutional amendment banning same-sex marriage, which would eventually divide the U.S. population before the national elections that year. The political move outraged militant groups, with some activists calling it a declaration of war on gay and lesbian Americans (see Jacques, 2004).

In Europe, according to ILGA-Europe, same-sex marriage, partnership, and parenting have usually been respected as issues that fall under the aegis of national legislation. Because the EU is more and more interested in creating common ground in legal matters for all the countries within the union, this respect for national norms has been undergoing changes that might eventually result in common laws that will apply to all EU participants. As a result, the boundaries between international, national, and regional legal competency are being gradually blurred. These changes were documented in the 2003 report *Families, Partners, Children and the European Union* that was released by the renowned European Region of the International Lesbian and Gay Association (ILGA-Europe). It states that the situation of GLTB European people is far from symmetric within all the countries of the region. Some European countries that are members of the union, including Italy, continue to oppose new policies regarding the administration of the family and parenting (ILGA-Europe, 2004).

Apart from the already-mentioned Strasbourg Resolution, other texts with equal emphasis on recognizing the human rights of sexual minorities were drafted at human rights conventions. They agree on advising authorities in European countries of the extreme importance of securing equality of treatment and parity of opportunity to sexual minorities and same-sex couples. These documents are explicit about the need to offer guarantees that protect individuals in a same-sex relationship so that they do not feel discriminated against and so that they are treated before the law as heterosexual couples are (see Danna, 1999). The European Parliament has affirmed, in addition, that it is opposed to any form of discrimination, either cultural or legal, based on sexual orientation. Further, it encourages all member countries of the union to address and resolve any impediments to the guarantee of equal rights for same-sex matrimony, parenthood, or adoption (see ILGA-Europe, 2004).

It is most unfortunate that these documents have failed many times to be fully appreciated in some countries, including Italy, and that they have not always had long-term practical repercussions, particularly in the case of securing same-sex unions. The current absence of fully comprehensive national laws in Italy in this respect is quite disturbing. Indeed, while it is clear that each country has the power to administer and interpret these documents in its own way, the fact that there is a corpus of documents advising legal recognition of same-sex couples that in practice are not followed or enforced, might confirm Urvashi Vaid's (1995) perception that gays and lesbians continue to be mainstreamed, condemned to live in a state of virtual equality:

> The irony of gay and lesbian mainstreaming is that more than fifty years of active effort to challenge homophobia and heterosexism have yielded us not freedom but "virtual equality," which simulates genuine civic equality but cannot transcend the simulation. In this state, gay and lesbian people possess some of the trappings of full equality but are denied all of its benefits. We proceed as if we enjoy real freedom, real acceptance, as if we have won lasting changes in the laws and mores of our nation. . .[b]ut the actual facts and conditions that define gay and lesbian life demonstrate that we have won "virtual" freedom and "virtual" equal treatment under "virtually" the same laws as straight people. (p. 4)

Vaid's testimonial, written the same year the Strasbourg Resolution was released, continues to be applicable in Italy a decade later. According to ILGA-Europe (2004), the Italian penal code is blind to the issue of anti-lesbian or anti-gay discrimination, and the Constitution does not make available anti-discriminatory protections regarding sexuality and sexual orientation. In addition, the penal code does not offer legal shelter for sexual minorities. Same-sex couples, partnerships, and unions are not legally recognized by Italian jurisprudence in any definite form, anywhere in the country (ILGA-Europe, 2004).

ILGA-Europe (2004) also reports that Members of Parliament have presented several proposals for civil unions, the first in December 1993 by the PDS (Partito Democratico Socialista or Social Democratic Party), the PR (Partito Radicale or Radical Party), and the RC (Rifondazione Comunista or Communist Reformist Party). The second proposal, always following the ILGA-Europe's document, was presented by the Green Party to the Tenth and Eleventh Legislatures. Finally, in the Thirteenth Legislature, a proposal for civil unions was presented in three bills: two in the Chamber of Deputies and one in the Senate. It is worth emphasizing that only married couples are currently granted the right to adopt; for example, the *affido familiare* (the custody of a child) is a right usually bestowed upon single or married people. However, in practice, homosexuality is more an obstacle than a vehicle to being granted custody. Finally, while some local authorities from cities like Pisa or Bologna have tried to introduce partnership registries, these are symbolic registries that do not specify the gender of the parties involved and are not granted the protection of the rights of a civil union, partnership, or marriage (see ILGA-Europe, 2004).

In 1994, the Strasbourg document generated much discomfort within Italian mainstream society. Former Pope John Paul II, for example, declared in front of a crowd gathered in Piazza San Pietro that

> what is morally inadmissible is the juridical approval of homosexual practice. . . This parliamentary resolution is asking to legitimate a moral disorder. . .The union of two men or two women cannot constitute a true family. What is more, the right to adopt children that are deprived of a family cannot be attributed to such unions. These children are therefore at risk of being hurt, because in these "surrogate families" they would not find a father or a mother, but "two fathers" or "two mothers." This is most dangerous. (Cited in Rossi Barilli, 1999, p. 220; my translation)

The current pope, Benedict XVI (Cardinal Ratzinger during the 1990s), is also vehement in his anti-gay pronouncements. For instance, he has been instrumental in the creation of orthodox writings of the Congregation for the Doctrine of the Faith, a document that surprised even U.S. Catholics by its intransigent repudiation of the United States's anti-discrimination laws regarding homosexuals. Interviewed about his position, Ratzinger affirmed that

> there are spheres where it is not unjust to discriminate against sexual orientation: for example, in the case of adoption or step-parenting of a child; in hiring teachers [of all levels] or instructors of physical education; or in the military. In fact it is not only licit [to discriminate against them], but mandatory. (Cited in Rossi Barilli, 1999, p. 213; my translation)

Mani Pulite

Italians witnessed the debacle of the fall of the First Republic following the *Mani Pulite* (Clean Hands) investigations that dated back to 1992. These investigations revealed that a number of Italian politicians had been conducting business illegally and that a number of well-known personalities had been involved in the laundering of money, or had used funds from the public administration to benefit their own affiliates and businesses. The episode had the unfortunate effect of strengthening ideas about *familismo*, bribery, bureaucracy, *partitocrazia*, and meritocracy in the nation (see Eve, 1996; Ginsborg, 2003). Although there had been reports about possible misdeeds taking place in Parliament and public offices (Testa, 2002), it was not until

1992 that investigations yielded results. That year, businessman Mario Chiesa was found trading bank notes in his office, Testa reports. This was just one of the first cases to become public, but after Chiesa's there followed innumerable accusations and trials that extended as a *Tangentopoli*, that is, with subterranean roots.[7] Chiesa confessed and provided the names of other administrative parties involved in money laundering. Soon a number of the individuals arrested, all related in some way to the administration, began to incriminate more and more politicians and businesspeople, creating a sort of domino effect that implicated the leaders of the Socialist Party (see Eve, 1996; Testa, 2002). In assessing corruption in Italy, British political analyst Michael Eve (1996) calls for prudence:

> There is no real reason to doubt that Italy has been exceptional among Western nations in the extent of its public corruption. However, we should be clear that it is only under certain conditions—fostered partly by the awareness created by newspapers, academics, and political polemicists, by changes in the conceptions of how far it is acceptable for an investigator to go in probing suspicions, and by many other ultimately social factors—that many forms of corruption emerge to the light of day and are successfully proved in court. (pp. 38-39)

Eve's caution is justified in light of the tendency to judge the Italian political system using an implicit comparison with the United States or Britain, thus failing to notice the many historical, cultural, and ideological differences between the countries. Stereotypes of Italy as backward and corrupt usually rely on idealized visions of other "advanced" capitalist societies. For Eve, these visions suffer from anachronism and reductionism in that they reinforce the misconception that there is only one polity that is valid or democratic. Indeed, Eve clarifies that corruption cannot be interpreted without examining the laws that make certain acts illegal. Therefore, some cultural historians (Doumanis, 2001) are inclined to evaluate with some optimism the cultural effects of Tangentopoli. In this interpretation, the end of the First Republic might signal the beginning of new forms of identification that depict Italy as a nation that requires the reconstruction of its political and civic bases, a process in which citizenship and commitment would play a crucial role for the first time in the history of the country.

Visibility or Desexualization, Again

As suggested earlier, following Vaid's (1995) model, one of the adversarial consequences of the AIDS pandemic for the gay movement was that, in order to unchain homosexuality from the disease, some GLBTQ movements' representatives were challenged to make queer life more mainstream. This has had the effect of appeasing the earlier radical political basis of the movement. On the other hand, at a time when most providers of health care were public in Italy, mainstreaming AIDS had the advantage of making sure that an equal infrastructure of resources, services, and treatment options would be provided to all individuals, no matter what their sexual orientation.

While the AIDS pandemic forced activists to un-queer gayness, Vaid teaches, it also served to queer heterosexuality—it has made gayness a more pervasive lifestyle, a highly aesthetic condition, a widespread *fin de siècle* commodity. By bringing up Vaid's (1995) criticism of *de-gaying*, I am not implying that there is an essential gay identity. *De-gaying* homosexuality means that conceptions about homosexuality are made to appear as a condition that is genetic, or it appears as an innate psychological orientation (pathological or not); concomitantly, it is an acritical perspective that eclipses inquiries about the social structures that produce and modify sexuality (see Vaid, 1995).

In the above sections, I have briefly discussed the progress and challenges to making homosexuality (and, more generally, non-normative sexuality) visible. For queers, this has meant sustaining strategies that could offer us the opportunity to express ourselves by means of activism and by the creation of new spaces for participation and sharing. Nevertheless, making queer closer to normal has also implied desexualization of queer politics. Clearly, this is one option facing the extremely difficult task of countering stereotypes and queer panic. And it has not been in vain, for we have won many struggles, first through activism, later through theory, educational programs, and literature. Following Vaid's (1995) model, it could be argued also that in Italy we now live in a cultural space of virtual acknowledgment, which entails deep paradoxes. For example, we now have a larger number of publications (though minimal in comparison to academic journals and educational programs in other countries), and we even count with important publishing houses like Feltrinelli and smaller editorial projects that create and publish books on queer theory and queer life in Italy, replacing the semi-clandestine publishing output of older, smaller publishing houses that were active during the 1970s (such as Kaos, La Tartaruga, and La Salamandra) (Consoli, 2000; Rossi Barilli, 1999). Nevertheless, queers are still minimally present in the academic and research system (either "out" as producers of knowledge or "queer" as a topic of research) and are usually constrained to hide their sexuality in workplaces, social meetings, and religious assemblies. The increasing appearance of gay characters and themes in films (a particular issue that I will discuss in chapter 6) is a positive development, yet it has been accompanied by the increasing mercantilization of sexuality and, in some cases, the vulgarization of queerness in reality shows. Representations of homosexuality in television and films continue to be deeply homophobic, although importing and adopting the global network gay.com or creating local venues like Gay TV, Italy have had a tremendous impact on erotic and personal life. Queers struggle for a PACS agreement in Parliament, and there are official representatives, like Vladimir Luxuria, engaging in intense and significant political activity. Yet laws protecting queer rights at work or the right to form a queer family are still withheld.

As Vaid's (1995) model suggests, sustaining a paradoxical existence might be the result of supporting visibility, a reasonable approach to resisting silence and ostracism. In fact, Vaid explains that, in the North American case, mainstreaming gayness was perhaps a reasonable strategy that aimed at reworking and debasing social prejudice against homosexuality, making a whole population aware of the importance of speaking out. But mainstream visibility has entailed immense costs. As Vaid (1995) suggests, by the mid-1990s, "as we have won the slow battle to secure coverage of AIDS and gay issues in the straight media, we have suffered from a collapse of critical thinking and a retreat from political analysis" (p. 80).

I began this chapter by discussing the domestic and international circum-stances that eclipsed FUORI! and gave birth to Arcigay. Now, in evoking the radical liberationist politics of the 1970s, I do not want to linger in nostalgia. Instead, I am evoking the potential of earlier gay liberationist practices and ideas for the practical use and the ideological potency that they have for current gay activism in Italy. In chapter 5, I will continue my discussion of these processes, this time with a particular emphasis on gay marriage and family. In agreeing with Lehr's (1999) and Vaid's (1995) discussions, I also want to emphasize that in Italy queer activism has been deeply influenced by the power of white men with financial resources and political connections. A queer movement that is minimally interested in paying attention to ethnic and racial identities is, however, a deficient queer movement. It is important to think of an alternative, more energetic, and more inclusive basis for our politics. In times when same-sex marriage and parenthood are at the center of the Italian gay organization, to keep our hopes in being queer and not normal is more than an act of rebelliousness—it is an orientation toward resistance and active Otherness.

cs **Chapter 5** so
Redefining the Meanings of
Marriage and Family

After the "Clean-Hands" investigations, Italians faced the challenge of building a Second Republic. Koff and Koff (2000) suggest that political parties had to consider what major reconfigurations their organizations and the country would have to undergo in order to assure the electorate that corruption had finally been eradicated. Party politics after the *Mani Pulite* investigations would never be the same, as new, more severe mechanisms for continual control of the political activities were initiated inside each party and Parliament. The First Republic, formed in 1948 with the ratification of the post-war Constitution, appeared now to have been eroded by the cases of corruption and the resulting social discontent with the ruling groups for their dishonest political behavior and under-the-table financial alliances (see Koff and Koff, 2000). By the 1990s, the fall of the Berlin Wall and the extension of capitalism as a way of life (individualism, consumerism, materialism) had very much diminished the influence of communism, and its meta-narrative was not as influential as in the past in determining the choices that many Italians made at the ballot box (see Cento Bull, 2001). The collapse of communism fostered a post-state political subjectivity, enlarged private ownership of previously state-administered services, and decentralized in part the organization of regions. Authors indicate three forms of agency that influenced the March 1994 elections in the creation of a Second Republic: political groups—including a new coalition of center-right ruling parties, private agencies, and governmental decentralization (Koff and Koff, 2000). The Second Republic also represents a turning point in the economy of Italy, characterized by the progressive expansion of multinational corporations within the country and by a more aggressive role for Italy as a player within the European Union. This dynamic has had important repercussions in different areas of social life, from consumption to labor to social relations (see Ginsborg, 2003).

Concomitant with the transition to the Second Republic has been a modification of conceptualizations of intimacy and sexuality as reflected in the increasing visibility of gays and lesbians in the media; a number of gay parades; a certain androgynous form of eroticism in fashion design and art; and the great political investment of gay organizations in legalizing same-sex unions. Beginning in the 1990s, the issue of legal unions turned into a pressing political issue on human rights and gay organizations' agendas, including those of Arcigay and Arcilesbica. The discussion of this political choice and its concomitant effects are at the heart of this chapter. In particular, I will explore here the way in which the family as an evolving social construct has and is being redefined through narratives and signifying practices.

Global/Local

In a book published at the beginning of the AIDS pandemic in the United States, Dennis Altman (1982) delivered a legendary commentary on the relationship between sociopolitical change and identity. He situated the 1970s as the decisive decade in the homosexualization of America. Curiously, this period also coincided, Altman suggested, with the beginning of a worldwide Americanization of homosexuality. Looking back at those years, Altman was puzzled by the direction in which sexual mores evolved. The breaking of rigid norms governing sexual life could have made sexual preferences irrelevant, he argued. Instead, these rules seemed to become progressively more inflexible, and civic and religious morals more oppressive, proving that "in Western societies homosexuality is far more than a matter of whom one goes to bed with; it is rather something that affects the whole fabric of everyday life" (Altman, 1982, p. viii). What captured Altman's attention was that this happened during the same decades (1960s and 1970s) that gays and lesbians became highly visible internationally.

Altman described the American gay identity that materialized during the 1970s as the product of patterns of behavior, use of symbols, and group cohesion. In addition, he argues that in the United States, racial, ethnic, and religious markers have historically enabled individuals to identify with others and join their struggles. In this interpretive model, these forms of identity can be said to precede the formation of a gay identity that evolved during the

1970s in the United States. Until the 1970s, identity politics was the "trademark" of American social movements. Among other reasons, the high visibility of American gays and lesbians served to extend identity politics' notions to other nations where queers had also begun to organize. Identity politics did not always thrive in other countries, though; the philosophy of this politics sometimes supposed the existence of separate, stable homosexual identities, at odds with the social background of a number of European[1] and Latin American countries where identity does not form the grounds for social life or political activity.

Michael Warner (2002) explains that:

> The Anglo-American world sports a heavily identitarian culture. . . .Consumer culture, to begin with, accustoms us to link up choice, affect, display, and identity. . . .In this context queerness reads as a public affirmation of the expressive/affective complexities that underwrite personal singularity. (p. 213)

Instead, notions of class and ideology might be more significant in the social composition of countries like Italy or Argentina, and might be (or might have been for some time) at the center of GLBTQ movements' agendas like FUORI! The rise of a consumer society during the 1980s and 1990s coincided with the demise of these movements and the attempt to incorporate identity politics. In the case of FUORI!, as I have suggested, its collapse activated the creation of Arcigay, which sometimes emulated foreign political strategies, in particular the defense of civil rights like PACS.

Arcigay allowed the queer movement in Italy to survive and grow, although over the years, and due to internal as well as external circumstances, the GLBTQ movement softened its political bases. Nevertheless, the internationalization of gayness has not proceeded mechanically, and since Italy is a country with rigid class differences, class and ideology continue to be central issues for all political groups (Dickie, 1996).

Indeed, Italian queer politics is inseparable from the nation's complex colonial past, a live history in which race and sexuality are deeply interconnected. The history of Italy's colonization by France, Germany, and Spain meant that for years, parts of the country were retained or claimed as territories (see de Lauretis, 1988). Colonial stories have been recoded in foundational myths about the regions, in the emblems and flags for cities, and in chants and dances, and they feature quite prominently in the strong linguistic, architectural, and culinary variations seen in cities such as Aosta, Trieste, and Naples. Teresa de Lauretis explains:

> Many Italians today refer to themselves as citizens of a Third World country, which they are in many ways, not simply economically. And I would add that part of the appeal of Gramsci for the critique of colonial discourse may come from his consciousness, as a Sardinian (an islander), of colonial economic oppression within the Italian context. When people here [in the United States] speak of Europe as synonymous with the West, as the homogeneous place of origin of white supremacy and imperialism toward "the rest of the world" (as it is typically put), they ignore the histories of internal colonization, not to mention various forms of class, sexual, and religious oppression, within Europe and within each country of Europe. So that words like Eurocentric (vs. Afrocentric, for example) are highly relative to the United States context and to assume otherwise is to put the United States at the center of the world no less than Reagan does. (1988, p. 1)

Similarly, as I noted in the introduction to this book, there is a particular history of homosexuality in Italy that is not linked accidentally to its colonial past. Once upon a time, Italy was a country regarded as highly homoerotic (Nardi, 1998). Ideas about the *Italian vice* tinted homoerotic fantasies about the Mediterranean's sexual liberty, from ancient Rome's orgies to the persecution of Florentines during the Renaissance, and to the late nineteenth century, when the southern coasts of Sicily were visited by wealthy and adventurous British gentlemen.

In the last decade, queer writers, once criticized for their historical amnesia (Jagose, 1996), have turned their attention to the cultural evolution of sexuality (Hawley, 2001). In this effort, we try to complicate the meanings of sexuality in an attempt to demonstrate the political, cultural, and psychical production of desire as social labyrinths where, for instance, heterosexuality and homosexuality are just two of the many modes of intimacy/love/sex. Redefining intimacy is indeed a battle to extend the barriers of everything preconceived as given by nature, tradition, or secured order, so that something formerly nameless or whispered with shame conquers the realm of legitimate speech. According to Barbagli and Colombo (2001), Italian queers are participating in this process as never before in the history of the country. They

> do not define their behavior as active or passive. . . they no longer have asymmetric relationships based on superiority and inferiority, domination and subordination, but relationships based on reciprocity and equality. They do not live in the secret of an endured isolation and do not meet in clandestine places, but count with a wide net-

work of associations and organizations exclusively for them that supports their identity. (p. 13; my translation)

The globalization of queerness poses new challenges for the remaking of intimacy, though. While for Altman (1982) the Americanization of homosexuality implied "the adoption [by other nations] of styles and fashions associated with an increasingly visible and assertive gay minority" (p. xii), discussions about the internationalization of gayness should incorporate the historical and social distinctions of each country where the gay movement took particular forms.[2] The American version of gay activism has become a cornerstone for many Italian gays and lesbians, illustrated by the use of U.S. erotica, the adoration of pop-music divas (which replaced the cult for the more voluptuous kind of diva, like Sophia Loren), the display of symbols like the rainbow or the pink triangle instead of the *manifesto rivoluzionario*, and by the use of English words like *gay, pride, queer,* and so on (see Nardi, 1998). What is more, queerness has not remained detached from the dynamics of consumerism and market globalization. This has been pointed out by several queer-theory writers. Following author Carl Stychin (2005), for example, it is possible to argue that consumer capitalism has generalized a gay identity—usually around liberal values like freedom of choice, individualism, and rationality—although it is dangerous to assume that the queer politics of advanced capitalist countries are mechanically copied in other parts of the world (Herdt, 1997; Plummer, 1992).

Examples of the way the American gay consciousness is negotiated in Italy are clear in (gay) popular culture. During a visit to Milan, my partner and I went to a gay club with some friends. At the entrance, we were presented with the March 2005 issue of a gay-friendly magazine. The issue did not differ from previous ones in the excellent variety and quality of articles, nor in the number of advertisements, probably the most important source of financial support for this periodical. A third of the pages in the issue were full-page ads, including half-page ads. There were ads for gay saunas, G&L tourism, hot chat lines, rainbow cell phones, drags and strippers, queer-friendly bars, discos, and clubs. All of the ads had at least one foreign language mark; most were partially written in English, and some could have been taken from any gay magazine in the world.

Particularly interesting is a two-page ad for an American pornographic film company. Within the last generation of Italians, a product once clandestine has become corporate, a click away from a home PC screen or available in hotel rooms, saunas, and even discos. Gay porn consumed in Italy is mostly American: porn companies enjoy the profits that come from the $10 billion that consumers of porn spend yearly in adult entertainment in some countries (Porn in the United States, 2004). Interestingly, the advertising in the magazine displays the boxes of the DVDs with their original name in English, but next to them there are small reviews telling part of the story in Italian. I mention this example to illustrate one way in which the internationalization of homosexuality includes patterns of consumption, production of aesthetics, and uses of the body that are always hybrid. One of the effects of global capitalism is the reduction of individuals to consumers of commodities. Capitalism creates, through the act of interpellation, a subject of consumption, producing not only goods and services, but the consumers of these items as well.

Transforming Intimacies

Italy, though profoundly different and distinct from other countries in Western Europe, shares with them some structural changes regarding population, demographics, aging workforce, and fertility rates that I will be discussing in this chapter. Italy is far from being the only country in which GLBTQ advocates are pressing for legal unions: in fact, it is one of the few Western European countries where these unions have not yet been granted in one way or another. But whereas in countries like the United States political debates for legal same-sex unions have been framed sometimes in terms of marriage (Warner, 1999), in Italy discussions have mostly centered about the legitimacy of domestic partnerships and on proposals for a civil pact of solidarity. This is interesting because one would wonder why, in a country where marriage has many times worked as the cornerstone for the family, queers have attempted to distance themselves from such a model. Indeed, as was explained earlier, it would have been quite futile to advocate anything like marriage, exactly because marriage as an institution continues to be considered a privilege of heterosexual couples. Instead, framing discussions around a contract for civil unions has the advantage of soothing debates and making the point that the rights we long for do not constitute a threat to the more traditional, nuclear family. The contract of civil unions—similar to the French Pacte Civil de Solidarité (Civil Pact of Solidarity, or PACS), which I will discuss below—is a legal agreement that binds two people independently of their sexual orientation or relationship. For the most part, all major

Italian gay organizations have agreed to pursue the parliamentary approval of an Italian Patto Civile di Solidarietà, modeled after the French agreement. This is not to suggest that all gay parties agree with the main points of PACS, as political and theoretical perspectives on the question of same-sex relationships vary from fierce opposition to fervent endorsement of state legitimacy. Nevertheless, sufficient concurrence has existed among gay representatives to present to Parliament a draft of PACS. As discussed in the introduction, although similar bids were made earlier, this is the first time in history that the Italian Parliament might agree to consider a proposal on gay unions, although (as I mentioned earlier) in the summer of 2006 authorities suggested that the proposal does not constitute an urgent item on their agenda. Given this context, it is imperative to question the social conditions in which this proposal is being presented and considered in Parliament. So far, the proposal has not been approved. If it were to be passed, however, it would perhaps reaffirm variations in the understanding and remaking of intimacy, sexuality, and family.

At this point, it is useful to define some terms that I will be using throughout this chapter and that might clarify the tension between local and global in relation to queer issues in Italy.

In the context of my discussion, globalization refers to a sustained process that takes time and in which the world's physical, political, and economic frontiers are challenged, renegotiated, and oriented to the strengthening of a world-system consciousness (Robertson, 1992) based mainly on North American capitalist values. In this process, following Barker (2004), national and international, global and local, do not have independent value, but constitute more and more an uninterrupted progression of interconnections sometimes referred to as *glocalization*:

> The idea of the local, specifically what is considered to be local, is produced within and by globalizing discourses. This includes capitalist marketing strategies which orientate themselves to differentiated "local" markets. An emphasis on particularity and diversity can be regarded as an increasingly global discourse. (Barker, 2004, p. 174)

Global and local are slippery constructs when examining the domain of identity. In this interpretation, identities are not given as a natural datum. Instead they are dense psychological, social, and cultural constructs that change over time and which are therefore influenced by processes that escape the sphere of rationality of the individuals, whose identities might be reshaped, oftentimes without them taking complete notice of the process in which they are immersed. It is important to keep in mind that cultural studies scholars stress that meanings, signifiers, images, institutions, practices, emblems, objects of consumption, and even behaviors are often not mutually and symmetrically negotiated by all the parties involved in the course of making identity, but rather they are imposed, sold, exported to, or appropriated from the center to the periphery (see Barker, 2004). This chain of appropriation/negotiation/remaking of the self describes relationships that develop between countries as well as *within* countries, particularly in nations like Italy, where there are deep economic and social discrepancies between urban centers and small villages, between North and South, and between the continental part of the country and the islands.

Second, the increased visibility of queer life internationally is often linked to the postmodern condition, wherein the over-saturation of media substitutes for past or local meta-narratives. There are multiple, contesting implications in the term *postmodern*. Some authors use it as an economic marker, denoting the passage from Fordism to post-Fordism (Barker, 2004). Sometimes the word *postmodern* is used simply to refer to the opposite of modern or, conversely, to indicate its ultimate form. For Dennis Altman (2002), a "*modern* society retains particular assumptions around sexuality and gender derived from earlier periods, and often enforced through religious and cultural ideologies" (p. 3). This passage seems to suggest that earlier understandings of sexuality are very different from those in neoliberal or consumer societies. In other circumstances, however, postmodern refers to a more progressive extension or culmination of modernity into the present. For instance, in his analysis of non-marital and non-reproductive intimacies, Anthony Giddens (1992) terms *pure relationships* the culmination of a gradual change that transformed the eighteenth century's courtly love to the current experimentation with pleasure and sexuality. At other times, the term postmodern describes fluidity and uncertainty at the center of current human relationships. This uncertainty contrasts with past, romanticized, linear relationships (Stacey and Davenport, 2002).

Working in unison with several connotations of a word like postmodern avoids reducing its multiple meanings. For example, I use Giddens's description of postmodern intimacies when stressing that contemporary relationships are formed independently from reproduction. In addition, I sometimes refer to the break between linearity and uncertainty as suggested by Stacey and Davenport (2002). Similar to Altman, I also use the term *postmodern* to suggest deep interrelations between political economic processes and sexuality. Following Vincent Rocchio's (1999) analysis of post-war Italian cinema, I use the term *postmodern* to refer to a widespread, yet quite unspecific feeling of disorder. Among other manifestations, I believe that this disorder is implies the absebce of speech, and it exists, therefore, not without psychological consequences. A body suffers the absence of speech as the fail of the symbolic framework of reference. In postmodernism, Rocchio suggests, the uniformity of signifying practices has collapsed and has been replaced with contending yet failing efforts to represent a new historical social domain: "cultural instability is precisely those moments when a historical balance toward uniformity in signifying practices breaks down, replaced with competing attempts to symbolize the social domain" (p. 25).

Bringing together queerness and postmodernity, some Italian cultural studies scholars use the term *omosessuali moderni* (modern homosexuals). Let me discuss two reasons why the term *omosessuali moderni* is highly problematic. First, it is a signifier that does not account for the unlimited possibilities of human desire. As I have suggested before in this book, any attempt to classify desire with heterosexual/homosexual divides is a form of methodological reductionism with political implications. Further, it is a sociological classification that probably emanated from heterosexual researchers and that may not necessarily reflect the experience and language of queers. Barbagli and Colombo's (2001) research is clearly useful in its effort to identify changes in subjectivity that they link with the image of the modern homosexual. While Barbagli and Colombo have struggled to pursue their research within the still-homophobic Italian university circuit, the following quotation is indicative of the persistent reductionisms that could be avoided if there were more funding and space for queer and gay and lesbian studies:

> Modern homosexuals do not make love with heterosexuals or with the opposite sex, but only with other homosexuals. They no longer assume the roles, dressing codes, or movements of the other gender; men do not show off effeminate and women do not show off masculine, but they all present themselves as gays and lesbians. (Barbagli and Colombo, 2001, p. 13; my translation)

The two signifiers that make up the term *omosessuali moderni* may carry with them the same symptoms of queer panic that I have discussed in this book—for instance, in my discussion of antiquity in the introduction, the examination of medical and homophile discourses in chapters 2 and 3, the analysis of Sibilla Aleramo's letters in chapter 2, or my discussion of Vattimo and Grillini's pronouncements during the 1980s in chapter 3. In this case, implicit in the term *modern* is an attempt to reference an emerging subjectivity that struggles to surface in Italy in dialectic opposition (but not in complete contradiction) with the more oppressive, asymmetric, and even clandestine characteristics of earlier modes of homosexual love.

With the term *homosexual,* the act of naming that legitimates this subjectivity might entail a particularistic gesture of closure, an impressive apprehension that denies the potentially radical discovering of queerness of all human desire. Of course, I take it that the intention of the writers was exactly the opposite, that is, to name a group of individuals who have received very little attention within a country that tends to display homophobia. What is more, by conducting research on homosexuality in Italy, Barbagli, a most serious scholar, inaugurates a whole new chapter in the history of sociological research in Italy. Nevertheless, this is the paradox implied in writing about queerness: that any form of naming creates categories that tend to shape culture. The act of naming has an effect on what was nameless (made invisible, unspoken). That is, the effect of naming implies that the impersonal and in-formed real, if the reader allows me the use of this characterization, becomes spoken. In this case, the term *modern homosexual* might bring to the symbolic realm something that was silenced before. Hence my point is not to criticize the research itself or the motivations of the researchers (indeed the point that I am making might apply to my own writing as well), but to attempt a move forward that complicates matters a bit further. In this light, an understanding of queerness under the term *homosexuality* takes for granted a psychological conceptualization of sexuality, one based on the idea that all sexual beings are oriented toward two possible sexual objects. In doing so, the objects of choice might delineate and subordinate sexuality to a gendered system in which subjectivity is compulsorily inscribed into gender systems of order (male/female, and their derived gendered classification of behaviors, language and social markers. Furthermore, a view like this might be dangerous in assuming that dichotomist heterosexual/homosexual classifications translate into or stand for a solid reality that exists before or beyond its linguistic construction, a process that Stuart Hall has examined in depth throughout his work. In doing so, we here encounter a language that pre-scribes certain forms of acting, doing, and speaking, and certain forms of sex (gay, lesbian), while excluding others which, therefore, could be interpreted by some as disposable, or less adequate, or abnormal. To make my point one more time, I pose a question: what options are we left with? If naming always introduces distinctions, and if distinctions carry the contexts in which a naming is made (as Butler would put it), how can we invent forms of talking and doing that are all-comprehensive of the human condition? The key word in my criticism is doing and speaking, as queer can unveil the instability of all identity (and not only that of *homosexuals*). If one wants to unmask the modern myth of essences and being, one must be able to admit that there is no solid identity behind social performance—but that is a thought that will always cause anxiety in the heterosexist mind.

Pure Relationships

What most clearly distinguishes postmodern sexuality is, perhaps, the break from reproductive sexuality, romance, and monogamy. This is what Giddens (1992) seems to convey with the term *pure relationships*, a notion that describes transformations in intimacy affecting both heterosexual and non-heterosexual individuals. The exploration of modes of love or sexuality independent of parenting and even monogamy,[3] he suggests, coincided with the increasing use of contraceptive methods in the United States and Western Europe, and with the achievements of feminists and queers. As Weeks et al. (2001) emphasize, these groups challenged relationships based on romanti-cism and continuity to widen the meaning of sexuality to include the produc-tion of the self, the search for pleasure and interconnectedness, and the confrontation of gender/sex dichotomies. New relationships exemplify that identity is always sexual identity, in the sense that it is grounded in a body of pleasure, in a relational self, and in forms of eroticism absolutely singular and yet dependent on our relations with others. Sexual identity "can be molded as a trait of personality and thus is intrinsically bound up with the self. At the same time—in principle—it frees sexuality from the rule of the phallus, from the overweening of male sexual experience" (Giddens, 1992, p. 2). By making sexuality plastic, pure relationships unfix the self from the demands of perpetual love or reproduction. Since these relationships break the connection between sexuality and parenthood, they can produce an alternative self, one not defined by the morals of courtly love or matrimony (see Stacey and Davenport, 2002; Weeks et al., 2001).

In their inclusive study carried out with non-heterosexual individuals from Great Britain, Jeffrey Weeks, Brian Heaphy, and Catherine Donovan (2001) found at least three interrelated themes that cut across their intimacies: more freedom, experimentation, and opportunities to choose; the irrelevance of heterosexual models in understanding queer relationships; and the larger reflexivity of non-heterosexual relationships. All three themes underscore the continuous negotiation of love and sexuality. Although heterosexual couples also renegotiate their relationships, the research suggests, their sexuality and love are oftentimes less reliant on social judgment, observation, and condemnation. Under constant scrutiny, queers have invented forms of connecting that are unique. Miriam, an interviewee in the study, says: "it is also about being creative and being pioneering; about not wanting to be defined. . . not wanting to conform in terms of what family needs to look like" (cited in Weeks et al., 2001, p. 111).

Two different Italian studies (Barbagli and Colombo, 2001; Bertone et al., 2003) confirm that the search for long-lasting yet creative love relationships is also a preoccupation among Italian queers. The studies demonstrate, however, particularities of this population that distinguish it from non-heterosexual groups in other nations. Rigid gender divides tended in the past to classify homosexuals according to their sexual practice (passive/active); according to gender roles (feminine/masculine); or according to the modality of the rapport (partner choice). This classification system mirrored asymmetric gender roles in Italy. These researchers emphasize that increasing visibility of GLBTQs in Italy correlates with a more flexible understanding of gender and sexuality. More than ever before, Italians who identify themselves as *gay, lesbian, bisexual,* transsexual, or queer are coming out to families and in public.

In a sociological study conducted in the city of Turin involving 514 individuals, 69 percent of the interviewed men and 35 percent of the women self-identified as exclusively homosexual, while 39 percent of the women declared themselves bisexual (Bertone et al., 2003). The research reveals that the role of the family and community is fundamental: they provide individuals with networks of support that challenge stereotypes and broaden the possibilities of alternative self-identification. When such support is missing, the process of creating a queer identity is harder and sometimes painful. As

Vicenzo, a forty-two-year-old, states in an interview: "My process of self-identification occurred in complete and absolute isolation in a social environment that is always potentially hostile" (cited in Bertone et al., 2003, p. 29; my translation).

The majority of Italian gays and lesbians prefer long, stable relationships to occasional ones, and they wish to live with their partners. However, the number of cohabiting partners is much smaller than in other countries. For instance, while 30 percent of lesbians live with their partners in France, only 3 percent do so in Italy (Barbagli and Colombo, 2001). Approximately 40 percent of gays and 33 percent of lesbians formalize their unions with symbolic rites. Usually, these are parties or dinners celebrated with friends but excluding relatives when participants have not come out to their families. Also, 52 percent of women and 28 percent of men use a ring as a symbol of their love (Bertone et al., 2003).

As with heterosexual couples, social rituals like the sharing of a house or meals are important markers of the new status of the relationship for Italians. Interviewed couples in these studies highlight the importance of eating together at least one time a day but, if possible, they share all meals. Private life is characterized by the use of familial language, personal symbols, nicknames, and affectionate body language that might change or be directly repressed once the couple is in public. One participant in the research, Nadia, comments that:

> If I could, I would get married. I'd love to get married, have a beautiful wedding reception, and spend a lot of money on it. By the way, to make it official is to sanction this thing [relationship]; it would mean that it is done once in a lifetime. This is my desire and I think about it very often. I usually talk about how I would make it, where, in what ways. (Cited in Barbagli and Colombo, 2001, p. 205; my translation)

Division of labor is probably the most visible marker that distinguishes heterosexual and non-heterosexual couples in Italy: "There are no divisions of domestic chores in a pre-established way; of course in practice we do different things, but as a general rule we do those things that we dislike less. . .there are no rules actually" (Pierluigi, cited in Bertone et al., 2003, p. 135; my translation). The authors of the study stress that freedom to experiment with roles is a way of contrasting with the more asymmetric roles perceived in heterosexual couples. In married couples, during the week, husbands devote 46.8 hours a week to work outside the home and 9 hours to

household chores, while wives spend 18.8 hours working outside the home
and 45.5 hours on household chores. Non-heterosexuals distribute the
household activities more equally and in ways that are more interchangeable
(Barbagli and Colombo, 2001). Finally, it is interesting that while 80 percent
of heterosexual Italians agree that the most important value within a relationship is *reciprocal fidelity*, non-heterosexuals amply disagree that monogamy
is a valid value *per se*, or see it even as an ideal necessary to comply with,
for societal reasons. In some interviews, 51 percent of gays and 29 percent of
lesbians declare having had at least one sexual encounter outside their
relationship, and most of the time it happened with the consent of the partner
(Barbagli and Colombo, 2001). Nevertheless, to some non-heterosexuals,
fidelity seems important. As Domenico, twenty-nine years old, explains:
"We had become the discourse of betrayal: He tells me that he can't assure
me he had not cheated on me. So, I thought he didn't love me any more. We
entered into a deep crisis for some months. . .it was the only time he betrayed
me, also because I would not have forgiven a second one" (cited in Bertone
et al., 2003, p. 130; my translation).

These assertions need to be situated within the symbolic universe of a
country in which the language of (heterosexual) marriage is absolutely
overwhelming. This symbolic encompasses not only the therapeutic ethos of
scientific, religious, and psychological discourse, but advertising for family
consumer goods like the Barilla pasta campaign ("where there is Barilla,
there's home") or Ferrero's Nutella and Mulino Bianco's nutritional advice
for families (constantly depicted as around a breakfast table, enjoying the
serenity of stable family cohesion) and, more important, the heterosexist
provisions at work, school, or in hospital, all designed to favor the straight
family.

As I suggested in my discussion of nameless intimacy in chapter 3,
whenever venues for queer coalitions and public visibility of queerness are
sabotaged, queers might choose either to silence their relationships and
desires or to draw on the heterosexist chain of signifiers around them in
everyday life. None of these solutions is really fruitful for the subject. By
drawing signifiers from a heterosexist linguistic ground, queer life is reduced
to a replica of straight life; by silencing subjectivity, we create reversed
homophobia. What is important to notice here is that the exchange of rings or
the wearing of an article of clothing does not suffice to make a symbolic
inscription on queer life. These are signs that belong to a particular (*particu-*

lar being understood here as a noun), a set of rituals and norms and language that has its own history and inscription in the symbolic realm. To be completely clear: the moment in which a new particular can emerge is not when some rituals from another particular are copied, but when there is a new inscription of the law that guarantees that the universal is enlarged and contested. Instead, the making of a wedding reception suggests assimilation and reinforces, in fact, the particular that queers might want to contest. Some readers might be tempted to criticize this point by arguing that identity is never mechanically modeled to follow one and only one set of rules. In this view, there is always a process of negotiation that occurs when a group adopts a segment of signs from another particular. While this could be the case, I am more interested in discussing here the possibility of making gestures that have the effect of widening the universal or symbolic as a whole. To be sure, my reading is not to suggest that queers have mechanically assimilated the language of heterosexuality. Instead, it is to highlight the enormous psychical effort required to continually contest such language or invent another one altogether,[4] an effort to remake one's own identity continually. And while from a psychoanalytic perspective such an effort to remake or resignify one's subjectivity constantly may not be differential of queer subjectivities, it is undeniable that certain cultural conjunctures can be devastating for the psyche.

Postmodern Italian Families

During a trip to Italy, I stayed at the house of Concetta and Michele, who married in Calabria thirty years ago and came to live in Turin, where I met them. They left the southern region of Puglia seeking better job opportunities and an improved educational environment for their two kids, Francesco and Pietro. Now professional adults in their thirties, Francesco and Pietro live with their parents and share a bedroom "because it is a family custom," Francesco once told me. He is planning to get married to Angelica, his fiancée since high school. Pietro is a gay man who had only come out to his mother under great pressure after she discovered gay erotica hidden in his closet. He is also in a long-standing relationship with an immigrant to Italy.

The family lives in a three-room apartment overlooking one of Turin's busiest avenues. They own this apartment thanks to savings that were lent to Michele and Concetta by their families. Concetta feels comfortable in her home, but dislikes the small size of the kitchen. A green, home-made, embroidered comforter with the initials of the family, kept in the master bedroom, is one of the precious items owned by the family, a reminder of their origins. There is a television in each bedroom and the kitchen, a laundry machine in the bathroom, and a computer in the sons' bedroom.

Raised Catholic and fervently devout, Concetta prays the rosary every afternoon, right after cleaning the livingroom and before she starts preparing dinner. While I stayed with them, she would pray the rosary listening to Radio Maria, the official Vatican radio station that broadcasts Vatican news and the rosary for the handicapped who cannot attend mass. Sometimes, Concetta would watch the television in "mute" mode so as to allow her to pray. She alternated the rosary with vivid conversations with me, or would interrupt the prayer to answer a telephone call from her sister in Puglia. This sort of multitasking was not for lack of respect or devotion; on the contrary, she felt her devotion was an integral part of her life, no matter what she was doing. Although she is now a housewife, Concetta was a professional nurse for many years. After she was diagnosed with a bone condition, she retired and has been living in her home for more than twenty years. She barely goes out, due more to lack of interest than the occasional physical pain. Grocery trips and other errands are run either by the sons or her husband. She does go on vacation to the South, where she returns to her family home to visit her sisters.

Concetta and Michele's marriage did not end when Concetta discovered Michele's relationship with another woman, even when Michele began to stay elsewhere some nights. Although this is not a veiled family secret anymore, there has been no more discussion about it for years.

Of course, Concetta and Michele represent one extremity of the spectrum of families I met in Italy. Antonia and Mario, for instance, are a young, unmarried couple in their forties who live together and are expecting a baby. They do not own a house but rent an apartment, have two small cars that somehow symbolize their independence, and are big fans of video games. In their apartment there is a high-tech studio for Mario. The couple broke up twice in the course of four years, but they expect that the baby will unite them forever.

At a social gathering, Mario and Antonia introduced me to three friends. Cecilia, Nilla,[5] and Marco. Cecilia, twenty-six, is a recently graduated lawyer; she lives with her mother and rarely sees her father since he left home. Marco, twenty-two, is currently doing community work to compensate for military service. His boyfriend, Nilla, is a self-identified *femme fatale* gay man in his early twenties, of great wit and the kindest disposition. He works as a drag queen and singer for a disco while struggling to complete his studies in architecture. Despite a very difficult economic situation, Marco and Nilla decided to move in together a year ago, and they reside now in a four-bedroom apartment with two other queer couples with whom they share expenses and household responsibilities.

The individuals in these very different relationships, as Chiara Saraceno (1991) points out, correspond to generations that have experienced, within a period of less than a hundred years, accelerated transformations in their daily lives. These include the negotiation of the limits between the public and the private spheres that Saraceno (1991) describes as the remaking of the Italian family. The last two generations grew up seeing the increasing political and cultural visibility of queers in Italy, but only the last generation has seen the public struggles of GLBTQs.

The historical transformation of families in Italy is difficult to assess because, as Marzio Barbagli (1984) explains, Italy's household system differed not only from region to region, but it was also different from that of other European countries. Notwithstanding this heterogeneity, researchers agree that after 1940, the number of agricultural households[6] decreased. This meant an increasing number of smaller family units dispersed geographically (Saraceno, 1991). Unlike their parents, the offspring of these smaller families did not always become peasants. Instead, many of them left the rural villages in which they grew up and moved to industrial cities looking for jobs. During the 1950s, those who had settled in large cities made a transition to behaviors of consumption in response to the urban pace. Decades later, their offspring became consumers of items and entertainment never imagined by their grandparents (see Barbagli, 1984; Ginsborg, 2003; Saraceno, 1991).

Industrialization meant not only the shrinking of the family unit, but also a reconfiguration of family roles and individuals' identities. Before the women's emancipation movement granted them more equality of rights at home and at work, women were subordinate to their husbands within a social structure that compounded their exploitation as mothers and wives. As explored in chapter 2, researchers in Italy indicate that important advances were made during the 1960s and 1970s, during which the educational level of women increased, and many found full-time or part-time jobs that they alternated with the household chores. Children, once viewed as an asset as help with labor, were now conceived in an atmosphere of love and care. Increasingly, parenthood was planned and assisted by means of contraceptive methods (Ginsborg, 2003; Saraceno, 1991).

Moreover, the increasing use of contraception, along with the slow increase in maternal employment, correlated with post-industrial relations that were characterized in several Western countries by mobility, gender equality, and independence from reproduction (Stacey and Davenport, 2002). The 1980s accelerated these trends, particularly in the context of an Italy increasingly oriented to market and service economies, as illustrated by the Benetton model of just-in-time production or D&G advertising campaigns. In this context there have been, in theory, more positions available for women in the market and fewer asymmetries in gender relations. Today younger women constitute a significant percentage of university students and prefer not to remain at home even after having children. Women have become economically independent, although asymmetries in salaries remain, together with fewer top executive positions for women. The once-fixed meaning of the word *famiglia*, the stereotype of the *casalinga*, and the image of the mother caring for the child have been challenged by the legalization of divorce and abortion, as well as the questioning of the experts and the Catholic Church's authority in matters of sexuality. These changes have been examined by Monica Bonaccorso (1994), who suggests that Italian families have been experiencing a drastic metamorphosis. Interestingly enough, she identifies these changes in the language of parenthood:

> The *single* mother substitutes for the young mother; we talk about *surrogate* mothers and fathers, about *non biological* mothers and fathers, about *artificial children*. We talk about *monoparental, binuclear,* and *artificial* families. In one word, we are talking about *alternatives*. (Bonaccorso, 1994, p. 3; my translation, emphases in original)

This linguistic turn is interesting in the context of changing gender relations, for it highlights the fact that the strong links between family and reproduction in Italy are not gender-free. According to David Kertzer and Richard Saller (1991), these links reflect the complex history of the relations between each parent and each child. What is more, as Philippe Ariès (1987) demonstrated, the history of family relationships progresses from a relative indifference to the overwhelming concern, in the present time, for creating a psychologically healthy environment for children.

Reproduction. There was once an image of the extended Italian family as a large number of members living in the same unit, but this image does not communicate the complexity of Italian families any longer (Barbagli, 1984). Today, few families resemble anything like a large assemblage of relatives living in one agricultural home. According to ISTAT[7] (2006d) or Istituto Nazionale di Statistica, before 1964 dating before marriage lasted an average of three years and four months, while after 1993 dating extended up to five years. The same source indicates that during the 1960s couples met at the house of relatives or friends (20.3 percent), or in their neighborhood (21.3 percent), or in communal festivities (17.5 percent), while after the 1990s they met primarily at friends' parties (19.7 percent), at friends' and relatives' houses (13.2 percent), at their workplaces (9.3 percent), or in pubs and discos. While only 1.4 percent of marriages were preceded by cohabitation before 1974, between 1984 and 1993 cohabitation without marriage increased to 9.8 percent, and to 14.3 percent between 1994 and 1998; finally, cohabitation without marriage makes up 25.1 percent of the cases between 1999 and 2003 (ISTAT, 2006d).

Nevertheless, the family in Italy, as in other countries, is still a dominant social institution, and Italians are still very fond of this arrangement. Paul Ginsborg (2003) suggests that today almost the entire Italian population lives in families (56,594,021 people out of 57,500,000). Indeed, most Italians report living in relationships that they identify as family, although it does not automatically follow that they live in *nuclear* family arrangements, that is, in a household unit comprised of a man and a woman united in a stable marital relationship with children[8] (Bilton et al., 1996). For instance, studies like Barbagli's (1988), Cecchi Paone's (2004), and Ginsborg's (2003), among others, show that in the last decade there was between a 5 and 7 percent increase in the number of people living alone, the so-called *mono* or individual families.

Nowadays, according to ISTAT, one in four Italian families consists of one member only, making up 24.3 percent of the total of families (ISTAT, 2004). In addition, the number of individuals in each Italian household unit has dropped in the last decade. Whereas the Italian national census of 1971 reported 3 individuals per household unit, ISTAT reported in 2004 that in thirty years the number had dropped to 2.6. Curiously, in the decade 1991-2001, the number of families did not diminish but increased from approximately twenty million to approximately twenty-two million (ISTAT, 2004).

This would appear to contradict generalized opinions about the crisis in the family. Nevertheless, the reduction in the number of members in each family has become a constant throughout the country. The region with the smallest mean number of family members is Valle d'Aosta (2.2 individuals), while the largest families are in Campania (3.1). These figures are consistent with the distribution of the birth rate in Italy, suggesting that Italian families in the South are larger than those in the North (see Barbagli, 1984; Cecchi Paone, 2004; Ginsborg, 2003; ISTAT, 2004).

In the last few decades, there has been a gradual decline in birth rates[9] in all European countries. Italy did not present a different distribution of birthrates from that of other European countries for years, but rates then began to drop fast, authors report. Throughout the 1990s, Italy had the lowest birth rate in the world. According to Ginsborg (2003), the average number of children per woman (calculated per 1,000 women and per region) was 2.42 in 1970; by 1980 it was 1.64; by 1990 1.30; and, according to ISTAT it was 1.18 in 1995 and in 1998. In recent years there has been a slight increase in these figures. By 1999, the average was 1.23; by 2002, it was 1.25. These statistics should be interpreted by keeping in mind the great divergences between the Center-North and South, Ginsborg (2003) suggests. Birth rates in the South have been higher since the beginning of the 1900s. According to the sources referenced here, the North-dominant reproductive model has remained that of families with one child and a mother in her thirties or older; in the South it has been that of families with two children or more. Today the South still has the highest birth rate (1.344 in 2002), while the region of Campania shows the highest average of the country (1.487), followed by the North (1.200 for the same year) in the region of Trentino Alto-Adige (1.461). The lowest average is in the Center-North region of Liguria (1.057). These trends suggest that southern Italian families are usually more extended and that children live longer with their parents. This might be considered evidence that parents prefer to keep older marriage traditions, including celebrating weddings earlier in life and having a larger number of children (Cecchi Paone, 2004; Ginsborg, 2003; ISTAT, 2004).

Italy was not the only Mediterranean country to undergo this reconfiguration of birthrates in the last decades, authors suggest. The populations of Greece, Spain, and Portugal have behaved in similar ways. Indeed, Spain's birth rate in 2002 was the lowest in the area (1.1). These trends can be of deep concern if work opportunities continue to decrease while the number of *pensionati* continues to grow. The indicators suggest an imbalance in the age structure of the Italian population. To this we should also factor in the arrival of immigrant populations. In the summer of 2006 it was reported by national newspapers that one out of ten students in Italy came from immigrant families. Finally, Paul Ginsborg (2003) estimates that if an inverted pyramid is to represent the future of Italian population (at present birth rates), in 2038 there will be twenty-five people aged sixty or older for every ten people younger than twenty years of age (Ginsborg, 2003).

Labor Market. The authors I consulted seem to agree that a low birth rate can have immense repercussions for the Italian society. For instance, it can indicate that new couples show less interest in procreating because they cannot afford to raise and educate more than one or two children. Conversely, it can also indicate that the individuals in a relationship find that their main investment should be in their careers or professions. Finally, it can also mean that new couples prefer to spend more time alone, find pleasure in living together, and share long relationships without experiencing parenthood (see Barbagli, 1984; Cecchi Paone, 2004; Ginsborg, 2003; ISTAT, 2004; Livi Bacci, 1997).

Religious authorities and politicians are less inclined to see these new trends as positive changes in labor and sexuality. They fear that individuals reclaiming their bodies and their freedom to explore non-parental relationships might lead to sexual libertinism. Historians have always been interested in the role of the Catholic Church in shaping old marriage practices and family arrangements. As David Kertzer and Richard Saller (1991) argue, declining birth rates in Italy do not minimize the importance of religious dictates because Italy is, among its neighboring countries, the nation with the lowest non-marital cohabitation and divorce rates. When Pope John Paul II addressed the Italian Parliament in November 2001, he implied that the birthrate crisis in Italy was a cause for severe concern for the future of the country (Bruni, 2002). In fact, a higher percentage of old people might help preserve more conservative values. As a result, following Ginsborg (2003), Italian society would have to depend on its young, less conservative individuals to support a large bloc of old, traditionalist people; but this older generation would probably continue to be more influential in the values that guide the society at large. According to Ginsborg (2003), this is a new paradox that Italy will have to deal with.

Further, since the Italian labor market has been contracting steadily, new job opportunities might be distributed more equally within the smaller, more youthful, segment of the population. However, job redistribution does not benefit the working population as a whole, for although several changes in family policies and new work opportunities for women are noticeable, the Italian labor market is still heavily gendered. In addition, as Bruni (2002) suggests, job opportunities might be taken by immigrants, either from other countries within the European Economic Union or from other parts of the world: North African workers and immigrants from the Balkans cross national borders to find better job opportunities in Italy, but they are poorly compensated with low salaries, daily surveillance, and harsh lifestyles associated with their illegal immigrant status. Among foreigners in Italy, 52.6 percent are young, between eighteen and thirty-nine years of age (ISTAT, 2006b). The same immigrants who are seen as threatening young Italians' job opportunities are also the ones who are usually available to fill positions that often do not provide the same benefits as do jobs of people working under a contract (what Italians call *lavoro in nero*) or industrial positions that might be regarded as mediocre or second-class by some Italians (see Bruni, 2002). It is interesting to note that during the second trimester of 2006, the ISTAT (2006a) estimates, work opportunities showed a 1.3 percent increase (more than 320,000 new jobs) in comparison with the same period in the year 2005. The number of individuals employed rose to 23,187,000, a 2.4 percent increase in comparison to 2005, and partly due to an increase in the workforce coming from foreign countries (more than 162,000) (ISTAT, 2006a). According to ISTAT (2006c), at the very end of 2005, the population of Italy was 58,751,711, while a year before it reached 58,462,375. The 0.5 percent increase (289,336 individuals) represents, the ISTAT researchers suggest, an increase in immigration.

These rapid changes in population can sometimes be followed by new anxieties. This situation struck me on a very personal level while I was doing my preliminary research in Italy. The day before leaving Turin in August 2004, my partner and I went to say good-bye to our next-door neighbor Andrea and his family. We engaged in small talk about the city, the way it was changing, and the multiple attractions it offered. I mentioned my interest in returning to Italy to carry out more research or, eventually, to settle down. I pointed out that although I was from Argentina, I had reclaimed my Italian citizenship some time ago and was now expecting all documents to be ready by the time of my return to Italy. Eventually, the topic of street violence came up. For some reason (maybe my identity had confused him, or probably because I do not look as *dark* as he imagined South Americans to be), Andrea mentioned that, every day, while commuting by car to work, he has to deal with "this bunch of Peruvians, Colombians, and Paraguayans who wait for a red light, then ask for some coins in return for an unwanted windshield wash." He complained about this and added, "Here, every day there are more and more like them. They come, don't work, and still expect you to give them money." He concluded by stating, "Ma le Lire non piovono dal cielo" (but Lire don't rain from heaven). He immediately got a startled look on his face and blushed, suggesting that he realized he was talking about South American immigrants like me. So he added: "Look, this by no means implies that they are not welcome here. In fact, they do a lot of small work that most Italians are not ready to take on, like house cleaning and cooking in restaurants."

They and *I* are, in this case, strong linguistic markers to identify otherness. Put in the language of chapter 1, they create what Homi Bhaba (1994) calls the *third space*, a transitional space traversed by those with an ambiguous identity: immigrants and queers; queers that are immigrants. The conversation with Andrea questioned the location of my self within this "third space," the complex status of being an Argentine grandson of Italians, living in the United States, traveling to Europe. Thinking of myself as a vagabond, a queer, and a tourist, I got dizzy. It was sad to confront Andrea, because I had heard other folks express similar confusion over immigrants coming to Argentina from neighboring countries. Bolivians, Peruvians, and Paraguayans are racially marked by many *porteños*,[10] stigmatized as street vendors and dark delinquents. This conversation with Andrea was deeply embarrassing for me, however, because I had imagined Italy as a land of warm emotions, welcoming families, and unconditional friendliness. In this fantasy of racial integration, I had constructed my own imaginary Italy, a nation and *terra madre* (motherland) waiting for me as the offspring of the Italians who had immigrated to Argentina just a few generations ago.

Cohesion, Marriage, and Gender Relations. According to Barbagli (1988), after World War II, a progressive decline in the number of agricultural families triggered changes in gender relations in Italy. Since there were fewer agricultural jobs taken up by women, they stayed at home more often.

But these changes were not just a question of the amount of time spent inside the house; instead, there was a redefinition of women's roles and in the quality of the relations they established. The significance of this redefinition of roles was noteworthy in rural settings such as Trentino or the island of Sardinia. For instance, in 1921, agricultural households duplicated the number of other household systems in these two areas (Kertzer and Saller, 1991) and were deeply dependent on female coordination. This gave women a degree of authority in everyday decisions. Even today, locals refer to the past of Sardinia as a matriarchy. Between the 1940s and 1960s, however, women became *housewives*. This had the curious effect of privatizing the family and the house (Saraceno, 1991), in some cases loosening the community's networks of interconnection while tying the family to the state and subordinating women to husbands. For instance, the old Civil Code's characterization of the Italian family, the only legislative reference to the subject until the 1970s, defined families following a patriarchal and vertical structure headed by the male (Menniti et al., 1997). Women were supposed to be inferior to the male authority. It was the role of the husband to supply the economic support for the family, and it was the role of the wife to raise the children and care for the house. In case of absence or death, the husband had the right to leave detailed instructions on how to raise the kids and take care of the house (see Menniti et al., 1997; Kertzer and Saller, 1991; Saraceno, 1991).

This domestic politics shifted during the 1960s, coinciding with the struggle of feminists. There were more full-time jobs available for women, and feminists pushed social changes that materialized one decade later. In 1975, there was a consistent change in the symbolic: laws passed in the period stressed the equality of rights and obligations for both parents and established that it is the obligation of both parties to negotiate in what ways they desire to raise their children and provide for their support (Menniti et al., 1997). As a result, the patriarchal authority of the father was progressively challenged, although the subordination of women in Italy is still far from reversed (see Passerini, 1996). Nevertheless, gender, sexuality, and family roles are being symbolized differently than in the past, and have materialized in dissimilar arrangements.

While there has never been a "normal" or traditional family structure in Italy, the current instability of the Italian family illustrates Judith Stacey's and Elizabeth Davenport's (2002) claim that the postmodern family "represents no new normal family structure, but instead an irreversible condition of family diversity. . ." (p. 356). Since the 1990s, in several Western capitalist societies, there is evidence of a tendency toward growing flexibility in family arrangements, particularly in the domains of sexuality and affection, the authors suggest. For instance, starting in the mid-1980s, separations and divorces started to become more and more frequent for Italians—for example, it doubled in the period from 1982 to 1988, and it increased more than three times again through the year 2000, without significant differences between regions (see Ginsborg, 2003; ISTAT, 2004). "Monoparental" households have doubled since 1985, and reconstituted units composed of divorced parents are probably a very common phenomenon in family arrangements in Italy today (Bonaccorso, 1994). Furthermore, gay and lesbian couples move in together more often: up to 49 percent of gay males and up to 70 percent of lesbians live in stable, prolonged relationships in Italy, including cohabitation (Barbagli and Colombo, 2001).

The growing number of lesbians maintaining a stable relationship can be taken as an important sign of the changing status of women in Italy. It is a phenomenon that has occurred at the same time that women made effective the struggle of feminism, reclaiming their rights and choosing not to have children if so they prefer, or giving preference to their university careers and having children later in life. In 1972 the typical age of first-time mothers was 24.9 years, but in 1990 it had risen to 29.0 (Ginsborg, 2003).

Postponing paternity or maternity are related phenomena, both influenced by the adjustments individuals make when they move from their parental families to their own families, and to a highly competitive job market (see Ginsborg, 2003). In the case of men, this transition is being made later than ever before. As in Greece and Spain, prolonged youth education and persistent youth unemployment in Italy are incentives to remain in the parental home until the third decade of life (Vogel, 2003). This is indeed a social phenomenon with strange particularities in Italy, and which has been given the name *mammismo*: "A mammone is the Italian equivalent of a "mama's child," a son or daughter often of adult age who refuses to let go of his or her mother's apron strings" (Ward and Larner, 2003, p. 16). The opposite of the *mammone* is the *figlio di papà*, a term that describes a young and usually shallow man who depends on his parents' funds. Although these two extreme stereotypes hardly reflect the real life of any individual, they might be useful in describing ways in which male subjectivity has been affected. In a shrinking and increasingly competitive labor market, men feel the pressure to be attractive, to remain young, and to keep their beauty as much as women do. Labor opportunities, however, may be increasing. In 2006, ISTAT (2006a) showed a slight decrease in the rate of unemployment—to 6.5 percent—one point below the second trimester of the previous year. Nevertheless, top managerial positions are very few. The image of a young entrepreneur with shallow values contrasts with the 1960s image of the FIAT *operaio*. It is not, of course, an image descriptive of all male Italians, although it is somehow helpful as a parody of the upper classes' younger generations and "media-icon *wannabes*" from cities like Turin or Milan. These men are heavy consumers of cellular phones, gyms, fashions, and style products. Many of them want to remain single to explore their sexual and romantic life with whomever they choose before marrying. This phenomenon is related to the making of the self mentioned earlier and implies a redefinition of the relationships among men, women, and children. Many men start thinking of becoming fathers only later on, and do it not without fear that it may restrict their freedom and professional competence (Bech, 1997). Again, this is reflected in linguistic changes, particularly in the adoption of English terms such as *single* or *partner*. When they do become fathers, it appears that the rigid respect that once characterized the father-child relationship has faded away (Saraceno, 1991). In its place, a new psychological ethos has developed, teaching fathers how to behave, what to expect, and how to maximize "quality time" spent with children. Open demonstrations of care and love are encouraged and expected, redefining previous gender roles.

Remember Me, My Love

When you watch a film by Muccino, you never know whether it is serious or not, suggests film critic Roger Ebert (2002). Ebert confesses that he is confused by *L'Ultimo Bacio* (The Last Kiss, 2001), because it is both sad and funny, or neither at the same time. In *Ricordati di Me* (Remember Me, My Love, 2004), Muccino combines the suspense of a thriller with the human dilemmas of a drama and some aspects of *commedia all'italiana*—the ability to expose the changes, contradictions, and humors of Italian society (Bondanella, 2003; Landy, 2000). In so doing, *Ricordati di Me* provides metaphors and representations for further discussion of the postmodern family.

Ricordati di Me, released in 2004, is the last film in what could be considered Muccino's trilogy, which is completed by *Come Te Nessuno Mai* (But Forever in My Mind, 1999), and *L'Ultimo Bacio* (The Last Kiss, 2001). While all of them talk about the breakdown of the family, *Come Te Nessuno Mai* is narrated from the perspective of caustic teenagers; *L'Ultimo Bacio* from the view of desperate young adults; and *Ricordati di Me* from the viewpoint of frustrated, middle-aged adults.[11]

Muccino's films were all made within the last six years and have the advantage of being witnesses to the latest political and social developments in the country. All of them portray middle-class, urban families living (or, better, surviving) in the Italy of a service economy, in a new millennium where the society has become sardonic about its own fate, in an Italy where social bonds are breaking down and where everybody is an anonymous citizen. Indeed, central to Muccino's films are the protagonists' struggles against these particular conditions. They seek refuge in their families and friends but, strangely enough, they do not often search for community networks, perhaps because Muccino wants to suggest something about the fragmentation of the social system. This is an Italy that became modern, technocratic, and mercantile all of a sudden, perhaps too rapidly for the characters whom Muccino depicts as stressed and overwhelmed. This stress is reflected in the frenetic rhythm of Muccino's films, which seem to document the accelerated pace at which we live and work, a tempo that leaves little time for intimate relations. Muccino is infatuated with representing the new speed of life, the makes of cars, the styles of clothes and music that the youngest generations follow, and the agony of their parents. Although the drama of the protagonists is central, Muccino's films are not psychological dramas; instead they are inquiries into the sociocultural dynamics or circumstances that are remaking Italian identity.

Ricordati di Me (like the other two films in the trilogy) is a film about Italy, but it is also about other contemporary societies. While there are of course markers of nationality throughout these films, locations and settings do not particularly capture the essence of Italy but, instead, draw similarities between Italy and other postmodern societies. While of course the viewer knows that the protagonists are Italians, there are not many geographical identifiers that anchor the protagonists' dramas in a national space that would be unique to Italy. Muccino acknowledges that he wanted to make films exportable to other countries. (Eventually, his films led to two contracts with

Miramax [Cavagna, 2005].) But Muccino also stresses that his films aim to confront the viewers with the possibility that the circumstances narrated in the films could take place in New York or Paris or Rio de Janeiro:

> As a director, I'm very universal. The story is [universal]. But also the way it has been told reaches different audiences. Obviously we are becoming very much globalized, so we have the same problems; we have the same TV shows; we have the same terror problems. Obviously, the background, the cultures are still different, but not so much. The families' problems are mainly the same. (Cited in Cavagna, 2005, paragraph 21)

In this interplay of local-versus-global, Muccino can be isolated from other contemporary, esteemed film directors who exploit the beauty of the Italian landscape as an integral element of the plot, with an excellent example being Emanuele Crialese's *Respiro* (2003).[12] In contrast, Muccino suggests that most contemporary, middle-class, urban families experience the same fears and problems, because a form of economic and cultural panic has become global. For this reason, as critic Dave Kehr (2002) declared, Muccino is the cinematic ambassador of the Berlusconian Italy, and he clearly knows it when he has a male character in *Ricordati di Me* say: "We [Italians] are now the simulacrum of a petit-bourgeois civilization, hypocritical and fraternizing. We have this desperate need to appear without being! Protagonists of a society aware of its own superficiality."

Much of Muccino's work consists of commercial films that viewers around the world have come to love (Cavagna, 2005), but which some critics have come to distrust. Steffano Della Casa (2004), an important Italian film critic, indicates that Muccino's work "has had the largest number of passionate adversaries. . . none of them wants to accept this nobody who suddenly becomes a success in Italy and abroad. Particularly recalcitrant for the local industry is his contracts with the United States" (p. 76; my translation). Perhaps, criticism about Muccino's work might originate in the fact that he has been an advertising consultant for companies like Nestlé, and that he constructs his persona as a celebrity icon, allowing papparazi to take photographs of him romancing women on the beach or appearing repeatedly on the cover of summer gossip magazines. Marco Giusti (2004) explains that his films are directed in exactly the same frenetic way as his commercials, but he excuses Muccino by reminding the reader that Alan Parker and Ridley Scott also worked for advertising companies.

Ricordati di Me was the most successful film of 2003 in Italy. It was nominated for ten David of Donatello awards and won Best Producer, Best Screenplay, and Best Supporting Actress awards from the Italian National Syndicate of Film Journalists. Released in winter, it made no less than €10,276,060.43 and captivated an audience of 1,718,971 spectators (see Della Casa, 2004).[13]

Marriage Wrecks You. Ricordati di Me begins with a zoom shot of Carlo (Fabrizio Bentivoglio) and his wife Giulia (Laura Morante) lying asleep on their bed. The shot then turns into a close-up of Carlo's face, wrinkled from exhaustion more than age. Even though the married couple is asleep, one can tell that they are distant from one another. They look toward opposite sides of the room, as if they start the day going in different directions.

Beds and mirrors are significant objects in some of Muccino's works. Beds are iconic of marital relationships. (They are of course iconic of infidelity as well.) Hence the opening shot of the bed repeats throughout the film, but it progressively signifies different things: emptiness, rage, death, reconciliation. At the beginning of the film, a matrimonial bed (a most private space shared by spouses) is "dead," with the bodies lying next to each other suggestive of corpses. Because the bed is mainly a place for pleasure and rest, this dead bed implies the absence of love and sex. I read this image as a critique of the private space shared by spouses and sanctioned by the marital agreement of intimacy. This agreement implies at least three parties: the two spouses and the state. Michael Warner (1999) has shown that once marriage is sanctioned by the state, the spouses grant it the power to regulate their sex lives, make decisions, and impose obligations. Marriage is not simply an act of choice between two people; it carries consequences for the whole of society, the author argues. In agreeing to confer the power of the state upon their relationship, the spouses celebrate the forces of the regulatory state upon the rest of society as a whole. For instance, as Warner (1999) suggests, marriage "celebrates" that the state that allows them to unite is the same state that prevents others from enjoying that status.

Muccino uses beds as signifiers for the postmodern crisis of masculinity. A dead bed bears witness to the vulnerability of the postmodern men I made reference to earlier. Indeed, some generations ago, in some parts of Italy, the stained sheets of a newlywed couple's bed were shown the day after to the family as testimony that the man had taken the wife's virginity. Men are supposed to perform well in bed. But Muccino shows beds where men weep, slumber, or lay physically handicapped after an accident: one hour into the movie, Carlo suffers an accident that might leave him impotent.

Curiously, *Ricordati di Me*'s inaugural shot echoes the one in *L'Ultimo Bacio*, but in the earlier movie, the male protagonist cannot close his eyes after his wife has revealed for the first time during a family dinner that she is pregnant—interestingly, here the spouses' names are also Carlo and Giulia. While this Carlo wonders in bed whether it is time to abandon the dreams and freedom of youth, the Carlo in *Ricordati di Me* wonders if he can still capture those dreams and freedom after so many years of having settled down. In addition, while in *L'Ultimo Bacio* the marital crisis starts with the pregnancy of Giulia, in *Ricordati di Me* it overlaps with a time when teenagers Paolo (Silvio Muccino) and Valentina (Nicoletta Romanoff) are both struggling with the crisis of oncoming adulthood. It is not a coincidence that at this point in *Ricordati di Me*, Carlo and Giulia realize how much they have given up in the name of marriage's respectability: Carlo never finishes his pretentious book, and Giulia, once an aspiring actress, never stages a single play. Instead, Carlo starts working for a private corporation politically affiliated with an organization that might represent Berlusconi's party. Giulia is a high-school teacher who talks on her cell phone while teaching and does not seem to care much for her students (who clearly don't care about school, either).

In *Ricordati di Me*, it appears that the crisis of the adults originates in their unfulfilled goals in life, particularly in their careers, whereas that of the teenagers is related to the difficulties in defining their life projects. This can be interpreted, according to Elisabeth Beck-Gernshein (2003), as describing the inconclusive, unfixed status of individual identity, which continues to be constructed throughout life. Indeed, this couple seems to represent the last generation of Italians (in particular, women) who would sacrifice their profession to care for a stable family. Ironically, because they represent that *Generation X,* or transitional generation, they are uncomfortable with what they have surrendered but cannot attain what they wish for, either. This *being in the middle* illustrates one central point of Beck-Gernshein's (2003) discussion about what she calls the *post-family* family. These are families in which the imperatives of marriage and parenthood collide with the imperatives of becoming a productive individual: "The course of the processes of individuation is tensed by the aspiration to find space for creating one's life project, and the nostalgia for being part of a relationship" (Beck-Gernshein, 2003, p. 25; my translation). In *Ricordati di Me*, Carlo and Giulia belong to the generation that Chiara Saraceno (1991) describes as traversed by the most critical of gender relations, for women began to change their status but did not completely define their new roles until one or two decades later with the victories of feminism. Indeed, in Greece, Italy, and Spain, employment rates for women of this generation are low, and if there are children, the first option is to leave a job or to stay out of the labor market (Vogel, 2003).

In the case of Giulia, these transitions are reflected in her career choices. She is allowed to work as a teacher, but only because her job is stereotypically *feminine* and does not interfere with her domestic chores. She is to care for the kids, but she has had to learn, according to modern times, that it is important to give them sufficient freedom for self-expression. She likes driving her SUV, particularly in the rain; however, she will not surrender *her* kitchen to any of the guys in the house. Similarly, Carlo represents perfectly the vulnerable man whom Pat Gill (2003) characterizes as the center of a moral dilemma preoccupying a number of films of the last fifteen years. These men are "haunted by feelings of doubt and recurring guilt. . .uncertain of their own involvement in the gloom and despair, rage and denial, free-floating terror, and attempts at redress" (Gill, 2003, p. 158). He practices cycling at the most expensive gym, wears top-quality suits, and works for a multinational company. At the same time, he dreams of becoming something like a new Italo Calvino, hates his condescending boss, and is completely disoriented about his love life. Considering this scenario, it is understandable when confused teenage daughter Valentina shouts during a discussion with her mother: "I don't want to live pointlessly as everybody else in this home."

Two events finally bring Carlo and Giulia to their collapse as a couple. He finds an old "ex," Alessia (Monica Bellucci), at a company party. "Happily married?" she queries. "Married," he replies. She then looks at him, as if agreeing with him that marriage wrecks you. As expected, they are drawn into an affair that reawakens Carlo's passion for writing and makes Alessia leave her husband to meet Carlo at a beach shack.

Meanwhile, Giulia becomes self-absorbed when her best friend introduces her to a theater director who is willing to let her perform an important role in a play that somehow mocks Pirandello's *Six Characters in Search of an Author*. The role she plays mirrors her own drama, although she seems to ignore it. In denial, she substitutes her pain with transference love[14] for the director. Ironically, when she throws herself into his arms, she discovers that he is gay. Immediately after, she lets him know that she has had two affairs since being married: "One during the first crisis, one during the second. It's educational, you know. When you sleep with a man who runs away right after [sex], it makes your marriage seem decent after all."

Giulia is acting (out) in a play that reproduces her own drama. Since so much of the movie revolves around Giulia's *mirroring* performance, this might be the time to explain the role of mirrors in Muccino's films, to which I alluded above. Muccino usually plays with mirrors, both as material and in the organization of the plot. Mirrors are, of course, reflecting surfaces that echo the postmodern construction of skyscrapers and financial buildings. Mirrors are also surfaces that reflect the passing of time and the collapse of youth and beauty. In a memorable shot in *L'Ultimo Bacio*, for instance, we see Anna (Stefania Sandrelli) removing her makeup in front of a mirror in the master bedroom. The mirror's frame holds a photograph of Anna as a youth (indeed, I believe it is a shot from Bertolucci's *Il Conformista*). The photographic technique in this shot plays with the multiplicity of the image. Anna looks at her image in the mirror at the same time that she looks at her photograph. Interestingly, we look at Anna while she is looking at herself, thus evoking the mechanism of imaginary identification. This is important for the reason that the image (its superficiality, its illusions) has become a significant definer of postmodern identity.

In *Ricordati di Me,* this definition of identity through the surface of images is clear in Valentina's dependency on mirrors: there is a whole wall made of mirrors in her bedroom; she dances next to the mirror during the dance class; she even looks at mirrors while having sex (she wants to make sure she can fake an orgasm so that she can use it with whomever, provided it is beneficial to her acting career). I do not need further examples to suggest that I am thinking here of Jacques Lacan's (1949/2002) classic description of the imaginary constitution of the Ego. The Ego is the least coherent and independent psychical formation; it is alienated in the image of completeness and self-sufficiency. Lacan stressed that in the prematurely born human being, the pyramidal nervous system is not developed, and the human relationship with the world is mediated by the visual activity. But this initial biological immaturity renders the entrance into the symbolic order possible, as well: at first, the human subject does not distinguish him/herself from the image from which he/she is alienated. Later on, through the identification with the Other, the subject is introduced into the symbolic. Finally, mediated by the Other's desire, the mirror stage comes to an end when the principally imaginary *I* yields to social intersubjectivity. This last stage seems to be missing in the case of Anna or Valentina, captured as they are by images of perfection. It follows that this entrapment of identity in the surface of mirrors corresponds to narcissism and differs from the dialectics of desire (founded in the subject's relation to the Other or object of desire) (Dean, 2000).

The storyline can be interpreted as well as a mirror of society.[15] For instance, the crisis of the couple mirrors the moral crisis of Italy: in the gym, Carlo confronts his boss, who says, "We Italians have corruption in our DNA. We've lost our values. Really, do *you* have any [value]? 'Cause it's even worse if you think you do have any." In the case of Muccino, mirrors express the degradation of human relations and values in postmodernity: because societies have become corrupted, families become corrupted as well. In this construction, families mechanically mirror society. This is what Muccino seems to suggest when he says, "The humanity comes from the humanity that preceded it. We are what our parents transmitted to us" (cited in Cavagna, 2005, p. 1). As I will discuss in the next subsection, this affected understanding of life infuses many of Muccino's films with the lamentable consequence of holding off anxiety instead of producing alternative narratives about marriage or family.

Marriage Saves You. While I am not in a position to argue with the director about the best direction for the ending of the film, I am interested in discussing the mechanisms of representation and beliefs that allow for the neurotic displacement and fear of anxiety in cultural narratives about the family, marriage, and intimacy in contemporary Italy as represented by the ending of this film. This interest emanates from my reading of Vincent Rocchio (1999), for whom the containment of anxiety identifies "those moments when a historical balance toward uniformity in signifying practices breaks down, replaced with competing attempts to symbolize the social domain" (p. 25).

In *Ricordati di Me*, narratives about the cohesion of family relations are most clear at the end of the film. Eventually, Giulia discovers Carlo's romance with Alessia. Predictably, the couple starts fighting and reproaching each other. For some time, Giulia plays the part of the victim. She is in shock that her husband not only cheated on her, but that he quit the well-paying job that ensured the family's standard of living. Demonstrating how *machista* he is, Carlo despises Giulia's new acting career and plans to abandon her and the children. It is at this exact point that the movie could have achieved its most dramatic peak. For instance, had Carlo and Giulia left each other, the cinematic text could have exposed the anxiety of confronting their lack of sexual satisfaction: that no matter what they do or whom they sleep with, nothing can complete them; that the more they are compelled by the social system to enjoy (sex, consumption, etc.), the more they are consumed by an imaginary wholeness impossible to attain.

This is not to suggest that Carlo and Giulia are not entitled to remake their love lives or experience their sexuality free from the order of marriage. Quite the opposite, it is to suggest they will be able to do so only if anxiety is traversed instead of displaced or contained. Otherwise, as Žižek would have it, the protagonists alternate between narcissistic identifications and imperatives of endless enjoyment and consumption[16] while never really articulating their desire. This is neurotic fixation, for Carlo and Giulia are seduced by images of unattainable happiness. By not confronting their singular modes of enjoyment, they can only find containment of anxiety in the remaking of their family.

Let me explain this in some detail, since it is critical to my later discussion on PACS. As I have indicated, it is possible to read into the film the Lacanian register of the imaginary in the narcissistic attachment of the protagonists to the lure of images, social symbols, and so on. This order of identification must be differentiated from the order of desire, which is not imaginary and which entails a dialectic relationship between the subject and the object (or with the symbolic Other). In addition, there is a third register, the real, which characterizes the core of enjoyment. Lacan conceptualizes the relations between the three registers and defines each of their logics in a number of ways throughout his teaching. Here, when referring to enjoyment, I am thinking of *unlimited* enjoyment as an imperative that can be opposite to the dialectics of desire, given the fact that desire implies delays, decoys, and dissatisfaction. Lacan puts it in this way: "If the living being is something at all thinkable, it will be above all as subject of the *jouissance*; but this psychological law that we call the pleasure principle (and which is only the principle of displeasure) is very soon to create a barrier to all *jouissance*" (Lacan, 1972, p. 194). Desire can be dialectized (put into words or subject to the signifier) only if there are certain barriers to unlimited enjoyment, so that the relations between the subject and the object are mainly situated within the symbolic register.[17] Of course barriers incite transgression, but for Lacan, transgression has a place in human life because it is one of the modalities of expression of the signifier (in other words, transgression is not outside the symbolic):

> If I am enjoying myself a little too much, I begin to feel pain and I moderate my pleasures. The organism seems made to avoid too much *jouissance*. Probably we would all be as quiet as oysters if it were not for this curious organization which forces us to disrupt this barrier. All that is elaborated by the subjective construction on the scale of the signifier in its relation to the Other and which has its root in language is only there to permit the full spectrum of desire to allow us to approach, to test, this sort of forbidden *jouissance* which is the only valuable meaning that is offered to our life. (Lacan, 1972, pp. 194-195)

The signifier, as Tim Dean has explained, guarantees that there is a whole spectrum of desire that the human being has access to—including queer sexuality (Dean, 2000, 2003; Dean and Lane, 2001). Carlo's relationship with Alessia occurs within this spectrum, but when, at the end of the film, Carlo abandons Alessia and decides to return to the family, he eludes confronting the part of forbidden *jouissance* he has allowed for himself. He literally chooses to "not listen to" the subject of the unconscious, thereby eluding responsibility for his desire. Responsibility does not mean guilt or moral liability, but the allocation of the discourse of the unconscious within the flow of enunciation or speech.

The end of the film shows the reunification of the family in apparent happiness. This closure corresponds to what Robert Rushing (2003) calls *arrest,* the collapse of narrative possibilities, the

> complete closure as a kind of *oikos*, a point of reference that absolutely determines in advance the co-ordinates of our journey, as well as its ultimate destination (both psychic and epistemic). . . .This is the moment when travel comes to a halt—the traveler returns home, to the point of reference that organizes and orients the voyage and renders it comprehensible. (p. 315)

Notice that there is a paradoxical relationship between imaginary plenitude and enjoyment that is responsible for this *arrest* that Rushing identifies—the detention of the narrative corresponds to the detention of desire. Imaginary plenitude or wholeness supposes compliance with (observance of) the imperative to unlimited enjoyment: marry, procreate, consume, and be happy! But the more the imperative is observed, the more unattainable that imaginary plenitude becomes. And, incidentally, the more individuals comply with this cycle, the more they strengthen an ideal: that the social system works, after all. As Slavoj Žižek (1999) points out, the status of this imperative to enjoy *supposes* that the real of desire can be absorbed into an ideal form of the Law.

While the couple's crisis mirrors that of Italy, what becomes of this relationship turns into a metaphor for the signifying practices that society implements (or fails to implement) to confront that crisis. Freudian psychoanalysis helps us here to understand the holding off of anxiety and its consequences. Anxiety is another name for an invasion or irruption of energy within the psychical apparatus. What is experienced as anxiety is the encounter with the real. Another way of saying this is that anxiety forces the individual (the subject, indeed) into a zone of overwhelming proximity with something that eludes symbolization, something that cannot be psychically elaborated (Dean, 2000, 2003). Contrary to what is sometimes assumed, anxiety is not a reaction to the absence of the object, but to its overwhelming proximity. A typical Lacanian example is that a child does not cry when its mother is far, but when she is too close (see Fink, 1995, 2004).

When the object is too close, there is no space for desire. One can see this proximity in the opening shot of *Ricordati di Me.* On the marital bed, the distance between the spouses' bodies might suggest that the intimacy and body pleasure once enjoyed has given way to tedium and anxiety. Since human sex demands that something in the subject becomes the object of desire of the sexual partner, not having sex is one possible strategy that neurotics use not to confront the proximity of the object.

Ultimately, the object causes anxiety because it is inhabited by a traumatic hole or lack. Indeed, this is what the irruption of the real reveals: that, in the case of neurotics, there is an unavoidable hole in our daily passion for meaning. By complying with the imperative to enjoy, Carlo and Giulia prefer to be petrified within an image rather than confront this hole or void. As Vincent Rocchio (1999) puts it in his discussion of neorealism:

> What Lacan's work makes clear is that the impossibility of the real, its residue and irruption into the symbolic, is the site of anxiety for the individual subject: the affective state of an inability to symbolize the real. Instability of culture—the demise of a cultural signifying practice in dominance—thus brings the threat of anxiety insofar as the real protrudes and invades, lacks containment through symbolization. (p. 26)

In its happy ending, *Ricordati di Me* progresses in the interesting direction of saving the family. Just before Carlo runs away from home, Giulia holds him by his arm, begging him not to leave her and the children, not to quit his job. She is ready to accept his flirting:[18] "I don't care anymore who you spend the night with. . . .What matters is us and our children." Carlo hurries into the street and is run over by a car. While he is in the hospital, the family gathers around him to take care of him. Giulia shaves him, smiles at him, and tells him that she loves him. Carlo says he loves her as well. Finally, he returns home, where Giulia has prepared a surprise party for him. Of course, once the crisis is overcome, success is implied for everyone: Giulia plays her role onstage as never before, Carlo reenters the company he had quit abruptly, Valentina succeeds on television, and Paolo takes his first solo vacation. What is most intriguing about this ending is that Giulia and Carlo do not "fake" their mutual love—they really love each other. Read in the context of Rocchio's (1999) notion of ideological containment, this means that anxiety is not simply "covered" by a veil of performances. I am not saying that Carlo and Giulia are hypocrites who remain faithful to their passion in the "deep" corners of their personalities. Instead, and as Žižek (1989, 1999) would probably point out, ideology is a reality that brutally swallows the subject of the unconscious—including its discontents or anxieties.

Similarly, in *L'Ultimo Bacio*, Muccino resolves the marital crisis in a re-encounter between Carlo and Giulia, with the addition of an external narrative about the happy future of the couple. In both films, it is not easy to tell whether Muccino is playing with irony or if these endings intentionally affirm the safety of the Italian family at all costs. It is true that there is in both cases a very subtle way of suggesting that the problems are not over. In *L'Ultimo Bacio*, Giulia is running in a park when a man approaches and she smiles complicity. In *Ricordati di Me*, Carlo has a brief telephone conversation with Alessia in secret. Nevertheless, I do not believe that these brief insinuations have the power to convince all viewers that the couple will break up again. Instead, I read these endings as reifying the strength and union of the family. It is as if the family can catalyze any disruption, contain it, or hold it off. Just as in the famous shot of Pietro Germis's *Divorzio all'Italiana* (Divorce, Italian Style) where recalcitrant Fefé (Marcello Mastroiani) and Rosalia (Daniela Rocca) stroll publicly in pretended harmony, Carlo and Giulia may now live happily ever after.

The most sardonic commentary I have read so far about Muccino's films is probably that of Gilda Williams (2001). Writing as a British woman, Williams declares that Muccino's works are only understandable to Italians:

> Due to its strange plot mechanism, [Muccino's film is] comprehensible only to an Italian. In the first part, two main characters struggle with unimaginable effort to escape their unhappy personal situation. In the second, they then struggle even harder to restore their old trap. Viewers mystified by this modus operandi might recall how, when Italy finally rid itself of the one of the most corrupt and embarrassing leaders in the developed world, billionaire trash-TV magnate Silvio Berlusconi, it then re-elected him, unchanged and unrepentant, just a few years later. Do Italians actually wish to live under a repressive social order? (p. 56)

This is the way I understand the danger of this film: it has the potential to slip from a narrative about one particular marital relationship to a more inclusive narrative that neurotically displaces confronting a more profound anxiety related to a moment when the central component of the film—the family, marriage—is being contested by some segments of Italian society.

෬ **Part Four** ෭
Representations of Queer Italy

Chapter 6

Inversion, Defiance, and Activism in Italian Film

I would like to open this chapter by proposing an allegory relating families and cinema. When the lights in the movie theater dim, an existential darkness grows, encircling the spectator. One might then witness that the human gaze has its own life. As a film travels from the projection room onto the big screen, fictions from the soul unfold. These fictions also project onto another surface, one which is neither internal nor external to us. In a certain sense these fictions are ourselves: selves inverted, projected, or captured magically. In films, the fictions related can constitute a truth that is valid for a moment; a truth that is a sort of revelation, or an invitation to madness. One has to accept that an experience of that type is possible.

There is another location in which one finds madness of this kind: families. Families are privileged sites of fictions, of care, truths, and betrayal. Like the movie theater, we are immersed in them: families also have their own darkness. As in the case of cinema, our selves are shaped by the stories told in the privacy of the family space. One might say that if the social encounter that the cinema provokes is not surprising as an extreme type of madness, it is because it somewhat duplicates and reminds us of that of the family, so familiar to some of us.

Madness and queerness are close cinematic friends: one or the other has usually concerned film directors. The cinematic screen is, in this case, both a mirror and a symbolic space that reveals family ties and their associated psychodynamics. As Vito Russo (1987) taught us, *the homosexual* as a character and homosexuality as a "phenomenon" has been a preferred object of film inquiry in several classic and commercial movies, addressed either directly or somehow veiled (the funny sissy of *Broadway Melody*, the perverted villain of *Cruising*, the vampire *femme fatale* of *The Hunger*, the hilarious yet desperate theater producer in *Victor/Victoria*, the AIDS-infected gentleman in *Philadelphia*, the lesbian criminal in *Monster*, etc.). While always present, though hidden between the lines of old scripts, homosexuality finally became visible on movie screens when gay and lesbian groups of the 1970s moved into the streets. Ever since then we have gained more and more attention and been represented in a variety of roles. In Italy, however, homosexuality only recently became a theme of systematic *unveiled* cinematic exploration, and even more current is the exploration of queer desire and queer intimacy. Nevertheless, it should be pointed out that queer readings of films can occur independently of the actual representation of queerness, and hence we can always read queer desire into many films that date back to the silent era. Along these lines, for example, *Assunta Spina* could be watched as a film that presents the audience with a queer avenger, a woman who contradicts the gender roles and cultural dictates of Neapolitan society.

In the first part of this chapter, I will look into the representation of homosexuality and queerness[1] in classic and contemporary Italian films. Although there are several references to male gay sexuality (as in the other chapters of this book), my interest here is in making a statement about the instability of sexual desire that transcends heterosexual/homosexual divides. Arguably, there are many possible ways of reading a cinematic text (from its location in the industry to genre analysis or criticism of the acting performance) and many frameworks in which to interpret a film (spectatorship theory, feminism, Marxism, etc.). While all these views are useful, in the second part of this chapter I combine queer theory and Lacanian psychoanalytic theory to explore a number of films in which the issue of non-heterosexual desire stands out. What these productions have in common is a recodification of sexual identity that attempts to break free from common assumptions about sexuality and essentialism. Some of these films question the relationships among symbolic law, social norms, and desire. At stake in this question is a criticism of biological and normative reductionisms, an intervention to open up sites of resistance and to provide venues in which to think of relationships and sexuality. Other films interpellate the position of the subject as a subject of enjoyment, hence creating spaces for thinking about what lies beyond the margins of the symbolic, that is, for thinking about the real. In this same light, I will examine the work of Turkish-Italian director Ferzan Özpetek in the second part of this chapter, with specific attention to the representation of queer families as networks of political solidarity within the film *Le Fate Ignoranti* (His Secret Life).

This said, let me clarify what this chapter is not. While I am interested in the relationships among representation, politics, and identity, I will not catalog every single Italian film that includes a character or theme related to homosexuality. As in other parts of this book, I suggest here that queerness is not something essential. The mere mention of *homosexuality*, or the simple inclusion of a gay or lesbian character, does not suffice to make a film queer. In other words, it is generally accepted today in queer theory that it is the reading of the film (a relationship that involves the film, the reader, and the sociocultural context) that makes a cinematic text queer, not an essence within the film itself. Given the fact that, as I will detail below, there can be as many readings of any film as subject positions (but probably not unlimited readings), any film can potentially entail a queer interpretation, erasing dreams of a comprehensive gay film catalog. Attempts to complete such a catalog are many, however, and I highly recommend Pino Bertelli's (2002) *Cinegay* or Roberto Schinardi's (2003) *Cinema Gay* for a more comprehensive inventory of the depiction of homosexuality in Italian films.

Representing Omosessualità in Italian Classics

Vito Russo (1987) once suggested that "there never have been lesbians or gay men in Hollywood film. Only homosexuals" (p. 245). Nevertheless, in the last three decades, audience interest in lesbian and gay cinema has grown considerably, and so have productions, festivals, cinema reviews, and cinema criticism, which are nowadays increasingly oriented toward problematizing the meaning of making gay cinema. In some areas of gay cinema, we observe narratives that are structured and developed from a homosexual/queer viewpoint, whose concern is the depiction and problematization of queer/gay desire and whose obsession is locating queer desire somewhere in a culture and in relation to the power structures particular to a society (see Aaron, 2004; Davis, 2004). For some authors, talking about gay cinema is an oxymoron, or a mere byproduct of market trends. In order to avoid the mercantile appropriation of gay sexuality, critics like Jack Babuscio have preferred the term *gay sensibility*, which he characterized as essential for gay identity:

I define gay sensibility as a creative energy reflecting a consciousness that is different from the mainstream; a heightened awareness of certain human complications of
feeling that spring from the fact of social oppression; in short, a perception of the
world which is colored, shape directed and defined by the fact of one's gayness.
(Cited in Jones, 1996, p. 313)

In Babuscio's view, oppression is intrinsic to gayness, an epistemology
that Richard Dyer (2002) contested several times. For Dyer, we cannot
define oppression mechanically, but we need to consider the interplay of
sexual ideologies and institutions that are historically and culturally specific,
produced by heterosexist frameworks like the family, and cultural products
like film (Jones, 1996).

In this vein, there appear to be some salient approaches to examining the
gay film that are similar to those used to analyze any other film. One approach consists of reading the narrative, focusing on the representational
codes and strategies used to depict a subject of cinematic research, in this
case homosexuality. Another concentrates on the relationship between the
spectator and the text, and pays attention, for example, to the mechanisms of
identification at play while watching a movie. Yet another would be to
explore the market tendencies, the institutional constraints, and the ideologies surrounding them. Finally, another form would stress the aesthetics and
ethics of the self/subject on which a film elaborates, including, in the case of
Lacanian analysis, a reading of the three registers put forward by Lacan: the
imaginary, symbolic, and real, and their relationships and their effects. While
these levels of analysis are very different, they began to interrelate with each
other in Italian film criticism in more concrete ways during and after the
1980s. The relative absence of earlier cinematic representations and analyses
of same-sex desire in film might be related to the more general invisibility of
homosexuality in Italian culture. As was suggested earlier, it was the internationalization of gayness that created the discursive forms and practices that
allowed a sexual identity similar to American "gayness" to evolve in Italy, a
historical shift that compromised the culturally specific meaning of same-sex
desire in that country, but that had the positive effect of offering a more
audible voice to queer Italy as well. Indeed, although it is not impossible to
read queer desires into earlier Italian films, the central concern of those
productions is most often far from a radical criticism of same-sex/queer life
or desire as it is understood today in queer theory; instead, homosexuality is

usually depicted stereotypically or is used as a means of provoking the public's laughter or disgust (Schinardi, 2003).

Indeed, Italian film critic Roberto Schinardi (2003) argues that until 1960, Italian cinema represented homosexuality grotesquely, even morbidly. One example of these stereotypes is the pedophile professor in Roberto Rossellini's *Germania Anno Zero* (Germany Year Zero, 1948), portrayed as a Nazi sympathizer and a child molester desperate to seduce teenagers. I would, however, be cautious of any automatic generalization. As Dyer (mentioned in Jones, 1996) has shown, while cinematic stereotypes have generally degraded homosexuality, and while stereotypes might never reflect the heterogeneity of sexual practices or desires, they can, however, be narratively and visually complex pieces that raise valid political issues. In the case of Italian film, an example of this kind of complexity is *l'invertito* or *il frocio* (the inverted or the fag), whose sexual behavior contradicts the gender norms and codes of ethics implicit in his community of origin. Particularly illustrative is the legendary Italian comedian Totò, who sometimes appeared cross-dressing in films dating back to the homophobic 1950s: *Figaro qua. . .Figaro là* (1950), *Totò a Colori* (Totò in Technicolor 1952), *Totò-Truffa '62* (1961), and *Totò Contro i 4* (Totò against Four, 1963) (see Schinardi, 2003). Perhaps Totò's comedic, clumsy, or overexaggerated gestures are far from the drag queen's performances of gender. However, these films, seen by contemporary audiences, might have a power similar to that of a gender performance. Indeed, the film character(s) can be interpreted as remaking gender roles by complicating the relationships among the male body, social expectations, and everyday performances. Consequently, the films can be read as asking questions about true-versus-false/imitation that can evoke some of the questions intrinsic to queer theory. Read in the light of queer theory, Totò's personifications are not cheap imitations of an original Woman; rather, he draws attention to the idea that all genders are transgender. As Wilchins (2004) suggests, since identity is the result of a strategic positioning within discourse, we all, at some point or another, play and stretch the limits of gender—that is, we all break, whether we want to or not, the binary rules of gender we have never made (see Wilchins, 2004).

In early comedies, however, the comedy more often than not served the purpose of mocking and laughing at homosexuality. In drama, on the other hand, homoeroticism has been represented in a more subtle manner, usually as a way to make points about social and political issues surrounding the life of the characters. Criticism has usually come from leftist directors, and their subtleness has entailed a secret pact with the spectators, who then face the challenge of decoding veiled allusions to same-sex relations in the cinematic narrative. William Van Watson (2002) teaches this in his reading of Luchino Visconti's *Ossessione* (1943), an unauthorized adaptation of James Cain's *The Postman Always Rings Twice*, whose narrative, the writer suggests, allows for both heterocentrist and queer interpretations. Visconti's *Ossessione* anticipates the neorealist films of the post-war era in its analysis of dramatic social interactions that take place under fascism, in the utilization of open locations, and in the criticism of social inequity during fascism (Van Watson, 2002). In addition, Visconti's commitment to the Italian Communist Party and to partisan, anti-fascist struggles served as the prototype for the future involvement with social causes that was characteristic of neorealist filmmakers in general (Van Watson, 2002). At the same time, however, this is a very self-analytic and intimate film that allows a homosexual reading. Van Watson (2002) asserts that indeed "heterocentrist readings of the film have been remiss in failing to take into account the homosexual nature of the director's personal obsession" (p. 175) and stresses that Visconti's "homosexual sensibility in *Ossessione* both manifests itself and seeks refuge in a variety of closets" (p. 176). Visconti's *auteristic* gaze in this film, Van Watson suggests, is indeed highly (homo)erotic and derisive, with the film's narrative revolving around the tragic nature of human desire and involving four characters—three males and one female. They form complicated erotic triangles; one of them includes a homoerotic relationship between the male protagonist Gino (Massimo Girotti), Giovanna (Clara Calamai), and the *Spagnolo* (Elio Marcuzzo).

Emerging as one of the greatest Italian filmmakers of the 1960s (Bondanella, 2003), Federico Fellini would also encode homoeroticism within film narratives, particularly as a means of political activism. Apart from the participation of activist Giò Stajano (see chapter 3), in *La Dolce Vita* (1960), the great *regista* stresses Anita Ekberg's exuberant, curvaceous body. Her being possessed by the Roman summer heat can be interpreted as a drag-queen performance. In the famous scene shot in La Fontana di Trevi, she contorts her body in orgasmic ecstasy in the arms of Marcello Mastroiani, while the waters from Neptune's marble statue bathe their bodies. (I would go as far as over-reading the scene by saying that the statue virtually ejaculates on them.)

Social criticism and homoeroticism took the form of harsh poetry in the work of Pier Paolo Pasolini. Pasolini's films were not directly concerned with queer desire, but he directed a number of productions where sexuality plays a fundamental role in setting the story, either by being tied to the characters' personalities or to their destiny (consider, for example, the depiction of suburban male bonding, or the close-ups of half-naked male bodies, and the erotic tension in *Accattone*). As Bondanella (2003) suggests, Pasolini's films are weapons performing cultural criticism beyond the confines of sexual identity (Bondanella, 2003). Or, to put it differently, his work revealed heterosexuality as political discipline, and not only as a sexual norm. Same-sex eroticism in Pasolini's films is often intertwined with violence, death, or decadence, and although his films are sometimes tinted with shadows of melancholy, they stretch social conventions, challenging traditions and defying normalcy (see Bondanella, 2003). Pasolini's treatment of sexuality and sexual norms is influenced by his Gramscian reading of class struggle. Consequently, the spectator is sometimes confronted with a view of sexuality that is violent and depraved, or of social relationships that fall under the microscopic control of the church and the family. Pasolini's films can strategically induce anxiety. The viewer is recklessly taken to the point of demanding liberation from social and ideological power, but it is just then that Pasolini makes us understand that liberation is impossible unless we make it happen. This *grand* way of narrating frustrates the reader with the intention of mobilizing reactions of rebellion and disgust with capitalism. One can appreciate Pasolini's point of view by situating some of his films within the political atmosphere in which they appeared—for example, as was suggested above, from activism efforts like FUORI!'s and its intense interest in advocating the subversion of heterosexism and class. Pasolini's revolutionary energy is best illustrated in two films: *Teorema* (1968) and *Salò o le 120 Giornate di Sodoma* (Salò, 1975). In the first one, criticism is directed at the dismantling of a family by including a strange and, we could say, probably bisexual character (Terence Stamp). His intense vision (probably a reference to class/imaginary identifications) and charm unchains in complicated ways the madness and sexuality of all the members of an industrial Milanese family, including the father and his son. The film's progressive movement toward madness and death can be read as an allegory of the alienation and madness intrinsic to the bourgeoisie (Moliterno, 2003). Further, Pasolini investigates capitalist perversion in *Salò o le 120 Giornate di Sodoma* (Salò, 1975). As suggested by Bondanella (2003) and Schinardi (2003), Pasolini here finds inspiration in the Marquis de Sade and Dante Alighieri to castigate the structural excess of consumer capitalism. From de Sade, authors explain, he takes the storyline of four cruel fascists (each representative of a different oppressive social institution) who exercise violence without restraint during a vacation in their palace, located in the fascist retreat of Salò (the city where Mussolini founded a fascist state just before his downfall). From Dante, Pasolini travels the descending circles toward hell and recombines them in a quaternary structure (four male protagonists, four daughters, etc.; see Bondanella, 2003; Schinardi, 2003). More than making a particular statement about homosexuality, Pasolini criticizes the power of consumerism over social and individual subjectivity. By taking this issue to the realm of bodily excess, he is able to perform a visual deconstruction of the death drive inherent in mutual human domina- tion and objectification: pure bodies of unlimited desire and cruelty com- manded by an all-consuming death drive (see Bondanella, 2003).

Bondanella also explains that, together with Pasolini, another young filmmaker became the international diplomat of the Italian postneorealist generation: Bernardo Bertolucci, who had been Pasolini's assistant. Both received attention from critics and global audiences alike. In addition, both directors engaged in sociopolitical criticism through their productions, making use of neo-Marxism and psychoanalytic intellectual sources (Bon- danella, 2003). Just months after *Teorema* was released, Bertolucci produced *Il Conformista* (The Conformist, 1970), which presented Italian audiences with an original cinematic adaptation of the novel written by Alberto Moravia. In this film, Bertolucci elaborated on the relationship between guilt and sexuality, with a queer character whose unstable psychology is tied to the tormented culture of Italy in 1938 and to his own relationship with fascism.

Undoubtedly, Fellini also made use of psychoanalytic notions in portray- ing human desire. One is even inclined to find notions that Deleuze and Guatari would develop in the *Anti-Oedipus*, for there are memorable scenes in *La Dolce Vita* that speak quite sardonically about the Freudian *Es* (the orgiastic party scene being the most obvious). Nevertheless, the film is more generally interested in critically exploring liberal and capitalist immorality, leading to decadence in the Italian post-war upper class, and its dialectic opposite, represented in the desperation of fishermen (see Bondanella, 2003;

Landy, 2000). These issues are explored several times in the movie. For example, while a group of high-class eccentrics is partying around a medieval *castello*, exhausted farmers move their bodies repeatedly while working the soil. When the orgiastic extravaganza ends, the participants look like vampires being burned by the sunlight at dawn; they drunkenly wander around a Mediterranean beach while poor fishermen bring fish from the shore as part of their daily work. The last scene of the movie shows the irreconcilable division between these worlds. The main character stands on one side of the beach with his new group of friends, making it impossible for him to listen to what a young working-class girl says to him from the other shore. In other words, Marcello Mastroiani's character *cannot listen to her* anymore—he's been somehow deprived of what makes him most human, the possibility of listening to another human being, of identifying with somebody else's existence even if for only a moment. There are references in the movie to cross-dressing and homosexual desire, including Stajano's effeminate and extravagant performance. Nevertheless, since this character completes the repertoire of eccentricities and pastiches in the film, it is clear that the film does not intend to confirm anything about homosexuality *per se*, but tries to denounce the lightness of bourgeois morals (see Bondanella, 2003; Landy, 2000).

During the 1970s, a number of remarkable productions included homosexual characters or homoerotic relations: Liliana Cavani's *Al di là del Bene e del Male* (Beyond Good and Evil, 1977) presents tormented characters united in a bisexual triangle, and Salvatore Samperi's *Ernesto* (1979) reinterprets the novel written by Umberto Saba, which describes the homoerotic discoveries of the male protagonist (Schinardi, 2003). Finally, *Una Giornata Particolare* (A Special Day, 1977) by Ettore Scola narrates the besieged life of a gay radio host, Gabriele (Marcello Mastroiani), persecuted by the fascist regime. His neighbor Antonietta (Sophia Loren) sees her morals and nationalistic ideology challenged after they meet and develop a friendship (see Bertelli, 2002; Schinardi, 2003).

During the same decade, productions elaborated on the contrasts between normal and anti-normative sexuality, some of them in very tragic terms, some of them in humorous fashion: Visconti's classic *Morte a Venezia* (Death in Venice, 1971) and the internationally successful Italian-French comedy *La Cage aux Folles* (I) (1978) are probably the most renowned. Peter Bondanella (2003) situates *Morte a Venezia* among the most mature films to break with the neorealist "canon." Indeed, he claims that it is in the course of three movies—*La Caduta degli Dei* (The Damned, 1969), *Morte a Venezia*, and *Ludwig* (1972)—that Visconti "moves from analyses of Italian society in the post-Risorgimento or post-war periods to consider a broader view of European culture" (p. 203). In them, Bondanella suggests, Visconti explores the rise of National Socialism and its devastating impact on European aristocratic families through contrasts such as raw beauty and intolerable decadence, which is the main theme in *Morte a Venezia*. In Visconti's work, it is left to the family the role of performing a political criticism of traditional social formations:

> I tell these stories about the self-destruction and dissolution of families as if I were recounting a Requiem. . . .I have a very high opinion of "decadence," just as, for example, Thomas Mann did. I have been imbued with this spirit: Mann was a decadent of German culture, I of Italian formation. What has always interested me is the analysis of a sick society. (Visconti, cited in Bondanella, p. 203)

As Gerber (2005) states, *Morte a Venezia* is above all the narrative of a subjective collapse, that is, a moment when the symbolic coordinates are insufficient to frame the encounter with the real. The real can be read here in the plague, a metaphor for decay and death that advances inexorably, embracing the body and its organs. At the same time, one can read in this psychological collapse something of the Lacanian notion of unlimited enjoyment, a break with the stability of an individual's well-being that demonstrates the weak status of the ego. The film, Gerber suggests, is a narrative of forbidden homosexual desire as well, taking the form of love and creative madness. As the plague explodes, it takes back into the ocean all the values the main character believes in, as well as the politically correct conventions of bourgeois existence. The paradox is that, in order to live, Von Aschenbach (Dirk Bogarde) does not look forward, but somehow backward, trying to return to a primordial state that Freud would have described as the force of masochism. Following Gerber (2005), the protagonist desperately looks to re-encounter a mythical form of beauty, which he finds represented in the unattainable Tadzio (Bjørn Andresen), an *efebo* whose androgynous look might be described today as what Wilchins (2004) calls genderqueer.

Gerber (2005) also points out that against every rational consideration, von Aschenbach wants to return to the mythical origins of beauty and life, and finally abandons himself to a love that devastates him. Nevertheless, this encounter never takes place, in the sense that such a return to a primordial state is structurally impossible: it is a state of completedness that never existed. Both the object and the subject of such a mythical moment, Freud would have remarked, are constructions that happen *a posteriori*. What really torments the protagonist, therefore, is the anxiety related to the discovery that such an encounter will never or can never actually happen. In complicating the relationship between the subject and the object, Visconti's film can be read as the encounter of the lack that inhabits the self, a gap impossible to symbolize and which no relation can suture. In Freudian psychoanalysis, this dilemma is expressed in the (dis)encounter between the subject and the object, when the subject is *driven* automatically beyond the pleasure principle (see Gerber, 2005). *Morte a Venezia* thus uncovers the crossroads of the signifier, or the symbolic, and the drive as a continuous force working at the borders of the human body. Visconti contrasts such force with the force of the signifiers that are present in any culture and offers a criticism of bourgeois life as a symbolic framework that, ultimately, fails in providing the subject with significant experiences. Here, the incapacity of a culture to provide a network of signifiers to dignify human life demonstrates that the human subject is always also the cultural subject. In the origins of erotic life there is both, the encounter with the Other of language and the encounter with castration, the recognition of a lack that Von Aschenbach finds unbearable. "Lack" as used in this context also means lack of a sexual relation: although there is sexual intercourse, there is no object that complements the human subject.

Toward the end of the same decade, the Italian-French production *La Cage aux Folles* (1978) presented a very different approach to queer life. Whereas in *Morte a Venezia* spectators are offered a subtle reference to homosexuality, which appears sublimated in art or intertwined within a complex psychological drama, in *La Cage aux Folles* the narrative deals directly with homosexuality and presents a series of out-of-the-ordinary characters, ranging from the butch- acting gay to the disco-music drag queen. Italian comedy actor Ugo Togniazzi, playing a most uplifting and protective gay partner, Renato, easily won the hearts of a variety of audiences who came to love the messy life of a queer couple who are at pains to learn how to behave like straight men when they meet Renato's son's in-laws (see Schinardi, 2003). Although the sequels *La Cage aux Folles II* and *III* were not up to the original, this Italian-French movie is a crucial gay-cinema landmark for at least two reasons. First, it shocks the wide audience with controversial themes: the film shows, perhaps for the first time in the history of Italian cinema, a comedy equally appealing to gays and straights. What makes the characters so fascinating is their ability to rehearse gender construction and to mirror this rehearsal to us, the viewers. The performance the characters are so focused on is twofold: at the same time that they must rehearse straight life to save Renato's son, they also need to keep rehearsing their drag performances for the shows they stage every night as owners of an exclusive gay club. The comedy is ironic in its successful demonstration that we can or might have to spend all of our lives rehearsing gender performances to suit the Other's expectations. At the same time the film is also interested in showing the constraints to which gay couples are subject—for instance, when the couple rehearses heterosexual body language and politically correct "behaviors" during breakfast in an open-air café. In this sense, by imitating heterosexual behavior, the movie is a powerful critique of how the human body is constrained contextually to perform normative activities. The movie can be read as implying that at a certain level all human subjects cross-dress every day, a form of parody about sexual identity that would be theoretically explored years later by queer theorists.

La Cage aux Folles also anticipates controversies involving queer family relationships, insofar as Renato's child has been raised by the couple after being neglected by his mother, who only re-appears in the life of her son twenty years later. Now an adult, he confronts the dilemma of marrying a girl who comes from an upper-class, conservative, politically involved, Catholic family. The film documents in detail how disruptive it is for the couple to have to betray their own beliefs, identities, and lifestyles to make the son happy. Ultimately, it asserts that such an enterprise is impossible. Influenced by the increasing visibility of gay and lesbian activism in 1980s Europe, *La Cage aux Folles* is a political film about essential identities and, for this reason, it might be the European gay movie *par excellence* of its generation (see Cunningham, 2003; Schinardi, 2003).

Queerly Bent Italian Cinema: Themes and Anxieties

We can attribute to film critic B. Ruby Rich the term *new queer cinema*, first used to describe a number of independent U.S. and international films being presented during the United States's film festival circuit of 1991-1992 (Daniel and Jackson, 2003). What made these films extraordinary was the stories they told, which centered, perhaps for the first time, on simple stories of defiant characters who come out of the closet to confront social normativity and to explore forms of sexual pleasure beyond heterosexual boundaries (see Aaron, 2004; Davis, 2004). The innovative aspect of queer cinema was that the camera rejected the presentation of homosexuality stereotypically or in dramatic form. Instead, queer directors aimed to produce films that captured more subtle relationships among the body, desire, and society. Hence representations of same-sex desire as perversion or anomaly were contested and transformed by questioning the complex nature of human desire beyond the issue of sexual orientation; queer cinema made sexuality political and cultural rather than psychological and individual (see Aaron, 2004; Cunningham, 2003; Davis, 2004). In particular, new queer cinema challenged previous forms of gay cinema, which were usually centered exclusively on male-male desire with disregard for non-normative sexualities (see Aaron, 2004; Cunningham, 2003; Davis, 2004).

According to queer cinema experts, the making of queer cinema is to be understood in the context of changes in cinema, as well as within larger cultural shifts that occurred in several countries during the 1990s. These include the manifestation and struggle of queer subjectivities and queer politics, and the rise of other forms of political struggle against neoliberalism and corporatization. New queer cinema, in addition, offered an aesthetic critique that coincided with queer theory's questioning of naturalistic representations of identity, and constituted a symbolic site for contesting dominant representations about the intersections of race, language, and sexuality (see Aaron, 2004; Cunningham, 2003; Davis, 2004). Moreover, during the 1990s the word "queer" was used to define a kind of political identity that has to do primarily with ideological ascription and not necessarily with actual sexual practice (Dean, 2000). At that time, the word queer made reference to forms of subjectivities that are disregarded as secondary, as Teresa de Lauretis would say. Queer cinema brought new light to these subjectivities, offering them a symbolic space for expressing and unfolding their/our problematics autonomously or independently of their juridical, religious, and communal approval or disapproval. Queer cinema was successful in shocking the audiences and creating paradoxes and uncertainties that were not solved with a Hollywood-style "happy ending" (see Aaron, 2004; Cunningham, 2003; Davis, 2004). Finally, what helped make "queer" such a powerful signifier in the 1990s was its slippery nature, which avoided cohesive significations and could be deployed by many diverse social agents at the same time. Although sex is not at the center of "queer," sexuality is, as Dean (2000) has pointed out. In Dean's psychoanalytic view, the human being is a sexual subject due to the fact of being a subject of language, and hence at the crossroads with Otherness, no matter what the sex of the object toward which the sexual drive is oriented.

Some critics (Aaron, 2004; Cunningham, 2003) have noticed that after the first more rebellious productions, some queer cinema filmmakers adopted a language more pleasing for mainstream audiences. This was not a phenomenon directly associated with cinema but was more largely related to the commodification of difference as something "cool," as Naomy Klein would probably point out. Indeed, the increasing circulation of queerly bent movies in the media meant that large audiences were not only exposed to a variety of films, but also to television shows, advertising, and magazine articles where there appeared modes of desire that were not *prêt à porter*: they could not and cannot be easily packaged within anxiety-containing boundaries such as male/female or heterosexual/homosexual. Nevertheless, the fact that these forms of subjectivity were suddenly so attractive to large commercial media corporations and straight audiences is highly problematic. James Allan (2004) notices that since the 1990s, the formerly irregular presence of defiant sexualities, either in Hollywood movies or in independent films, has been rapidly reversed. Documentaries like Jennie Livingston's *Paris Is Burning* (1990) engendered immediate public and corporate repercussions (Allan, 2004). However, Allan notes that the emergence of independent films led to their mainstream "double"; these were high-budget, technologically mastered, and super-expensive Hollywood productions with megastar casts. Five years after the term "queer cinema" was coined, its subversive potential was already at risk of being devoured by mainstream cinema. As Allan (2004) notes, these productions attracted millions of spectators worldwide, usually by incorporating figures like Madonna (in *The Next Best Thing*), Julia Roberts (in *My Best Friend's Wedding*), or Jennifer Anniston (in *The Object of My Affection*) (Allan, 2004). A similar phenomenon has taken place in the last decade in Italy. On the one hand, we can observe increasing visibility for gay and lesbian groups in television shows and movies, including, for example, soap operas with gay characters and even reality shows with gay and also transgender and transsexual participants. On the other hand, what is surprising in the context of Italy is the speed with which these mass media products were so favorably received by large audiences or marketed as commodities. I am thinking, for example, not only of the box-office successes of Özpetek's films (see below) but also of major homoerotic advertising campaigns like the Dolce & Gabbana male underwear campaign launched for the 2006 World Soccer Cup Championship.

While during the 1980s the AIDS pandemic was timidly addressed by Italian filmmakers (see Bertelli, 2002), since the late 1990s the television and newspaper treatment of queer issues like civil unions in Europe has broadened and lent media attention to the rise of (mostly American) GLBTQ films in the country. Television visibility of same-sex desire has been coded in sitcoms translated into Italian, including *Will & Grace, Ellen, Sex and the City*, and *Friends* (where Ross's former wife discovers she is a lesbian after conceiving a child with him). These shows, however, are usually televised late at night, dubbed, and are oftentimes only available on cable television. Yet it is to be celebrated that new melodramas now disrupt the lazy television afternoon with the problems of gay people coming out (*Curoi Rubati* [Stolen Hearts], *Il Maresciallo Rocca*, or the more recent *Mio Figlio* [My Son]), and newspapers such as *La Repubblica* have devoted much space to the PACS project and the Rome Pride Parade (CulturaGay, 2005).

Are we, nevertheless, to celebrate increased visibility as something positive without noticing the irony that at the same time that this has happened, Parliament continues to delay legislative projects like PACS? One does not need to read *Dialectic of Enlightenment* to realize that while never before in the history of modern communication have the media devoted so much attention to queer sexuality and family relationships, mass-media products are usually acritical merchandise that respond automatically to the demands of diverse communities for more excitement and coolness (see Bernstein and Reimann, 2001). What is to be remembered, therefore, is that global media products like these are not simply commercial goods for spending free time, but rather have tremendous impact on identity formation, weighing upon bodies of suffering. Media products play a part in the social imaginary encoding of individual and group practices at a global and local level that direct, even if not mechanically, ideas and representations about subjects that still remain alienated (see Aaron, 2004; Allan, 2004; Daniel and Jackson, 2003).

As the authors cited above explain, mainstream media visibility can be problematic. The frenzy for queer cinema is not dissociated from the commodification of sexual identity, including the reinforcing of stereotypical representations and essentialisms. This is clear in the case of Italian cinema. Even before queer issues were at the center of Ferzan Özpetek's aesthetic sensibility or Antonio Capuano's social denunciations (see below), representations of homosexuality in Italian films flirted with homosexual desire. As was mentioned above, the works of directors like Bertolucci, Fellini, Pasolini, and Visconti were complicated for some spectators; they alluded to theoretical notions, exhibited high visual quality, addressed themes with density, and, in some cases, required theatrical performances. Of late, the highest standards of the Italian canon have been kept alive by independent and mainstream directors who try to compete in a market oriented toward the commercial box office. In the case of queer cinema, this is a particular problem, because the release of a large number of queer films, usually not so stylistically refined, tend to bend to the pressure of a market eager for (and shocked by) queer issues more than it is interested in complex criticism of sexuality and society. An example can clarify this point.

In *Uomini Uomini Uomini* (Men Men Men, 1995), director Christian de Sica constructs a stereotypical narrative about gayness, where being gay is equated with manly behavior, heterosexual clothing, and masculine bonding, leaving unquestioned the system of meaning that lies behind gender. The movie has the advantage, however, of problematizing in quite original terms the ticklish subjects of aging "gay" and aging "single." For Italy, despite the century-long struggle of the gay and feminist movements, heterosexual marriage still constitutes a foundational tradition, a signifier that metonymically stands for "heteronormative family," Catholic religious "faithfulness," and accommodation to a standard of living. However, marriage has also been a much-contested notion, not only because for over a century feminists have challenged it, but also because diverse regional and ethnic constituencies have constantly redefined the meaning of the "Mediterranean family." One positive aspect of the film, therefore, is that Italian males who do not want to get married might identify with the gay characters' loneliness and despair as they confront exclusion by a society that tends to consider unmarried men as second-rate individuals. Nevertheless, *Uomini Uomini Uomini* eliminates the traces of regionalism and strategically appropriates and stabilizes one meaning of sexuality and one version of "marriage." This happens three times in the film: in the marriage of one of the main character's former lovers to a woman, despite his being in love with his ex-partner; in the double life of one character, a married man who discovers that he is gay late in his life and laments the consequences for his child; and in the co-dependent relationship of a middle-aged character with his old mother, with whom he still lives until her death. Instead of questioning the language of the dominant to encourage radical ideological critique, the strategy at play in the film is to use the language of the resistance to constitute a form of ideological acquiescence to cultural domination, as Rocchio (1999) has perfectly explained in his discussion of neorealism. In Lacanian terms, marriage is used as a Master signifier that abstracts regional, sexual, and class differences. In this case, according to Rocchio's model, the narrative makes use of the same strategy as the ideology it is supposed to criticize, because it constructs one truth and one possible resistance to this truth—the fact that in this movie the characters are all professional white men from upper-class Rome invites any cosmopolitan audience to identify with such a Master signifier (Rocchio, 1999).

Nevertheless, to its credit, *Uomini Uomini Uomini* raises a disturbing question regarding the globalization of *gayness* as it is seen in the supposed codes, behaviors, likes and dislikes, dramas, and vicissitudes that a supposedly typical gay should ascribe to in order to fit into an European city. What is at stake here is what "being gay" means, how it is negotiated, and what consequences can be drawn from the materialization of an essentialist, global gayness. This is a crucial question for filmmakers and critics, since the representational codes that are used in constructing queerness, the narratives created for international audiences, and the way desire is encrypted in the script are never naïve issues, but always political viewpoints.

In this sense, queer films should provide signifiers that express what commercial movies repress (but never completely erase, as Vitto Russo's [1987] seminal study *The Celluloid Closet* showed). Accordingly, queer films can resist and reveal alternatives to representational codes that reify or reduce the complexity of human desire. Queer films can surprise the spectator who has been seduced by narratives of chromosomal homosexuality, educated by the myth of sexual orientation, or terrified by the psychological codes of pathology. Mainstream films that include queer issues because they are cool or simply because they are profitable remain antithetical to a politically useful queer vision if they do not engage, for instance, in a critique of the sociosexual construction of subjectivity or in an analysis of the pleasures, limits, and contours of human desire.

Whether new queer cinema represents only an Anglo-American aesthetic or an ideal type of queerness exceeds the scope of this essay. In the case of Italian film, however, there are a number of directors whose works are creating a new aesthetic and political sensibility. Among them, Andrea Adriatico, Ferzan Özpetek, Antonio Capuano, Pino Quartullo, and Gianna Maria Gabelli stand out. It would be impossible to do justice to all of these directors here. Instead, I would like to make brief reference to three films that share a particular concern for the issue of non-heteronormative unions and parenthood: *Il Vento di Sera, Nunzio Pianese,* and *Le Fate Ignoranti.* These films complicate the singular characteristics of the heterosexual, middle-class, urban Italian family by asserting the existence of wide regional, class, and sexual differences, and by criticizing the continuous unwillingness of the Italian state to legitimate families of choice.

The Quest for Rights

While queer film directors emphasize the changing nature of the nuclear, middle-class, heterosexual family, several individuals in same-sex relationships across Italy are seeking to obtain a state license that legitimates their unions. These relationships seek to transform and politicize the family, and the struggle is writing a new page in Italian history. Following the official norms of countries as varied as Argentina, Canada, France, Holland, or Spain, these activists are trying to pass laws allowing civil unions. It is imperative to recognize that this struggle takes place within a cultural milieu where gays, lesbians, bisexuals, transgender, and queer people continue to live in a state of what Vaid (1995) calls virtual equality,

> which simulates genuine civic equality but cannot transcend the simulation. . . .We proceed as if we enjoy real freedom, real acceptance, as if we have won lasting changes in the laws and mores of our nation. . . .[b]ut the actual facts and conditions that define gay and lesbian life demonstrate that we have won "virtual" freedom and "virtual" equal treatment under "virtually" the same laws as straight people. (Vaid, 1995, p. 4)

As an illustration of this virtually equal status that Vaid describes, Andrea Adriatico's *Il Vento, di Sera* (The Wind in the Evening, 2004) is instructive of the interrelation of social norms and individual subjectivity. The film begins with shots of interchanging cellular phones' text messages, interspersed with images of the protagonist, Paolo (Corso Salani) at his home, and his boyfriend Luca (Luca Levi) at a nearby train station. The text messages are in fact secret codes for shooting a politician. When the terrorist attack begins, Luca is shot just as his boyfriend comes out to the street to see what is causing so much noise. The film's narrative unfolds from the moment Luca is shot to the moment of his death in hospital and the following rituals of mourning. As Lazere (2004) has pointed out, director Andrea Adriatico takes advantage of his vast experience as a theater director to stage a slow-paced narrative situated within a dark night, where the characters' psyches are chased by the arches and alleyways of Emilia Romagna's best architecture.

Critics like Lazere indicate that the narrative is centered on the psychological effects of the horrifying political crime in Bologna that, sweeping away the life of Paolo's lover and partner, confronts the protagonist and the viewers with the fragility of the human condition. The sudden loss of the beloved partner unpredictably unmasks the fundamental void constitutive of the human subject. The loss of an object of love always reveals to the subject a more fundamental lack, the lack of an object-complement that fulfills or completes human sexuality.

As Arthur Lazere (2004) points out:

> Adriatico (along with co-screenwriter Stefano Casi) effectively makes these very real and legitimate points about the ways that gay couples are not equal before the law, but he doesn't dwell on them. Paolo's vulnerability to such unfair treatment serves only to rub salt in the wound of his profound loss. He is bereft; the structure of his life, the long-term loving relationship at its center is now broken and blown away like so many leaves in a windstorm. (parag. 4)

Because humans are symbolic beings, there is no *natural* relationship between the subject and the object, for the object only serves as a decoy for the course of desire. In other words, there is no object that 'regains' the impossible, mythical enjoyment the neurotic fantasizes with. The loss of an object—the lack of "the" object—appears in this film complicated, however, by the fact that with the terrorist killing of Paolo's lover, an abrupt hole in the symbolic network is exposed as a wound or cut that cannot be closed up by personal mourning. The working out of the loss—mourning—is interrupted when Paolo starts to search for truth, by finding answers about the attack. What is revealed through this narrative is that the fracture in the subject is not personal, insofar as the subject is not the individual or "self," but is instead a subject inscribed in the realm of culture. Hence the murder of his partner is also an attack on the whole community, shaken as it is by the reign of silence when no one wants to claim responsibility. In this light, *Il Vento, di Sera* is akin to Antigone's struggle to bury the body of her brother against the edict of Creon.

In Seminar VII, *The Ethics of Psychoanalysis*, Lacan asserts the impersonal character of the symbolic. The cultural rituals that accompany the mourning of a dead person are the logical culmination—and extension—of the inscription of the human being in the symbolic order, which starts when the subject is given a name through parental desire, and continues even after death, in the universal forms of rituals of bereavement. Like Creon, who moves against the symbolic by enforcing his own "particularistic" norm, in *Il Vento, di Sera* the representatives of the juridical order deny Paolo all possibility of mourning. In an act of extreme violence, he is not considered a relative of the deceased: he cannot enter the hospital where he rests nor is he granted any rights of succession. The protagonist's tragedy coincides exactly with the social drama—the drama of a society silenced, of relationships counter to what is considered the norm, of subjectivities violently pushed to invisibility. The assassination of Paolo's partner strongly affects the social bond, making the point that the struggle for the rights of gay and lesbian couples are not a "particularistic" or "personal" struggle but are at the level of universal human rights. Paolo's love for his partner, their "ordinary life," makes his pain a cause for the viewer's identification, not because the narrative revolves around the personal drama of the character, but because his pain is intrinsic to the human condition and yet absolutely singular. Just like all profound human pain, Paolo's testimony of the weakness of our existence is situated on the edge between private life and public life—hence making evident the central role of social and juridical institutions to articulate the symbolic.

Queers and the Catholic Church: Who Enjoys More?

Because religious life is central to the historical makeup of the Italian state and to ideologies about the family, the role played by the Catholic Church in Italy cannot be dissociated from considerations about the legal status of gay, lesbian, bisexual, transsexual, and queer Italian people. As early as 1999, Pope Benedict XVI (Cardinal Ratzinger during the 1990s) affirmed that it was sometimes important to discriminate against homosexuals (see Rossi Barilli, 1999). Later on, in March 2003, the Roman Catholic Church released a 900-page document, *The Lexicon*, which reaffirmed the key points of Catholic sexual ethics: its attack on civil and same-sex cohabitation, and its condemnation of homosexual parents. Homosexual parenthood is constructed in *The Lexicon* through a rhetoric that likens it to pedophilia: "The pedophiles, following the example of the homosexuals, have begun secretly and with firmness to fight for their supposed rights, in an attempt to make legal their actions" (Arcigay, 2003; my translation). In *The Lexicon*, homosexuality appears schematized as sadomasochism and pederasty, derived from psychical weakness or anxiety, and hence deprived of basic social and human rights: "There shall be no rights granted to homosexuality, which must not constitute the foundations of any juridical vindications. Homosexuality is not a subject of juridical right because it has no social value whatsoever. . .it remains a psychical complex which cannot be instituted socially" (Arcigay, 2003; my translation).

The role of the church is addressed in recent Italian queerly bent cinema, which suggests the alliance of institutional Catholicism with political power and corruption. This is the case in Antonio Capuano's *Pianese Nunzio, Quattordici Anni a Maggio* (1996, Sacred Silence). As critics note, on the one hand, there is in this movie a narrative from the point of view of a thirteen-year-old boy, Pianese Nunzio (Emanuele Gargiulo) (Queer View, 1997). He's a lively character who, like many teenagers, wishes only to be a pop star and to be in front of television cameras. He sometimes makes it to the screen in cheap commercials, but the film interprets this ironically, for unlike other teenagers who might become famous, he is exploited. Pianese finds peace only during his regular meetings with Father Lorenzo Borelli (Fabrizio Bentivoglio), his spiritual benefactor, who also gives other working-class children protection and food. The story is complicated as it questions the social and political value of Christian charity and solidarity. Indisputably, the priest is the bravest member of the community. He is the only one who seems to confront the *camorra* (a corrupt criminal society similar to the *mafia* but operating in the region of Campania) and asks the members of his church to help him stop the violence that is killing more and more children every day. The *camorra* leaders are depicted in this film as beyond the limits of the law, acting with total impunity, through a dynamic of power that exercises control and threatens the population by means of violence and terror. These groups represent organized crime, and might appear somehow connected to some members of the Catholic Church and the government. As a perverse Other, the *camorra* promises a better life for teenagers, while at the same time exploiting them in drug traffic (Queer View, 1997).

The priest can do very little to dismantle the *camorra* or reduce the incidence of innocent people dying in the streets day after day. Instead of renouncing his ideals, Father Borelli moves a step forward and decides to put his life at risk by mobilizing the whole population against the mafia. His sermons become openly political and controversial, and he concludes mass by denying holy communion to the members of the community. Interestingly, the *camorra* leaders meet and agree that they must get rid of the priest by exposing his sexuality and implicating him in the sexual abuse of Nunzio Pianese (Queer View, 1997).

Herein rests the crux of the film, which defies reductionism. A few lines above, I stated that the *camorra* appeared to be beyond the law, making it a group operating with impunity. However, just at the moment when viewers most likely have figured out who the good guys and the bad guys are, a dialectical turn inverts the order of things. The priest actually *is* abusing the child, a fact that destabilizes the narrative and makes it impossible for the viewer to hold on to any particular Master signifier. As Žižek would probably say, the film unmasks the whole in the Other, confronting the viewer with castration. The Father who was supposed to be the defender of the child suddenly appears to be instead the Father of complete enjoyment whom Freud describes in *Totem and Taboo*. The dialectical turn works because viewers are abruptly confronted with the fact that they had placed too much confidence in the priest, elevating him to the stature of the Ideal or investing him as representative of the symbolic, while in fact the Father is not only affected by the same castration, but even more, he appears to be a child-molesting pervert beyond the law. Throughout the movie there is a sense of anxiety that finds no resolution, for it is impossible to locate the symbolic coordinates of the victim—is it the child sexually molested by the priest, or is it that the child is already a victim of the corrupted social system? Is the priest a psychological abuser, or is his sexuality the ultimate form of contesting the private/public divide? Are his actions personal or symptomatic of the decadence of the social structure?

What is most fascinating about this film is its connection with the issue of parenthood. In the case of *Nunzio Pianese*, parenthood is *barred* (crossed by the bar of castration). This uncertainty might force the viewer to question the usual notions of parenthood. What is a parent? Who is the father? Is it the man who biologically conceived the child only to abandon him later? Is the parental function exercised by the social institutions, which are suspiciously interested in the welfare of Nunzio? Is the father the priest Borelli, who protects and teaches the child, but who also abuses him? Or is it the woman who is the child's current caregiver? Throughout the movie this question is never answered, thus rejecting objective, universal knowledge about parent-hood—a reminder of the Lacanian dictum that the father is pure uncertainty. This uncertainty comes to the front in the drammatic biography of Nunzio, and it confronts the viewer with his/her own anxiety—the way each of us, through our own biographies and neuroses, resolves the question about the father.

Here, following Lacanian authors like Bruce Fink, Tim Dean, and Slavoj Žižek, one could say that the Lacanian notion of a Master signifier is most provocative, for a Master signifier tries to represent the uncertainty of the parental function. That is, a Master signifier is an element that rises from the chain of signifiers to stand in the site of the Other, to veil the castration of the Other. The *name-of-the-father* (or parental function) determines the lack in the Other by inscribing the subject in an order of incompleteness. The symbolic is always ordered around a fundamental lack: there is no complete set of signifiers. Instead, the Master signifier promises completeness, a form of knowledge in which the big Other is neither barred nor castrated, discrediting the *pas savoir faire* that characterizes human sexuality[2] (see Fink, 1995, 2004).

One of the issues encoded by Capuano's movie, beyond the surface of Nunzio's psycho-social victimization, is that the neurotic *fantasy* is so difficult to examine because the "victim" is participating in the game of the Other, maintaining the form of enjoyment s/he complains about. Of course I am not here referring to Nunzio as a child, but to Nunzio as a metaphor of a society whose enjoyment is often projected as the radical enjoyment of an Other. When "homosexuals" are constructed as deviants, or as psychically ill people who must not raise children for the reason that they are pedophiles who might abuse the child, the underlying fantasy is that homosexuals are bodies of complete enjoyment, an exorbitant form of pleasure that contravenes all humanity (Dean, 2000). In the case of the Vatican document, this would be translated as follows: "is there someone who enjoys more than us?" Because such interrogation is impossible (because there is no extra-linguistic

Other), it can only be answered through the very same meta-linguistic affirmation that the statement implies. As in the case of Snow White's stepmother, whose question to the mirror always returned her own beautiful image (precisely because she was talking to a mirror!) until the day when the Otherness of Snow White broke into the story ("Yes! There is someone more beautiful than you"), here the homophobic fantasy constructs the Other that it is so desperately looking for: "Yes! There is one who enjoys more than you do" (in this case, homosexuals). Therefore, there is no representation of *homosexualities* in this religious fantasy. The erasure of singularity favors the fantasy of the homosexual, a radical Other of unrestricted enjoyment.

Although there are many issues that constrain gays, lesbian, bisexuals, transgenders, and queers in Italy, the arena of same-sex parenthood can be considered the most controversial one because of the signifiers and fantasies it stirs up. Homosexual parenthood is discursively constructed by state apparatuses and religious institutions with Master, sexist signifiers. In addition, it is constructed through the primacy of a binary logic of thought that serves to deny us most of the formal and substantive human, civil, and citizenship rights.

Italian queerly bent cinema shows a paradoxical interest in the question of parenthood that, as Rocchio's (1999) model suggests, engages the acute anxiety of a changing culture where the traditional model of family is not exempted from the crisis that this institution is undergoing in other Western countries. The question about parenthood that these productions encode, the search for redefining parenthood, is a question about the uncertainty of the symbolic, which characterizes the human world. However, nowadays this question is encoded in the cinematic experience more powerfully than ever before through the unfixed nature of human sexuality, its relationship with power structures, and its bond with political life. Refining conceptual understandings of sexuality, love, and intimacy in Italy enables a tactical interrogation of common assumptions about the Italian family, partnership, and parenthood. More important, it helps to distinguish the unfixed character of human sexuality, which differs drastically from the imaginary and social constraints in which it can appear misrepresented, distorted, or perversely manipulated.

Political Solidarity and Transgression in Özpetek's Families of Choice

Despite the fact that the Italian nuclear, heterosexist family has been systematically questioned by queers and allies for being a restricting model for understanding intimacies, a large number of Italians struggle for the legitimacy of their relationships as families. Following Lehr's (1999) model, though, it is possible to understand that queer families do not conform to the standards of the heterosexist, nuclear, middle-class, urban family; instead, they contest it while demonstrating that other arrangements (multiparenthood, multi-partnership, transgender unions, and interracial/interethnic/intergenerational same-sex couples, to mention just a few variations) are legitimate forms of human intimacy and relationship. What is more, some of these intimacies can challenge certain values derived from gender divides, norms attached to parental roles, hierarchies resulting from domestic asymmetries, emotional attachments to monogamy, emphasis on reproductive, genital sexuality, gender and sexual performance, and so forth (see Kirsch, 2000; Lehr, 1999; Stacey and Davenport, 2002; Weeks et al., 2001).

Contrary to these values, queer intimacies of the kind I am describing (including those of GLBTQs and non-heterosexist heterosexuals) are supported in an ethics of difference and care. By this I mean that the queer intimacies I have in mind (regardless of the sexual activity or choices of the persons involved) are forms of relationality that have the potential to recognize the foreignness intrinsic to human life, the contingencies of human biography. Care of the other and of the self imply recognition that the human condition is open to the unpredictable boundaries of each individual's biography, what Lacanians call the contingency of the real. Further, while these ethics preserve the unique symbolic status of the human being, they do not wish to codify in any system of norms any repertoire of behaviors—in other words, these are not prescriptive ethics or moral catalogs. These are ethics of intimacy founded on the unending flux of desire, not on the attachment to any particular object. Romanticized ideas about queer families of choice tend to obscure the fact that there is no domestication of the real—that the human condition moves dialectically toward its own insurmountable Otherness.

In his six films as a director, Turkish-Italian filmmaker Ferzan Özpetek explores some of these controversial issues. His often autobiographic narratives place emphasis on cultural and sexual transitional spaces and

identities while avoiding over-romanticized cinematic views on queerness. His films exhort queers to strengthen their commitment to political solidarity in several ways. These are ways of speaking and doing that were introduced in Lehr's (1999) seminal study of queer families: the need to create a communality of interests, responsibilities, and sympathies within groups of eclectic subjectivities that cultivate the intrinsic sexual and racial difference of each identity; and, we could add, to strive for a better world that is not deaf to radical Otherness (not only sexual, class, or national Otherness, but of that radical foreignness that constitutes the human condition as such).

Crisscrossing Trajectories. Özpetek's journey in the world of cinema started more than twenty years ago, when he began working as a correspondent for Turkish newspapers and as an assistant director to Julien Beck and Ricky Tognazzi. His six films, *Saturno Contro* (2007), *Cuore Sacro* (2005), *La Finestra di Fronte* (Facing Window, 2003), *Le Fate Ignoranti* (His Secret Life, 2001), *Harem Suaré* (The Last Harem, 1999), and *Hamam* (The Turkish Bath, 1997), have had international repercussions. *Hamam* was applauded at the 1997 Quinzaine des réalisateurs during the Cannes Film Festival, the same festival where, two years later, *Harem Suaré* became a favorite contender. *Le Fate*, a main attraction at the Berlin Festival in 2001, won four Nastri d'Argento awards. And, finally, *La Finestra di Fronte* was hailed throughout Europe, granting the director four Davids of Donatello awards (see CulturaGay, 2005).

Born in Turkey in 1959, Özpetek has much in common with others who were forced to or decided to live as expatriates. He moved to Italy, struggled for work, perfected his education, and began a career as assistant director in a variety of films, including television, short, and feature films.[3] It took fifteen years of hard work to perfect his vision and to start work on his own films. When it was the right time, he decided to shoot a film that addressed the thorny issues of death and sexuality—in other words, two issues that demand, probably, the most demanding psychological elaboration, as Freud would say. He named the film *Hamam*, and it became the first in a series of films in which the artist introduces the principal questions posed in all his later films (see Anderlini-D'Onofrio, 2004; CulturaGay, 2005). It is Özpetek's own transnational identity that allows him to do cinematic research focusing on those aspects of cultural behavior, sexuality, and queer performance that are sometimes taken for granted. Özpetek confronts the map of multiculturalism at times when the national self wants to be secured by new immigration and national policies. This is not to suggest that there is something essentially peculiar about his perspective solely because he was not born in Italy. Instead, it is to suggest that he is as foreign to Italy as to Turkey. To me, Özpetek speaks the language of the frontier, he dreams of transitional spaces that are neither interior nor exterior (the Turkish bath in *Hamam*,[4] Michele's terrace in *Le Fate Ignoranti*, the Harem in *Harem Suaré*, a ghostly house in *Cuore Sacro*, and an extended-family kitchen in *Saturno Contro*), and he depicts times that defy chronology. Where one would see only torn architectures, he envisions old-time scenarios, hidden pleasures, and sensual mysticisms. Defying the separation between life and death or between mine and yours (as in *Cuore Sacro*) his characters' souls are continually reelaborated in the actions and decisions that they need to take in view of their loved ones' destiny. Furthermore, by contesting gay/straight divides, Özpetek's films open spaces for an erotica reminiscent of Mario Mieli's *transessuale*, in the sense that his films complicate the cultural construction of femininity and masculinity as much as they complicate notions of nationality and national ideology (see Anderlini-D'Onofrio, 2004; CulturaGay, 2005).

When Özpetek puts to work his own experience as a border-crossing person, he composes critical ethnographic films, in the sense that the self is reinvented through an inquiry into one's choices in life. The wager of his films is invigorated by the creation of his public persona, for he is rarely seen in interviews or on television shows. While Özpetek has been acclaimed by gay and straight audiences, he is to be regarded as little concerned with evoking or representing earlier strands of Italian or Turkish cinema,[5] and little interested in making gay cinema (CulturaGay, 2005). My interest in briefly noting these aspects of Özpetek's identity has nothing to do with a deterministic analysis of his work in relation to his biography. Rather, I am interested in writing about an artist with whom I identify as a transnational queer person in Italy, for I suspect that viewers whose cultural identity is being complicated as they travel across nations, or whose politics or sexualities do not conform to standard norms, might feel attracted to this auteur.

His Works. Özpetek's interest in the ethics of care and political solidarity as created by some queer families is a common concern in his films. A most important source for understanding some of these films is Anderlini-D'Onofrio's (2004) essay, which clarifies the themes and destiny of each protagonist. Özpetek usually portrays ordinary characters who change in unexpected ways. For example, in *Hamam* there is a typical representation of a middle-class professional, an architect from downtown Rome who lives in a large *palazzo*. This man, Francesco (Alessandro Gassman), must travel to Turkey in order to accept a Turkish bathhouse his aunt had owned for years, after she started a new life far away from Italy (and far away from past love ghosts and melancholia), and which she wanted him to inherit. On his arrival in Istanbul, Francesco meets the group of people whom his aunt had adopted as her (one is tempted to say "queer") family of choice: a patriarchal man named Mr. Osman (Halil Ergün) and his wife, Perran (Serif Sezer); their teenage daughter Fusun (Basak Köklükaya); and her brother Mehmet (Mehmet Gunsur). While this family is not composed of gays or lesbians, they might be seen as queer if we are able to appreciate their everyday interactions, the way they care for each other, and the rituals they engage in. What is important here, I would underline, is not whether the family is made of queers, but the way they speak and do queer for Francesco. What I am trying to stress is that one should not come to Özpetek's films with the only reason of expecting to see gay/lesbian relations—though they sometimes are present in his films. Instead, one should come to appreciate the predicament or psychological crisis that the encounter with Otherness creates in either a main character (in this case Francesco) or, conversely, in the viewer. Read in this light, the family organization that Francesco finds in Istanbul differs from his way of organizing the world. In other words, the family he encounters counts for Francesco as a social organization that has arranged the signifiers available in the symbolic domain in a completely different fashion. This different way of arranging signifiers is crucial, for it informs the political potential of the film as it shows that social life and its derived subjectivity can be redone and challenged. Even if Francesco is Italian, the host family he finds appears *strange* to him at first, probably too united. One is tempted to see here an insinuation that Özpetek is making: depicting a Middle Eastern family that, ironically, resembles in some ways basic aspects of the Italian family.

In this family, Anderlini-D'Onofrio's work insinuates, Francesco's aunt might have been forced by her alien status to build a new, non-essentialist identity through the building of a transitional/transnational (and possibly) queer persona. Indeed, one would wonder if she had moved out of Italy in an attempt to escape a past of excruciating oppression by a heterosexist society, or if she had already experienced forbidden pleasures and was now trying to make sense of her identity in a new light. As Anderlini-D'Onofrio (2004) shows, in Istanbul she revived an old hamam and gave men access to other forbidden pleasures. Her hamam is really a reflection of her new non-identity, which Francesco confronts, as he is also adopted by the family that his aunt assembled in Turkey. They protect him and give him the comfort to start his own travel in the borderlands of identity, a process by which he has a glimpse into his aunt's pains and glories through letters preserved in a private chest, as well as through daily anecdotes told by her relatives of choice while they share their homemade food with him (see Anderlini-D'Onofrio, 2004; Due 2005). The delights of Turkish food and dishes, smoke, sensual dances, and colors are overemphasized in the film, to the extent that Özpetek's *Hamam* sometimes insists on an exotic representation of Turkey. As Bülent Diken and Carsten Bagge Laustsen (2001) put it, in discussing the Orient,

> the configuration of the self and other is not primarily related to the construction of differences within a symbolic space. Rather, the Orient functions as a fantasy space of that which is prior to social or linguistic differences. In this context the Orient demonstrates a remarkable formlessness: it is not only the Other but also the hyperbolic. (p. 761)

Nevertheless, I agree with Serena Anderlini-D'Onofrio (2004) that "accusing [Özpetek] of orientalism only belittles his creativity. Istanbul's sensual beauty in *Hamam* is better understood as a measure of Özpetek's nostalgia for it, as a transcultural person who now lives in Italy" (p. 165).

Anderlini-D'Onofrio's (2004) reading of the film is most helpful here in understanding that Francesco not only starts to enjoy his stay in Turkey, but he actually prolongs it indefinitely once he decides to emulate his aunt in search of his transnational soul. His wish to rebuild the deteriorated bathhouse might very well signal his decision to rework his own identity, also in a state of decay from the continuous dictates of a consumer way of life and an unfulfilling marriage. Of course one could speculate here that the film incurs a too-mechanical understanding of subjectivity, as it appears that, once distanced from Italy, Francesco begins his own liberation from sexual norms. This would imply that repression comes from afar and would situate the making of identity too closely attached to the symbolic systems of any social organization. While this is a possible reading, I have nevertheless come to be intrigued by (and can identify with) the way Özpetek represents the alterations of the self when one is far away from one's *original* national culture; this circumstance of being in a new transitional space challenges the making or remaking of one's own identity and sexuality. It seems to me that he is trying to connect geography and desire as crisscrossing spaces of the self. This self is therefore not essential, but open to the contingencies of one's own biography—the real. I use this Lacanian notion to suggest that there is more than a mere flux of desire in Francesco's decision. This is a political act, an unplanned cut in the chain of signifiers that has defined the life of Francesco. His decision to rebuild the hamam cannot be situated at the same level as his daily performance, as it is not part of his imaginary reper-toire of responses. This is a decision that is to be located at the level of responsibility: a moment when the subject gives a response to his position as a desiring being—His act does not give up his desire.[6] While in Istanbul, Francesco's aunt discovered that she was intrigued by men's private pleas-ures, and she wanted to partake in them (see Anderlini-D'Onofrio, 2004). This desire to participate in "male" body pleasures, critics like Anderlini-D'Onofrio reveal, puts a question mark to gender and sexual identity that serves to destabilize the viewer's identification. Further, they claim, her refusal to be catalogued questions her own identification as a "woman" and questions gender divides (Anderlini-D'Onofrio, 2004) to the extent that one is reminded of the Lacanian formula: she is not The Woman. Indeed, by staying in Turkey, she attempted to find an answer to the question: Am I a man or a woman?[7] Inversely, by identifying with his dead aunt's quest for freedom, Francesco seems closer to the question: Am I alive or dead?[8] This distinction renders the sex/gender of the object of desire absolutely secon-dary. Although Francesco begins a sexual relationship with Mehmet in the hamam, what matters is not that this is a same-sex relationship,[9] but the fact that Francesco discovers that he actually desires—in other words, that he is not *dead*.

While his new family cherishes the rebuilding of the hamam, private in-vestors who would like to tear down the historic place and build a five-star resort conspire secretly against Francesco. At the same time, his wife Marta (Francesca d'Aloja) reproaches him for not coming back to Italy. But her motives are not completely sincere at first. Indeed, she has a secret lover and has been waiting for Francesco's return to sign the divorce papers that will set her free. Again, one could question here why Marta waited for him to leave Italy to be in a position of demanding a divorce. In this vein, we are tempted to interpret that the *copula* Marta-Francesco represents a unity sanctioned by the state or Italian society as something organic, a gestalt where the image is primordial, whereas each subject's desire is erased. When Francesco leaves, this *copula* breaks into pieces as if there had been, for years, a totalizing image reflected in a mirror, the image of a perfect couple that now collapses with just a brief, temporal separation. But Özpetek's film allows for a more complicated interpretation. When Francesco's return is delayed, Marta finally decides to board the first plane to Istanbul and take the divorce documents directly to him—in this case we could read the gesture as a decision in the psychoanalytic sense of the term: it implies separation and confrontation with castration. Indeed, upon her arrival, she is surprised to discover another (an Other) Francesco and to realize that the radical alterity is not that of Turkey, but that of the man she thought she knew so well and for so many years. It is this transitional identity/space of Francesco and the hamam that now intrigues her as it had intrigued first his aunt, and Francesco later (see Anderlini-D'Onofrio, 2004). Once more, the family of choice plays a fundamental role in welcoming Marta and locating her symbolically within a chain of signifiers. This symbolic location seems to counteract the anonymity of the (speechless) bourgeois life and evokes the Lacanian function of the *name-of-the-father*: it is within this family that both Francesco and Marta can give *names* to their desires. In Italy, they were mere individuals; in Turkey, they are subjects of desire. Predictably, this leads to confrontation and quarrelling, leaving Marta in a very strange situation within the elective family. Care and support is represented here in daily rituals that the elective family performs to sooth the escalating tension between Francesco and Marta, illustrated in a scene when Marta has her coffee read by a Turkish psychic. How should one read these mystic elements? Maybe we could attempt a preliminary interpretation: reading the coffee works for Marta as the reading of signifiers in an analytic session: it shakes fixed significations and moves the subject to confront her desire.

Özpetek seems to respect Eastern principles, including an ethics of compassion and beliefs about the transmigration of the soul (Prono, 2001; Anderlini-D'Onofrio, 2004; Due, 2005). These ethics come into view, critics show, in his recurring exploration of life after death. These are social ethics that critics believe resemble, in some ways, Pasolini's and Rossellini's criticism of capitalism. This resemblance is much clearer in *Cuore Sacro*, where the director evokes intertextually these other Italian film directors. The film describes the life of a successful Milanese entrepreneur who abandons her consumer lifestyle to serve the poor (reminiscent of Rossellini's Saint Francis in *Francesco, Giullare di Dio*) (CulturaGay, 2005). *Hamam* begins when the aunt dies and leaves the harem to Francesco and ends when Francesco is stabbed and Marta takes over the hamam. Similarly, in *Harem Suaré*, a baby prince is killed, changing the fate of the whole harem; *Le Fate Ignoranti* opens with a tragic car accident and ends with the protagonist's pregnancy; *La Finestra di Fronte* is in part an homage to all queer loves that are forbidden and made forgotten, especially for those who were victims of oppression during dictatorial regimes like fascism. Also here, death structures a narrative in which the ethical guiding principle is the human need to remember loved ones despite the passing of time. Finally, *Cuore Sacro* depicts women within a family linked together by memories that have been repressed and need further elaboration. In all of these movies, the interaction between the past and present anchors new relations that come to life unexpectedly. The narrative's diegetic time is a non-chronological time, but a time measured according to the ability to connect with others and with ourselves despite the tragedies that change our lives. In this sense, the most provocative scene of Özpetek's *Cuore Sacro* is the one that takes place in the *metropolitana,* when the female protagonist reaches a turning point in her existence. She enters the train station in what could be described as an altered state of consciousness. Having realized that her life has so far been shallow and materialistic, this is a female character who seems to find no meaning in whatever she does. Similar to *Hamam*, there is also here a place that the protagonist, Irene (Barbora Bobulova) inherits. This house keeps memory alive. On the walls there are strange mystic symbols, on the furniture objects from faraway cultures and times. Her relative, it seems, had been trying to find some meaning in life, much as she does now. As Irene decides what to do with the house, she meets a young girl who touches he heart deeply. This girl is a street wanderer who sometimes steals food for the poor. Irene begins a friendship with her and, eventually, becomes interested in charity projects herself. While I agree with critics who have compared Irene's personal quest with Saint Francis of Assisi's personal transformation, to completely appreciate Irene's metamorphosis one should also compare her with the Indian prince Siddhartha Gautama, who came to be Buddha, or the illuminated. Irene's life after meeting the young girl resembles Siddartha's first walk outside his palace, which took him eventually on a journey of discoveries and teachings. Both of them connect for the first time with human suffering, poverty, and misery. Further, the moment Irene becomes illuminated, she decides (as did the Indian prince) to abandon the world's attachments. She does so in public, as she enters the train station and takes off her clothes. She is of course intercepted by police officers and taken to a psychiatric unit to be evaluated. Far from mystifying Irene, what a queer reading of the movie can offer is a critical recoding of this act in *public*. A close-up of a woman getting naked in the middle of a working day, in an overpopulated metropolitan station like Milan's, is a suggestive shot: this is a female body that comes to despoil a cosmopolitan public space, to expose her flesh as a surface of contact with others, with no class separations or clothes. This is not a body that is offered for others to see as a painting or a stripper, but a body that crosses the line of what is publicly accepted as normal performance. Finally, the fact that the scene is set in a train station underlines something about the transitory nature of the human condition and invites the reader to think about identity as a journey during which one's self is undone, undressed, and remade.

In the same way that *Cuore Sacro* offers an evocation of Siddhartha's inner journey or Saint Francis's conversion, others of Özpetek's works sometimes refer the viewer to the Middle East. For example, for *Hamam* he chose the use of profoundly hypnotic Islamic fusion music (composed by Genoese Aldo De Scalzi and Pivio, who go by the name of Transcendental), and for *Saturno Contro* he chose to add some Latin and South American melodies, all of which may be read as an attempt to dislocate the viewer's ethnocentric way of listening. Following Anderlini-D'Onofrio's (2004) model, we can say that these are films that dismantle the Western cultural and historical construction of identity, intimacy, family, and ethical norms, while at the same time they are deeply respectful of—although sometimes over-romantic about—a variety of non-Western or non-capitalist traditions. Sometimes, for example, close-up depictions of male bodies bonding and caring for each other, or massaging their sweating bodies (*Hamam*), or having sexual intercourse in a three-way relationship (*Le Fate Ignoranti*), sexualizes the spectator's gaze, subjugating the viewer to the role of voyeur, challenging his/her identifications.

Özpetek's *Harem Suaré* (1999) puzzled critics and viewers. Its non-linear, slow narrative and its abundance of subplots were, perhaps, partly responsible for its being misinterpreted by gay audiences. They were disappointed that the film did not revolve around same-sex desire as did *Hamam* (CulturaGay, 2005): this reaction repeated itself in 2005 when Özpetek announced that he was not a gay film director, right after the release of *Cuore Sacro*, a movie that also baffled gay critics. Indeed, it is both in *Harem Suaré* and in *Cuore Sacro* that Özpetek matures as a queer film director, hence departing from the expectations of both straight critics and gay male audiences.

In *Harem Suaré*, different time and space locations are intertwined. One possible storyline can be situated in Istanbul at the beginning of the 1900s. In this space, we see a sultan as the patriarchal head of one of the last and most sumptuous harems. Far from being interested in a historically faithful representation, Özpetek portrays the harem similarly to the intermediary space of identity that I characterized in chapter 1, following Winnicott, as *transitional space:* a third space located between the real world and the reality of dreams and sensual bedtime stories. The harem seems to rest in a state of eternal order and peace until the arrival of the political crisis affecting the Ottoman Empire. This crisis threatens the life of the patriarchal head and of his favorite wife, Safiye, an Italian woman who was sold to the harem to provide a male heir. Safiye and a black eunuch who takes care of her fall in love. Later, a child is conceived, who is taken to be the sultan's heir, but upon discovery of the affair, the child prince is killed just before the harem collapses with the whole empire. Another possible narrative within the film emerges if we concentrate on the segments in which, in the evenings, women gather in the main room with a storyteller called Gulfidan (award-winning actress Serra Yilmaz, who also has a main role in *Le Fate. . .*). She narrates empowering stories of female heroines to all the wives. A third reading emerges if we concentrate on a woman who tells her story to a female listener in a train station. This woman could be Safiye herself, who is now making sense of her past vicissitudes as she travels through different countries, probably escaping from her past.

Harem Suaré's temporality and spaces are an allegory of queerness; they disobey orders and evoke the transgression of gender and sexuality divides by combining different languages, spaces, and narratives. Özpetek's queer films, however, do not always include gay characters because, as in other queer films, "the text or the performer's star image does not have to have obvious (so-called 'denotative') non-straight elements to be termed "queer";

it just needs to have gathered about it a number of non-straight readings" (Doty, 1998, p. 150). This is exactly what critics have failed to recognize when they lament that the movie is not *gay*. Instead, in *Harem Suaré*, Anderlini-D'Onofrio (2004) seems to suggest, gays and lesbians can take queer pleasure in identifying with Safiye's search for sexual autonomy within a patriarchal regime; transgender persons and non-white queers can sympathize with the black eunuch's love for Safiye, while straight men and lesbians might feel stimulated by scenes of body contact between Safiye and her private masseuse, etc. *Harem Suaré*'s multifaceted, queer richness is only partly due to the performers' imagery; the plastic, fluid description of places and time also contribute to the creation of discomfort in the viewer, questioning his or her certainty about which is the central, "real" time of the plot. This questioning has the ultimate purpose of dislocating imaginary identifications of both queers and straights (see Anderlini-D'Onofrio, 2004).

Memory and Impersonal Desire. La Finestra di Fronte's temporality performs queer political criticism of normative views on human sexuality. In this film, Özpetek works out a notion of desire that is impersonal. In a shot reminiscent of Pasolini's *Accattone*, the young, married heterosexual couple Giovanna (Giovanna Mezzogiorno) and Filippo (Filippo Nigro) encounter Davide, an elderly man wandering across Castello Sant'Angelo. The man (the *opera postuma* of Massimo Girotti, famous for his portrayal of the John Garfield character in Luchino Visconti's 1943 *Ossessione*) does not look like a street beggar, but like an upper-class *pensionato* who has lost his memory and is now trying to go back home. Not having any information about him, the couple takes him home in a sympathetic attempt to help him and give him shelter for a couple of days. As in the case of Francesco in *Hamam*, he is adopted by a family, and, as in the case of *Harem Suaré*, the female protagonist begins a journey in time unchained by Davide's own search for answers about his own past. This time, the journey to rebuild identity goes back to fascist Italy. This personal trip reveals Davide's own identity. During the story, one learns that Davide is an Italian who escaped the horrors of the fascist persecution and concentration camps fifty years before. Back in 1943, he was an apprentice at a bakery. He lived his life hiding in the bakery but secretly loved another man. One night while he was baking bread he discovered a secret terrorist plan, plotted by fascist officers, who decided to exterminate members of Davide's community. Having only a few hours to warn the group under threat, Davide decided not to keep a date with his beloved one. In his attempt to save his neighbors, Davide lost the chance to begin a relationship with this man, and never met his life-love again. Davide is now an old man. The pain endured throughout his life and the effects of a degenerative illness have devastated his memory.

When there is a break of the symbolic, and the subject is prevented from articulating a full, personal speech, then it is the body that suffers. But it is also through the body that the *letter*, or the mark of the signifier, endures. Davide mumbles the signifier that has given sense to his life: Simone, the name of his beloved. Indeed, this only signifier stands in place of the Other as a guarantee of memory. While at first this name makes no sense to Giovanna, it comes to play a fundamental role in establishing who Davide is, and most important, it is a fundamental symbolic piece in establishing a lost page of communal history—the recreation of what happened the day Davide's community was terrorized. Interestingly, the temporal journey allows his host, Giovanna, to embark on a personal journey into the borderlands of time and desire as well. This travel includes anxiety. She elaborates on her life choices, including her marriage, as she fantasizes about a neighbor, Lorenzo (Raul Bova). Lorenzo and Giovanna spy on each other through facing windows, a flirtatious performance that gives the film its name. *La Finestra di Fronte* is a title evocative of the Lacanian notion of fantasy: fantasy can be understood as a framework for the drive, a framing fantasy that gives sense to the most intimate, singular ways in which a subject organizes his/her personal history. While the symbolic and imaginary are registers somehow shared by all human beings, the fantasy puts into play the drive, which is the most singular aspect of our biography, the way each person deals with the weight of the real upon his/her body. By alluding to the *facing window*, Özpetek's film has the immense value of making us note, almost as a provocation, that even this most personal, singular piece of our condition is nevertheless touched by our connection with others. My window opens up when I connect with you.

Memory as a journey without destination (see my discussion in chapter 1) is a main theme in *La Finestra di Fronte*. The image of a journey should not be mistaken with a discovery of a pre-existent identity waiting there to be discovered before the fact. Instead, all memory is an *après coup*, a symbolic and personal reconstruction of a mythic time forever lost in the past. Neither Davide nor Giovanna *finds* anything at all. They do not travel to an anticipated destination. This traveling without destination is also a theme that reappears in *Le Fate Ignoranti*.

Although viewers might feel comfortable believing that Davide remembers something forgotten and Giovanna remembers herself, in fact they all create something *ex nihilo*, out of nothing. It is difficult not to be reminded in this context of the Lacanian topological entangling of the three registers (symbolic, real, and imaginary) in the movie's knotting of desire and memory. In *La Finestra di Fronte* the signifier reveals its creative potency: the work of language creates a reality that is neither factual nor imaginary. Giovanna claims her identity, but the identity she claims does not exist before the fact: she needs to forge or *write it*. This need to write about the making of one's self reappears in *Hamam* and *Le Fate Ignoranti*. As in all these films, *La Finestra di Fronte* incorporates a particular view of the written word. The characters interchange written signifiers, either letters that come from a remote past, or letters written on the back of an object, or on walls (like in *Cuore Sacro*), that reveal personal secrets. In some early Lacanian conceptualizations of the signifier, the letter is placed as an interpretable and concrete mark, a representative of the symbolic that guides each person's destiny. As did Edgar Allan Poe in "The Purloined Letter," Lacan teaches that desire, as a letter, circulates, changing meaning according to its position and the reader/speaker. This movement of the letter is emblematic of the work of the unconscious, structured as a language. The letter is held in the hands of the protagonists of these movies as signifiers of desire for the loss of sexual relation (the loss of the fantasized intimacies of infancy). Since characters in these films sometimes write to dead people, the act of writing is a gesture that names or puts into *letters* what is not there: the letter stands for what is always (structurally) lacking; indeed, it marks the lack around which all the other signifiers come to acquire a specific value. As I discussed before, regarding the suicide of two young male lovers in Giarre, the letter is, also here, the herald of time that tells humans that we have lived and loved, for there is memory where there is the act of writing.[10]

Political Solidarity. In the interviews that followed the success of *Le Fate Ignoranti* (see, for example, Basoli, 2005; Due, 2005), Özpetek talks about the shifting meaning of families. On the one hand, he argues that the characters in his films are all human beings who need to learn to sleep alone serenely. The director suggests the dialectic between one's encounter with loneliness (probably closer to what queer theorists and Lacanians call *radical alterity*) and one's ability to connect with others. On the other hand, in October 2006, in some RAI-TV news shows where Özpetek spoke about his latest movie (*Saturno Contro,* released in 2007), the director presented the movie by explaining how important it was, in his view, to meet others and build new relations, to add instead of subtract. In this vein, there is an interesting dialectic in this director between loneliness and friendship that can be related to the social bond, insofar as there is never a complete form of identity (since neither the imaginary nor the symbolic order can suture the gap of the self), for identity is always in need of construction within the social domain. Here, connection means more than aggregation: it is a form of solidarity and openness to difference. This encounter with difference underscores Özpetek's notion of families of choice:

> I find the traditional family unhealthy. Too often, the parents project on their off-spring their frustrations as well as their aspirations. Instead, in the families that I put onto stage in my films, their coming together is a choice; it is crucial to have the ability to create a family for oneself, to choose some persons that can join you in life. [*Le Fate Ignoranti*] is a film that seeks to beat down the boundaries of sexuality and advocates tolerance. In this sense I believe it is an activist film. I am deeply convinced that we are living in a moment in which it is very important to learn to open oneself, to open the doors to our houses, the doors of the soul and of the body. In my life this opening is very important; I strongly believe in the possibility of the encounter with others. (Due, 2005, paragraph 1; my translation)

The film begins with a close-up of Antonia (Margherita Buy) walking around a room full of gigantic, virile Roman statues. A man approaches and flirts with her, whispering in her ear words of love. Antonia accepts the flirting but gently refuses to go with the stranger: her own lover is coming to pick her up. After a while, the camera zooms out; Antonia finally accepts the invitation, and through smiles and childish gestures, the protagonists reveal that they are indeed husband and wife, erotically toying with each other. This first scene is central to the plot, for *Le Fate Ignoranti* is a film about the instability of truth and the production of one's subjectivity. For Antonia, this production starts right after the first scene, when her husband Massimo (Andrea Renzi) dies after being hit by a car. After his death, Antonia finds out that he had kept a seven-year love relationship secret. Looking for answers, she embarks on a quest that destabilizes her own identity as well as the viewer's: when she meets her husband's lover, it turns out it is a man, Michele (Stefano Accorsi). He lives in a big apartment with other "hunky" and "pussy" gays, a "butch" lesbian, and a transgender/transsexual, all of whom, eventually, befriend Antonia. Özpetek shows a family of choice that offers Antonia psychosocial reference points for constructing a different self while she mourns. What she mourns is not only the loss of her husband, but ultimately the loss of every belief she had in love, sexuality, and herself. By encountering a group of people whose lives challenge Antonia's ideal of family and intimacy, *Le Fate Ignoranti* illustrates Valerie Lehr's (1999) point that we need to address queer family activism "in dialogue with others in a way that recognizes 'gayness' as only one facet of complex identities, and as a facet of identity that is not definable outside of practice" (p. 79).

Truth and Self. Filmed in Ostiense, the working-class suburb of Rome where Özpetek lived after arriving in Italy in 1978, *Le Fate Ignoranti* is highly autobiographical, quasi auto-ethnographic in approach:

> Something similar happened to me. I dated a man for two years having no clue that he was married. One evening at dinner with some friends, I met the restaurant owner, and she started telling us about her husband and her children. At around midnight he showed up. I took it in stride, but I started wondering what would happen if something happened to him that forced her to find out. The script evolved out of that idea. (Özpetek, cited in Basoli, 2005, n/p)

This was not the first time that Özpetek included himself within the narrative of a movie: *La Finestra di Fronte*, for example, is also based on an encounter between the film director and an old man he found wandering around the Ponte degli Angeli (the bridge leading to Castello Sant'Angelo in Rome). This time, however, the political content went deeper. Despite Özpetek's persistence that he dislikes politics, *Le Fate Ignoranti* is a militantly activist film in many ways.

First, it is a movie centered on the making of one's subjective truth. More specifically, it is a film that complicates the experience of being true to *our self*—the ways in which individuals make sense of the self and its place in the world. Antonia and Michele stand for two very opposite interpretations of what counts as true. In Antonia's bourgeois world, the truth needs to be defended at all costs: it is a basic, almost transcendental principle on which she bases her relationships with herself and others. She has moved so far in a world where the subject has agency and produces material changes. It is only after she discovers that her husband lived a double life and after she enters the world of his lover, Michele, that she can start thinking of truth as always

partial, never completely stated, and of subjectivity as a contingency produced by the relation of doing to speaking. In this way, *Le Fate Ignoranti*
illustrates Michele Foucault's critique of the self as a transparent, universal
notion:

> The central issue. . .is not to determine whether one says yes or no to sex. . .but to
> account for the fact that it is spoken about, to discover who does the speaking, the
> positions and viewpoints from which they speak, the institutions which prompt peo-
> ple to speak about it and which store and distribute the things that are said. What is
> at issue [is] the way in which sex is "put into discourse." (Foucault, 1976/1984,
> p. 43)

More important, Özpetek does not romanticize queer life, but instead
makes it clear that the making of subjectivity and identity implies active
engagement and politics that transform heterosexism and their discontents.
This is particularly clear in the scene in which Michele and Antonia carry on
an intense discussion in the rain. The tension has built from things unsaid.
Suddenly, they burst into accusations and reproaches toward one another,
insulting and hurting each other deeply. In showing each character's despair
and ire, Özpetek wants us to become detached viewers—to resist agreeing
with either protagonist. The quarrel between the characters is not intended to
mobilize another imaginary identification but to stress that all forms of
stabilized identity (such as homosexual or heterosexual) are the result of
knowledge production: "In Italian the movie's title. . .[literally the Ignorant
Fairies, although the word *fate* does not resonate with the word *gay* as it does
in English] does not mean that the characters are uneducated, but that they
can be rude and uncouth. They are not good-natured and polite. . .but they
know about feelings, and that's how they affect each other" (Özpetek, cited
in Basoli, 2005, n/p). This is an extraordinary passage, for it reveals that the
director does not think of queerness in any romantic way, but he does
nevertheless believe in its political potential. This is why I have chosen to
comment on these movies here, for I believe their political message contravenes the conformity with the state or the conformity with heterosexism that
is usually implied in the plea for civil unions.

Critics have suggested that Özpetek uses intertextual references to Italian
directors in movies like *Cuore Sacro*. There are also references in *Le Fate
Ignoranti* to other film directors, in this case Almodóvar and Kieslowski
(Mauro, 2001). Certainly the theme of love and death is not far from
Almodóvar's *All about My Mother* and *Talk to Her*. In both of these films the

Spanish director plays with changes in life triggered by extreme circumstances: the death of a son in *Todo sobre mi Madre* (All about My Mother);
the pregnancy of a woman in a coma in *Habla con Ella* (Talk to Her). Indeed,
as Nancy Blake (2004) notes, Almodóvar's concern with the definitions of
death and life have a starting point in a scene involving organ donors in *The
Flower of My Secret*. While these two directors have been acclaimed by gay
audiences in Europe, it is important to stress that Özpetek and Almodóvar
differ in many ways. In particular, it is interesting to observe the differences
in their female characters. Blake (2004), for instance, has analyzed the
position of female or female-identified characters in Almodóvar's movies by
exploring to what extent they relate to or contradict the Lacanian *pas savoir*
regarding female sexuality. On the one hand, the women, transsexuals, and
transgenders in some of Almodóvar's films mock the image of the Total
Woman and present a text that makes us consider the many possible ways of
naming desire and its object. Many of Almodóvar's female or queer characters are anti-heroic, sometimes ridiculous, and often tragic. On the other hand,
in Özpetek's films we usually encounter women elevated to the place of
sublime objects: they are heroines who transform their lives and the lives
they relate to. They are usually left alone with a decision that challenges a
symbolic order, and are sometimes doomed to suffer the consequences of
their acts in loneliness, judged and ostracized by Others. In some ways, these
women and their vicissitudes are evocative of other women in Italian cinema,
including divas of the silent era and gay icons like Sophia Loren and Gina
Lollobrigida.

At the same time, male characters in Özpetek's films are fragile and anx-
ious. In a scene in which all the characters are united for a toast, Michele
says: "To Massimo, because he was one of *us*!" In this same scene, while
explaining the reasons for living within an elective family, Michele explains
to Antonia that she has never had to experience segregation and hate. Living
in a queer family is a choice for survival. This choice is clear for Antonia
during a Sunday lunch, when she finally meets everybody in the "extended
queer family." Sitting on opposite sides of the table, Michele exhorts Antonia
to take sides—either with us (as queer) or without us (as straight). When the
Neapolitan transgender/transsexual shares with the others her anxiety about a
future trip to her home village where she will be seen for the first time as
male-to-female transgender, Antonia encourages her not to try to pass as a
man but to be herself. Michele then insists on his point, making Antonia

aware that the values that count for her as a middle-class white woman might endanger the lives of queers in a heterosexist rural community. While Antonia leaves the table challenged by a knowledge that destabilizes herself, it should be remarked that Michele's reaction is selfish rather than educative: it is not based on a level of discussion that would bring awareness to Antonia or others at the table, but it stems from his fear that Antonia breaks the unity of the family. In this sense, Michele illustrates an earlier point made here, that *queer* should be defined as a form of doing and speaking rather than as a form of *being*. In a moment in which Michele reifies binaries (either "with us as queer or without us as straight"), he shows the extent to which, potentially, anybody can behave according to heterosexism, for as social beings, we have all internalized some phobic tenets of heterosexual patriarchy. (And how can we not see here a reference to Mario Mieli's critique of heterosexism?)

Similarly, even when Antonia eventually becomes part of the queer family, she never does share with them her pregnancy. Film critic Luca Prono (2001) contends that this is an unacceptable narrative choice:

> There are several disappointing implications for a queer audience about Antonia's choice, but those very same implications will no doubt be praised by a conservative spectator. By deciding not to tell that she is pregnant, Antonia is implicitly judging the community of queers as unsuitable to share her news with. It also seems unlikely that she will let the soon to be born child be adopted by Michele's extended family. (n/p)

Clearly, readers of this cinematic text might be unhappy with its ending. Indeed, there are a number of elements of the narrative constructed by Özpetek that need to be assessed critically, and not only Antonia's departure. First, this is a commercial movie whose highly aesthetic depiction of queer sexual life intends to capture the attention of the wide international audience more receptive to queer films. In this sense, this movie should be situated at the crossroads of the demands of a global industry and the imperatives of queer politics that were outlined in a previous section of this chapter. Second, as in other films of this director, the choice of very popular (and good-looking) actors and the choice of sensual music seem to follow the construction of perfectly erotic scenes aimed at pleasing the heterosexist, voyeuristic gaze more than at queerly dislocating the position of the viewer. While watching *Le Fate Ignoranti*, one is more often captivated and seduced than forced to confront one's identification with ideals of beauty, sex, and romance. This does not help the ending of the film, which, it has been suggested, closes as a typical romantic Hollywood film (Prono, 2001).

Nevertheless, I admit being captivated by the decision of Antonia. I take her departure as a moment of liberation and resignification. Indeed, I take it as her final identification with queerness as a form of identity that is not stable. This is symbolized in her final choice of inventing a story about a trip out of Rome (indeed a trip without any destination) to pursue a love affair that serves to hide her pregnancy. Of course Amir is a very beautiful young heterosexual man, but this is not what matters for me. What matters is that she fictionalizes or, to use a Lacanian notion, elaborates a metaphor that empowers her: I do not want to reduce the ending of the film to the question of her being a *woman* who can make a *choice*. Instead, I want to emphasize that now the subject is in a position where something can be fictionalized. This fictionalization is the opposite of the imperative of enjoyment (as described in relation to *L'Ultimo Bacio*) and is certainly more critical than a mere reification of the ideals of romance and individual freedom. The way I read Antonia's decision, her leaving the group on the basis of a romance with Amir is not an act of egotism or a lie; hers is an act of detaching herself from either her family of origin (epitomized by her mother), her past as heterosexual *wife*, and even her attachment to the group of activists in Michele's family of choice. This act breaks free from true/false dichotomies, such as *we* versus *them* (implied in Michele's complaint) or *true* versus *false* (implied in Antonia's previous obsession with truth and epitomized by her career choice as scientist and virologist) and allows her desire to *come out*, reconsidering where she stands in each of the large spectrum of ethical decisions she can now make. This moment is very important to my argument about queer subjectivity in this book, in particular because it has the potential advantage of showing Antonia's subjectivity as something that can be redone, no matter what her age, sexual orientation, or gender. Antonia is, after all, engaged in a reconstruction of her identity as much as each of us. As Yannis Stavrakakis (1999) puts it: "we are necessarily engaged all the time in identity construction exactly because it is impossible to construct a full identity" (p. 4).

From Homosexuality to Genderqueer

In some thirty years, Italian cinema has moved from portraying homosexuality as deviance or something to be laughed about, to considering queer desire as an ethical and political dimension present in all human beings. In between,

Italian directors have been concerned with stereotypes of the homosexual as a sissy or as inverted, the psychopathic fascist pedophile, the excessive pleasure seeker of decadent bourgeois Italy, the global macho man wearing suits and hooking up in the gym's sauna, and the perverse priest. Not all cinematic representations are negative or stigmatizing, though. Italian gay and queer cinema has produced beautiful narratives of fluid desire, highly aesthetic films that complicate the links between identity, the social, and the political. I am not suggesting that these narratives have evolved evenly. The queer struggle against film reductionism and the search for cinematic languages that represent the whole spectrum of the queer community is not just one that moves accidentally or rhizomatically, but also one that is doomed never to end insofar as human language is not a system of absolute, mechanical denomination, but an open (or cut) structure that produces difference.

The point of intersection of the human body and language yields to an infinite number of subjectivities that no code can label. Queer readings of films like Özpetek's deal with this crossroads. One could say that, ideally, queer cinema should not seek totality or absolute knowledge about sexuality; it is suspicious of any attempt to categorize the experience of gender and sex in binary categories like heterosexual/homosexual. Instead, queer film directors experiment with these categories, deconstructing and questioning them (Aaron, 2004; Davis, 2004). For instance, there is a wide variety of sexual encounters in *Le Fate Ignoranti*, from the caricature of heterosexual romance in the opening scene of the film to the explicit and polemical scene where Michele engages in a threesome with two other men. It is in the scene where Antonia and Michele kiss where the film reaches its queerest pinnacle. In this scene, Michele is at Antonia's garden. He realizes, by looking at two patio chairs, one placed next to the other, that Massimo loved another person, not only him. He has to confront the fact that Massimo could love two people at the same time and in very different ways, neither of which is more truthful. Suddenly, Michele confronts his own words: Massimo is not "one of us." At the same time, Antonia has brought Michele to her home, confronting for the first time the fact that her husband did not find complete satisfaction in her. In Lacanian terms, she was/is not The Woman. In both cases Massimo's or Antonia's sexual orientation matters less than the fact that desire operates awry—tangentially to the individual, finding satisfaction in its movement more than in its objects. Predictably, Michele and Antonia kiss each other.

Had Özpetek finished the scene here, the spectators would be left at the simple level of mechanical, imaginary duplicity: hate turns into love, love into hate. But Özpetek shoots higher: as Antonia and Michele kiss, they fantasize about Massimo, and probably about Massimo's other lover. This very Lacanian reference to *the Other of the Other* can be interpreted as the director's attempt to show that human sexuality is structured around fantasy just as much as political ideology is (Žižek, 1999). Fantasy implies for human beings a continuous effort to represent what lies beyond the symbolic, in the contingent margins of the real.

C8 **Conclusion** 80

In writing this book, I have embarked on a journey that is as political as it is personal. Similar to the 1979-1989 *Choose Your Own Adventures* book series that I used to read as a kid just before going to bed, this book offers multiple ports of entry, but does not carry to reader to a single, final destination. I have attempted to write about queer Italy from a perspective that is close and personal, one in which my voice as researcher and person multiplies meanings and opens up spaces for discussion with the public and with other writers. This work is offered to readers who, it is hoped, will be willing to make new connections with other literatures or experiences, draw exciting conclusions, and carry out further research about queerness in Italy—and other countries, for that matter. Despite the variety of contexts explored in this volume, and the many possible readings of such contexts, there are some ideas that I consider central and which I would like to reprise in this conclusion.

Central to this book has been a question about the existence and potential of queer politics in Italy, an inquiry into the specificity of queerness in this country, and its relations to queer politics—in particular American queer politics. I have argued that queerness and queer politics are co-dependent forms of doing and speaking. In doing/speaking *queerness*, we invent forms of subjectivity that are counter-identitarian; in doing/speaking *queer politics* we rewrite heterosexist culture. By bringing together subjectivity, intimacy, and the contexts of history, representation, and politics, I have tried to demonstrate that heteronormative culture is maintained and promoted in Italy through a wide range of symbolic and material supports. This is as notable in the foundational discourses of marriage, monogamous love, and parenthood as it is evident in the overwhelming heterosexual architecture of culture that expresses itself through heterosexist marriage and family laws, the constitutional protection of matrimony as the foundational stone of the nation, the endurance of the private, domestic sphere (as opposed to a culture of public politics), and the language of romance. In some ways, this cultural organization does not differ much from other countries where religion and family are the cornerstones of society. Describing American heterosexism, two prominent queer voices, Lauren Berlant and Michael Warner (1998/2002), explain that while queers find it difficult to oppose the prevailing conditions of heterosexism, they have created a culture of resistance on their own: "Queer culture, by contrast [to heteronormative culture], has almost no institutional matrix for its counter intimacies. In the absence of marriage and the rituals that organize life around matrimony, improvisation is always necessary" (Berlant and Warner, 1998/2002, p. 203). In this study, I have shed light on the forms and meanings that queer resistance has taken in Italian culture, and I have suggested multiple directions in which it should evolve—directions that I recapitulate in this last chapter as well.

As shown in the course of this book, while queer improvisation and experimentation in intimate life have emerged in Italy as a result of a similar heterosexist alienation that Lauren Berlant and Michael Warner (1998/2002) point out, there have been only two preponderant forms of queer political activism and activist resistance, also described in this book. One emerged in the 1970s and was aligned with the radical left; it found inspiration in psychoanalytic notions and was much motivated by feminist struggles. While it trusted in mechanical resistance as a means of opposition, this first form of queer activism could be characterized as queer radicalism for its non-conformist and non-compromising politics, and was best exemplified in the works of Mario Mieli and by the first actions taken by FUORI!.

A second form of activism, which can be called gay and lesbian identity politics, emerged as a result of the extension of consumer culture and implied the application of Anglo-American identity politics frameworks. These frameworks invigorated the movement and provided queers with increasing visibility but oftentimes assumed the existence of detached individualities that can voluntarily group to transform the state. The identity politics framework operating in the background of this form of activism has encountered some difficulties in Italy because of the more extensive use of class as a form of political identification. It is a framework that helped to form, however, a national coalition of activist groups, and that facilitated the creation of awareness campaigns regarding human and civil rights, AIDS, and artificial reproduction technologies. The current plea for civil unions should be situated at this level of action.

Both frameworks have had to confront the fact that heteronormativity is an overwhelming infrastructure of Italian culture, one that connects the country and provides a totalizing backbone of experiences, language, rituals, and history. In the presence of an historically impermeable heterosexist social matrix and in the presence of a heterosexist model for family life, it is extremely difficult for Italian GLBTQs to explore modes of creative and culturally specific resistance, although efforts have never been absent. Therefore, the current plea for civil unions should not be interpreted mechanically as the abandonment or refusal to engage in queer radicalism, but as a possible means of dealing with the familial machinery of heterosexuality and Catholicism—although this is certainly not the only means of transformation available.

My interest in mapping contexts of queer Italy originates in the belief that an important step toward inclusive queer politics is to acknowledge the existence of a complex form of cultural and historical identity that differs from that of other countries. This identity has surfaced in relation to Italy's inclusion in the European bloc as a country that is a geographical and political bridge between Eastern and Western Europe. It has materialized in relation to its colonial and colonizing past, its regional and linguistic diversity, and even its situation within a global world where queerness is constantly being redefined or negotiated. In delving into the question of cultural specificity, I have struggled to avoid one-sided responses that would fix Italy or queerness as objects of inquiry. With this understanding, the queer Italy I write about is not solely the Italy of *froci, invertiti, lesbiche,* or *omosessuali,* but the Italy of anybody's biography situated in the borderlands of a culture in permanent and conflicting evolution.

The result of this work of inquiry is a map of queerness in Italy, defined as forms of personal, social, and political becoming, speaking and doing that are entirely cultural, reliant on their representation in discourse; they are positions in language that depend on other representations and signifiers. In this regard, a second understanding that has guided my writing and that can help design queer politics is that of identity as open and unfinished. Following Lacanian theory, I situate a fundamental exteriority at the very heart of human identity. This exteriority poses the question of a lack that is not limiting but enabling of better social and cultural relations inasmuch as it recognizes that Otherness is constitutive of the human kind. In affirming this, I have tried to counter prevailing essentialist views on identity that permeate

Italian gay activism, and that are at the center of the current defense of civil unions.

From Marriage to Civil Unions

A major conclusion of this research about queer Italy is that the present discussions about civil unions are, nevertheless, inseparable from the symbolic and imaginary realms that have defined the preponderant role of the Italian family. Anxieties about the future of *la famiglia* are constantly raised in public by conservatives and Catholics, who blame queers for undermining traditional moral values (Rossi Barilli, 1999). Ironically, though, more than demonstrating the existence of one typical *famiglia Italiana*, research data presented in this book suggest numerous variations in the way Italians organize and give meaning to family relations. The decline in the rate of heterosexual marriage and the plea for civil unions, for instance, need to be assessed in this context of flexibility and negotiation about meaning, the result of complex sociopolitical and symbolic transformations.

At the time of this writing, gay unions had never before been so thoroughly mediated, talked about, publicized, advocated, and repudiated in Italy. Interestingly enough, the public debate oftentimes leaves important questions unconsidered. Although the meaning, benefits, and political consequences of PACS are widely analyzed on television, issues like gay parenting, the status of partners who are foreigners, multiracial queer families, and even AIDS are not a frequent subject of inquiry. Defenders of PACS argue that the document will provide individuals with choice, but they overlook the power the document accepts from the state as a mediator in enforcing certain behaviors and dismissing others. Many queer writers would agree today with Warner (1999) that defining gay unions as a simple exercise of freedom of choice conceals the potential consequences of such legalization for those queers who "choose" not to marry and might also substantiate the bigoted viewpoint that non-united/unmarried straights and queers are deviant or pathological perverts.

Until today, debates about gay marriage have not been as numerous in the public sphere and in the media in Italy as in the United States, in part because GLBTQ groups did not pursue the legalization of marriage *per se*, but followed the French model of PACS. Or it may be that, decades after fascism, queer life continues to be somehow silenced or made invisible. In fact, to appreciate the advantages and disadvantages of PACS, it is important to bear in mind that narratives about the family in Italy encompass religious, moral, racial, and historical values, as well as representations that are different from those of the United States, some of which have been introduced in this study: honor, faithfulness, sanctity, cohesion, natural motherhood, and so forth.

Having been critical of the ideological evolution of the gay movement in Italy, from its liberationist roots to its present conformation, I want to conclude this volume by highlighting the benefits of the struggle for civil unions. One of the main advantages of PACS is that, in conjunction with other proposals presented to Parliament regarding discrimination and parity of opportunity, it heightens the urgency to provide legal protection for gays, lesbians, and queers in Italy. The status of the human rights of queers in Italy is so fragile that there is no time to waste: changes in law cannot wait any longer. However, that a changing international context might favor these changes does not mean avoiding critical confrontation of the terms we use when we redefine intimacy. The language of PACS does not preclude the continuity of past struggles, but guarantees that options are open to those who seek the protection of the law:

> The present proposal does not intend to be an authoritarian imposition upon all the unmarried couples who want to remain free from any legal binding, but it intends to offer a possibility of choice to those who want to make use of it. *It is time to grant those who do not want to marry what the so-called pluralism of our society has not guaranteed them so far, unless they paid the price of serious and useless social costs*, of imposing upon the non-traditional family the obligation to choose between two options only: the traditional marriage or the absolute absence of any legal recognition and even protection. (PACS proposal, p. 1; my translation, my emphasis)

It is clear that the proposal hopes to contest the status quo of a normative legal framework. However, it is also worth pointing out certain passages where the proposal reinforces the ideology of the family. Again, this is another example of ideological closure or queer panic, similar to the ones mentioned earlier. For example, the text refers to homosexuality as a natural condition, and it stresses sameness over difference: "the Italian homosexuals, who *as any other human being* have not chosen their sexual orientation. . ." (PACS proposal, 2005, p. 1; my translation, my emphasis). In addition, by forcing human sexuality to adapt to a pre-existent dichotomist homosexual/heterosexual map, this document might reify a two-gender system and interpret sexual choice as a question of sexual orientation more than as a cultural and political complex. The document might have the negative effect of excluding transgendered persons or those who do not identify with this system of classification. Moreover, it also suggests that a stable relationship between two individuals might guarantee human fulfillment or happiness: "The present law guarantees the inviolable right of man and woman to find their full realization within a couple. . ." (PACS proposal, 2005, Article # 1; my translation). Article #2 establishes that the pact is the union between two people, hence casting away non-monogamous unions. Although it does entail patrimonial benefits, it fails to fully discuss the intricacies of parenthood, tutelage of children, interracial/transnational unions, or adoption. Article #21, for example, does grant citizenship to a foreign partner, but only after five years' residence in Italy. This is an extraordinarily long period of time for any immigrant, but particularly discriminatory to lower-class, immigrant queers who are therefore forced either to live as dependants of their partners (hence reinforcing gender asymmetric divides) or to work illegally (hence being subject to deportation or state persecution).

The Italian PACS is also timid concerning parenthood. At this level it is far behind the legislation of other European countries that have passed some laws allowing legal adoption by same-sex couples (see Fisher, 2003). In addition, although the Italian PACS presents some advantages over ideologically and institutionally reinforced marriage, it should be more critical regarding the potential power of the state to regulate sexual life (see Kitzinger and Wilkinson, 2004).

Compared to studies produced in France and the United States about French or American queers, there are very few interpretive studies on the Italian queer family. Although some regional and statistical studies on Italian homosexuality have appeared in recent years, no comprehensive, interpretive national research has been carried out in Italy either on queer Italian families or their children across time and space. In addition, I am not confident that statistical or sociological studies would suffice, for what we need in Italy is the development of interpretive models that are bold and that incorporate critical cultural studies methodologies that give voice to a population usually invisible, alienated, and ridiculed. This includes the need for more studies that are carried out by and/or focus on queers, immigrants (two sectors very much invisible within the Italian academe either as producers of knowledge or as a focus of studies), women, racial "minorities," and non-whites. Together with other studies mentioned in this book, Monica Bonaccorso's

1994 research is one of the few research works centered on this subject. What distinguishes Bonaccorso's study is that she does not try to compare homosexual and nuclear heterosexual families. Instead, she begins by arguing that the Italian family is changing, and that today there is nothing stable within the family. She terms a heterosexual *alternative family nucleus* those families with heterosexual parents who deviate in one or more characteristics from the nuclear heterosexual family. And she argues that homosexual families are just one more alternative nucleus. The traditional heterosexual family is here a married couple, a man and a woman, with at least one natural child. Instead, an *alternative family nucleus* shows parents who might be gay with children from previous relationships, or divorced, or parents who used reproductive technologies to conceive but do not live together any longer. Bonaccorso (1994) argues that the *only* difference between homosexual and heterosexual families is the *atypical* lifestyle of gay parents:

> Contrary to what is usually believed, there is a similarity between the homosexual and the heterosexual alternative family nuclei. Indeed, in some aspects it seems that the homosexual family is, point by point, a copy of the alternative heterosexual one. A first common denominator is mono-parenting (children live in both cases with one parent only) and binuclearity (children spend their lives between the family of origin and the new reconstituted family). (p. 67; my translation)

In this quote, Bonaccorso seems to match and compare queer families to heterosexual families, but I am not convinced that this is a constructive movement, for it might privilege sameness over difference. The use of heteronormative language to assimilate queers and their relationships to straight relationships and families might therefore obliterate the fundamental quality of humanity, that each subject (and relationship) is unique and different. Unfortunately, when any ritual, like marriage, acquires its cultural value from excluding certain groups, defending that ritual only perpetuates and even produces more exclusion (Kitzinger and Wilkinson, 2004):

> The radical critique of marriage—much of which applies equally to civil partnerships—is abandoned with the change of name. The campaigns to promote civil partnership legislation focus on "deserving" lesbian and gay couples in "marriage like" relationships (co-resident, long-term, assumed monogamous, often with children), while those of us who live outside these heteronormative ideals for coupledom are sidelined. (Kitzinger and Wilkinson, 2004, p. 145)

As this paragraph suggests, the language or symbolism of marriages camouflaged now as civil unions compels queers to adapt themselves to the dominant language of heterosexuality. Bernard Shaw's *Pygmalion* is illustrative of the effects of this therapeutics of the self: the speech therapist Henry Higgins successfully transforms Eliza Doolittle, a *draggle-tailed guttersnipe*, into a high-society darling. After effectively being passed off as a Dutch princess, she feels she belongs to the upper-class world. Instead, never before has she been farther away from being a true English lady. All the time she has been manipulated by Higgins to prove his reputation as a speech therapist. Shaw suggests in subtle ways how Eliza shares responsibility for what has become of her: her dreams of being loved, her ambiguous interest in Higgins, her objectifying relationships with her father, and so on. Similarly, there is something absolutely symptomatic in the will some queers show in adopting the language of the family, even though it may be a complete oxymoron. Poignant French queer theorist Marie-Hélène Bourcier explains that

> the moment gay identity seeks the integrationist politics of rights, the moment that identity settles, solidifies, then it leads to the logics of exclusion. . .[that segregates] transsexuals, SM and, in a particular way, lesbians. To demand the PACS, or the right to adoption, is to segregate. Thirty years ago, [queer] militants critiqued the heterosexual organization of society. Today, we imitate it completely. From the moment when we want to adopt children, we will not be able to say that every Sunday we go fist-fucking. (Cited in Rambach and Rambach, 2003, p. 148; my translation)

The ultimate sign of this act of constriction was celebrated in Rome's Piazza Farnese last Valentine's Day, in commemoration of the patron saint of (straight) lovers[1] and in defense of the Italian PACS under parliamentary consideration. That day, thousands of pairs of lips tried to make a political statement using the most heterosexual symbol of romantic love throughout the centuries: kissing in public. The strategy was acceptable perhaps because it is not offensive, and because it makes our sexualities look like heterosexual sexuality—the image of the kiss evokes representations of romance and faithfulness, but what representational systems would dildos, leather, and chains evoke? A kiss is not dangerous for the onlookers, however; instead, it is politically correct, coy in showing the queerness of all human sexuality, and, certainly, so naïve!

Radical Difference

I agree with some strands of queer theory that contend that homosexual/heterosexual dichotomies are cultural constructs which do not reflect the complex unsteadiness of human sexuality. Nevertheless, I have been discussing the reasons why psychoanalytic conceptions of subjectivity (less reliant on constructionist frameworks) can also benefit gay and lesbian frameworks in Italy. A comprehensive view on queerness should realize that sexuality is about politics. This motto takes two main forms, as Berlant and Warner (2002) have shown: queerness is the sexualization of politics, or queerness is the politicization of sexuality. In both cases, queerness is a form of speaking and doing that remakes the social bond by locating contingency and difference at the center of any political dialogue. Both contingency and difference are categories of political praxis that need to be situated at the center of GLBTQ politics in Italy.

In the context of this book, I have provided examples that show that contingency refers to the inscription of the symbolic law (law that is different from the variable cultural norms). Such inscription is always erratic, transitory, or incomplete. The political operates through norms that need to refract incessantly the universal. In other words, the symbolic—that is, the law of mediation *par excellence,* as Žižek (2001) would have it—can only operate refracted in particular norms or cultural codes. Law does not operate in a void, but on the material supports offered by cultural codes. However, because cultural norms can never encode the symbolic completely, the refraction in codes is always erratic, incomplete. There is no code system that encodes the universal completely, for the reason that the symbolic always represents a surplus regarding the particulars (Lewkowicz in Fariña, 1999). Law is then not something given from the beginning and for always, but something *always being* inscribed and necessarily recoded. The universal is not *something* but a constant work of coding difference, of dealing with contingency demanding permanent symbolic testimony, a witnessing on the part of the subjects—their political gestures. The symbolic is not a given datum for the human experience. It is, on the contrary, the result of a constant work of inscription of the law. Another way of saying this is by pointing out that neither imaginary nor symbolic identification (neither rivalry not totalizing ideologies) provides a stable basis for identity, which remains always open, incomplete, lacking something.

The other axis of political praxis—difference—alludes to radical alterity in the sense of a form of politics that has no guarantees or guarantor. This politics implies the recognition of Otherness: that each human being is different and exists beyond the confines of intersubjectivity. As Dean and Žižek have explained, whereas the Lacanian "other" corresponds to my neighbor as my *semblant* (think, for example, of the response of Michele in *Le Fate Ignoranti:* "He is one of us!"), the Other (capitalized) is the set of rules that corresponds to the instance of socialization made possible by the mediation of laws. And yet, these authors teach that there is a third Other, the radical face of alterity, with which there is no possible relation at all. This form of Otherness is "a zone of irreducible alterity" (Dean, 1997, p. 916) that within me is neither me nor you, but *It.* What I call queer politics is, therefore, a form of dialogue that does not disavow this radical alterity under imaginary *us* versus *them* or straight/gay divides, but a gesture, an act that erodes the fiction of being *normal*, the reverenced mythology of the average being living within the average family and having average sex. This gesture by no means implies that queerness must necessarily turn into anarchism or fear everyday life or materialize into organized boycotts against the family (although that could be quite an interesting agenda!). The conception of queers as threatening Others or bodies of total enjoyment, Dean also suggests, is a fantasy strategically mobilized to impede full-speech dialogue.

If queer politics is invoked to cause panic in the heterosexist mind, it is because the lack of guarantees of queerness can potentially result in anguish against difference: *You are not me in any possible single way.* In the political dialogue that I am advocating, the political subject is therefore confronted with a realm of impersonality, because the political gesture of doing/speaking queer is not intended to gratify anybody (any Total System). I am not arguing that queer politics is best done in nostalgic isolation. Paradoxically, while in the past I have explored the politics of the act done in solitude, over the years I have come to realize that the political gesture that is most respectful of difference is that which most strengthens the social bond as well. To paraphrase Hannah Arendt (1959), the human being can only achieve "happiness" when happiness is realized in political action—through the political dimension of the act—a living form that is and participates in the political act of de-subjection from any order of determinants.

The Otherness I am describing here is, in my view, that part of our psychic or historic biography that is unknown by oneself and which opens one's life to contingency. In this openness, I am evoking one more time the idea of a journey without a destination. Although these ideas emanate in part from my training as psychoanalyst, they have materialized for me during the last decade, coinciding with my coming out as a queer person, my traveling to other countries, and my relationship with an Italian person.

Id and Entity. The signifier *identity* carries within it two main, yet opposing images: Id and Entity. These are two very contradictory forms of understanding subjectivity, and both have been central to cultural and queer studies. While the image of the *Id* suggests discontinuity or flux, impersonality (*it*), and non-Aristotelian logics, the image of the *Entity* evokes continuity, solidity, self, or individuality. For strategic political reasons, I have tried to explore the usefulness and limitations of both these notions as they emerged in the Italian context. For instance, I have devoted entire sections to looking at the ways feminists appropriated and reclaimed the notion of the self while combining it with psychoanalytic notions that empowered their struggles during the 1960s; or I looked into Mario Mieli's criticism of the notion of identity, which he considered insufficient to explain the interconnectedness and impersonal status of queer desire. At the same time, I have situated my own self and identity in this project to emphasize that identity is a form of doing and speaking, not a substance or thing. As I see it, identity concerns both self-identity and social (cultural, political) identity insofar as human beings are constituted in relation to an Other. This Other, to borrow from Dean, is on the one hand the location of intersubjectivity, but also the site of language or the symbolic law *par excellence*, and it is also the Other of radical difference that inhabits fantasy.

All the forms of alterity render identity a permanent dialogic construction (and also a struggle), performative and interdependent on the social bond. It is this interdependence and dialogic status of identity that I accentuate as the political nature of human identity. In my view, queer politics should seek the realization of *human dignity* through political action. Following Wilchins's (2004) and Lehr's (1999) models for the American case, this means that queer politics in Italy has an important role in re-manufacturing society, conceiving of it as the making of a public space where citizens can question any norm or decision not originating in their own activity. In other words, politics is not an exclusive matter of the state or social institutions. Rather, it is also a question of the political and psychical subjects that make it happen. As Hannah Arendt (1959) stated, "speech and action reveal this unique distinctness. Through them, men distinguish themselves instead of being merely distinct; they are the modes in which human beings appear to each other, not indeed as physical objects, but qua men" (p. 156).

Public, private, borderland. Central to this book has been an analysis of the historical and current relations among intimacy, politics, and culture that examines the opposition between public and private. I have suggested notions like transitional spaces, borderland, and confines as more serviceable images for rethinking these relations. The transitional or borderland space could be interpreted as the site where our lives become invested with words to the point of remaking citizenship and subjectivity, the site constitutive of the *social bond*. Politics can only appear with the recognition of the Other as a different subject, with whom a particulate dialogue (a dialogue where truth is always partial) is potentially possible. The current plea for civil unions in Italy is such a wonderful case study because it shows that politics should not be understood as the struggle between social groups or political parties to defend particular interests, but that politics should be a collective enterprise whose object is the change of the institution of society as a whole. Paraphrasing Arendt (1959) again, for human beings action is a choice. It is essential, then, that queers do not adapt to the language of heterosexuality but critically advocate a vigilance of the political and keep observing the possible consequences of reinforcing, through our own demands, heterosexism any time that the potential of queer life and intimacies is taken as secondary to the importance of state legitimacy.

Going back to *Le Fate Ignoranti,* at some middle point in the narrative, Michele and Antonia realize that Massimo had met Michele in a bookstore while desperately looking for a volume written by Salonic poet Nazim Hikmet that Massimo wanted as a gift for Antonia. Michele was looking for the exact same book, a rare volume not easily found, and started to chat about the poet with Massimo. Both Antonia and Michele then understand that in a sense *they are the same*, regardless of their sexual orientation, gender, and social class. This sameness is a particularly delicate matter: on the one hand, it is clear that the ultimate message of a commercial film like this is, quite straightforwardly put, that we are all human beings made of the same human *stuff,* and we therefore endure similar pain and happiness. Yet, to fully appreciate this movie, we need to read the text from a different perspective altogether: difference instead of sameness. Of course, in saying difference, I am invoking here once more the three Lacanian registers that have been used in these pages to criticize the notion of identity. At the level of imaginary identification, Antonia recognizes Michele as a rival, which triggers her anger for not being The Woman she had imagined she was (the mysterious lover of the first scene, the keeper of Truth, the exceptional daughter, and so on). Similarly, Michele discovers that Massimo is not *one of us* simply because he is not everything he had imagined him to be. Michele, in this respect, had elevated the queerness of Massimo to the level of a Master signifier. This image of complete unity with Massimo and the other members of the family of choice is finally broken into pieces when he discovers that Massimo loved Antonia profoundly. In both cases, Michele and Antonia confront the failure of the imaginary to provide them with a solid identity. At the level of the symbolic, things are not much easier, for while both protagonists make themselves a place for symbolic recognition within a family of choice, this recognition is not stable. At the end of the movie, we see Michele wondering if he will ever see Antonia again. He therefore needs to accept the loss of a member of his family of choice, which indeed resignifies the site of the primordial loss introduced by the signifier. The entrance to the symbolic order implies this structural loss, which can be simply put in the following words: *not everything is possible*. While queer families provide networks of care and support for their members, all human affiliations are inhabited by this insubstantial, irreducible loss. Following Stavrakakis's (1999) model of political analysis, this is therefore another second register that fails to provide a totalizing sense of identity and that fails to encompass or symbolize the real, the third and final Lacanian register:

> What are the implications of the constitutive alienation in the imaginary and the symbolic for a theory of subjective identity? The fullness of identity that the subject is seeking is impossible both in the imaginary and in the symbolic level. . . .Symbolization, that is to say the pursuit of identity itself, introduces lack and makes identity ultimately impossible. . . .Identity is possible only as a failed identity. (Stavrakakis, 1999, p. 29)

The ultimate message that the movie offers for the purposes of this book is, therefore, beyond the personal or even intersubjective level of identity; it is a message about the sociopolitical consequences of the continuous making and failing of identity that Stavrakakis (1999) points to in the above quotation. Since the making of identity is always incomplete and unstable, political, familial, and religious ideologies and other socially constructed discourses function as objects of identification in adult life, providing images and signifiers that promise the closure of the irreducible split of the human subject. As I have stated, in some of Özpetek's films, including *Le Fate Ignoranti*, a queer family provides a symbolic matrix that locates the protagonists in relationships of care and support. The ending of *Le Fate Ignoranti*, however, is particularly intriguing. While Antonia's leaving could be read as a nostalgic, Hollywood-like ending, to me it represents an ending that bothers viewers who have identified with the promises of family love and care portrayed in the film. One could even say that the gesture of Antonia is an ethical one, for it detotalizes the unity of the queer family, legitimizing the lack of identity and the lack of social utopias. To cite Stavrakakis again, "what is clearly at stake here is the possibility of enacting symbolic gestures that institutionalize social lack, that is to say incorporate the ethical recognition of the impossibility of social closure" (Stavrakakis, 1999, p. 134).

The ethical gesture Stavrakakis suggests can take place by locating symbolically something of the real; that is to say, by putting into signifiers and representations that which is, by its own nature, beyond the symbolic. This logical impossibility implies a work or demand on behalf of the (universal) symbolic to recognize difference (particulars) and to give it a political status (Stavrakakis, 1999). In the case of queer politics, this translates into seeking ways of representation that do not elevate the family or matrimony as a Master signifier, but which legitimate the existence of the alterity or lack which inhabits all human beings. In that sense, the human condition is a queer condition.

Moving Forward

In this book I have argued that the plea for civil unions demands contextual analysis. The challenge of the Italian GLBTQ movement is that this appeal is a call for the state to normalize queerness, and yet is also a necessary instrument of struggle that emerged out of international and domestic transformations that I have described here. Demanding state legitimacy is, however, a movement highly problematic: It can reify the already-existing exclusion of queers who do not agree with the labeling of their intimacies. Following queer theory writers like Warner, I agree that legalizing same-sex unions can make queers surrender to the power of the state, the symbols of heterosexuality, and the patriarchal law—and indeed I have cited research suggesting that, sadly, queer conformity to the language/norm of heterosexuality has already begun.

My intention has been to provide a practical case study—queer Italy— and apply multiple methodologies and sources that demonstrate at a pragmatic, not just an abstract or theoretical level, that (id)entity—sexual, political, or ethnic—is a non-essential quality of our subjectivity constantly traversed by the forces of language and power relations. An essentialist view on sexuality relies on positivistic and/or biological claims that limit political activity. At the same time, homosexual/heterosexual dichotomies cannot account for desire, which is always queer, independently of the sex of the object toward which a person is attracted. Throughout this book, it has been explained why queerness is not a matter of sexual orientation, but a form of strategic positionality that occurs in intersection with a diversity of contexts.

Understanding identity as fluid has the advantage of allowing one to build a strategic common ground that creates commonality, and to build alliances among people of the most diverse social background and interests, regardless of their sexual preferences (see Wilchins, 2004). The Italian queer movement can only benefit from a politics that reaches out, seeking others who can organize against xenophobia, whiteness, and heterosexism. Furthermore, as queer writers cited in this work have suggested, non-essentialist views on sexuality and identity can bring awareness of the need to forge non-separatist politics leading to overcoming gender/class/race/national divisions within the wide spectrum of Italian GLBTQ organizations. An example of these divisions is the continued rift between the gay and lesbian movements, discussed earlier in this book. As Wilchins (2004) would put it, a male, gay-centered movement is not only blind to the all-encompassing strength of the two-gender cultural system currently prevalent in many countries, including Italy, but reductionist of the complexity inherent in the human condition.

Because the construction of sexuality is not independent of judgments about class, ethnicity, race, and nationality, a queer politics framework demands that activists address these issues within their agendas (Wilchins, 2004) with the same intensity with which they are actually addressing the need for civil unions. Indeed, they need to be addressing them *as part* of the plea for civil unions, not independently of it. I have illustrated this point by referring to my own journey and experiences in Argentina, the United States, and Italy in an attempt to shed light on the multiple determinants that traverse the self. While sexual identity is a flexible construct for many queers in Italy, issues like sexual orientation, nationality, religion, and class continue to be sites of exclusion and the exercise of power and discrimination. While I am aware that the language of queer politics has surfaced in Italy as a result of changes in the economy and culture in the present global world, it can serve Italians by criticizing powers interested in creating solid dichotomies, and by contesting their control of the body and their infliction of shame and fear. For this reason, it is important to move from the realm of the symbolic into the realm of the contingency or the real.

The experience of transnationals living in Italy, or new citizens (legally registered or not), either from inside or outside the European Community, has to be acknowledged, praised, and incorporated into the current Italian movement, which has been guided for the most part solely by male Italians. Because we have experienced isolation, ghettoization, and language barriers, many migrant queers have direct experience that can benefit the movement's need to build a community based on difference.

For queer politics to prosper in Italy, we need to move from the advocacy of civil rights to the creation of new *social* and *human* rights, as activists around the world are maintaining. In this I follow Wilchins (2004), who criticizes the limited scope of current civil rights, which in evoking the language of heterosexuality can maintain the functioning of a gendered law while at the same time marking which forms of behavior are still not acceptable. "It is now acceptable to be gay, but it's still not yet okay to be a fag. You can be a lesbian, but not a dyke" (Wilchins, 2004, p. 19). Valerie Lehr agrees. According to her, rethinking the claims that the queer movement is making can place political activism's emphasis "not on demanding that rights be extended, but rather on demanding that they be redefined, since guaranteeing rights for those previously excluded requires new understandings of the rights constructed around exclusion" (Lehr, 1999, p. 96). In truth, the title of this book, *Queer Italy*, originated in several conversations with colleagues and friends from different regions of Italy and in dialogue with my partner and sister. We have envisioned a utopian day when human rights in Italy and elsewhere are all inclusive and respectful of the radical diversity at the heart of humanity.

How do we express the connection between our theories and our everyday politics? By inquiring into an imaginary, personal *Queer Italy*, I have tried to answer this question by pointing out that theory without personal and social commitment is academically imprudent. Instead, when theory is committed to questioning social orders, and when the researcher includes the self as an interpretive gesture of reflexivity, then our work can become a practice of emancipation by offering unusual versions of history that oppose any coherent, imposed, self-regulated, or self-conscious version of who we are, what we desire, and how we behave. *Queer Italy* is a challenge to think the often unthinkable, difference, in a universe inhabited by plurals: cultures, languages, memories, and, of course, Otherness.

๛ Notes ๛

Introduction

1. The French PACS was passed in Paris on November 15, 1999.
2. Intercrural intercourse involves placing and rubbing the penis between the partner's thighs, either from the front or rear.
3. Currently the linguistic unification of Italy remains a problem. There are several languages and dialects spoken in the country: Italian (official), French (Valle D'Aosta), Slovene (Friuli-Venezia Giulia), German and Latin (Alto Adige), Sardo (Sardinia), Friulano (Friuli), Franco-Provençal and Arpitano (Valle D'Aosta, Piedmont), Occitanian and Provençal (Val Argentina), Catalan (Alghero), Greek (Salento and Aspromonte), and Albanian (mainly in Sicily and Calabria). I will refer to the issue of language in different ways throughout this book.
4. As Rictor Norton (1997) points out, homosexuality and language have a long history of camouflage, disguise, and concealment.

Chapter 2

1. Indeed, what Lévi-Strauss discovered is that it is the exchange of women that maintains the stability of the social system. This has been a highly contested claim that I cannot discuss here, although my engagement with feminism and queer theory will make clear my position on this subject.
2. I will return in chapter 4 to the significance of having a relationship named by the community. For now, I would like to point out that to name is a power conferred by a third party who *represents* the symbolic. Indeed, one of the roles of the witnesses who are present in ceremonies like those of marriage is that of assuring that the agent represents, but does not *embody*, the symbolic. Notice that there is more than one register superimposed in this problem. Since I will be using psychoanalytic terms in this and the following chapters, I would like to briefly discuss them here. The first register is that of the imaginary. The recognition by the community, the identification triggered by the rituals of marriage, the ennobling that comes with making a family, the gratitude to ancestors, the planning of a happy future in family, and so on are all effects of the imaginary. The imaginary constitutes, therefore, an order of dual relationships characterized either by recognition or misrecognition (*méconnaissance*). The second register is that of the symbolic, which is foundational of subjectivity in Lacanian psychoanalysis. The symbolic register is introduced with the world of language—or, more precisely, with the workings of the signifier as such. As a register, the symbolic antecedes and is dialectically opposed to the imaginary register. The symbolic is beyond any agent that represents it. Nobody can *embody* the symbolic or name it. Rather, subjects are named by the symbolic; they find their place in this world by being allocated within the symbolic. Finally, there is a third register, which describes the constitutive limits of the symbolic. This is, of course, the Lacanian real. The real can be understood as that which, precisely be-

cause it is not part of the symbolic, allows the symbolic to work. What matters here is that imaginary recognition is not confused with symbolic sanctioning. It is generally accepted that human family survival depends on a pact with a social body of other families and institutions (for instance the state) which appeal to a number of procedures to gain recognition. This recognition is mainly imaginary, and not symbolic, insofar as it is historically and culturally specific, and it depends on a body or regulatory norms or codes made by individuals. Insofar as individuals can never completely translate the symbolic into codes, these codes stand for the symbolic only partially—and oftentimes mistakenly. In other words, the sanctioning of certain relationships and not others based on the particularistic favoring of certain sexual codes and behaviors and the exclusion of others as improper does not belong to the realm of the symbolic. The symbolic stands for human diversity, not for favoritisms. As Lacan puts it: "All that is elaborated by the subjective construction on the scale of the signifier in its relation to the Other and which has its root in language is only there to permit the full spectrum of desire. . ." (Lacan, 1972-1973, pp. 194-195). Nevertheless, queer politics needs to address the limit of the symbolic and move toward politics that take into account the real: as Žižek (1999, 2001a) has demonstrated, the whole fabric of ideology and politics relies on the structure of a fantasy whose kernel is real, not symbolic. I go back to this issue several times in this book. For a complete analysis of the registers in Lacanian theory, see Fink (1995).

3. To cite a number of examples, in Sparta it was the community that parented individuals, not the biological parents of the child (Le Fur, 2004); in early twentieth-century northern Morocco, religious groups of mountaineers required that married men have sexual intercourse before learning the Koran; and in early societies in New Guinea it was acceptable for a man to substitute a woman when no sister was available for exchange in marriage (Greenberg, 1988).

4. A lovely Italian way of referring to the nation is to call it *bel paese*, or beautiful country.

5. During the Reinassance, Italy was divided into city-states that were continually threatened by occupation from neighboring powers. *Risorgimento* (revival) is a term that describes the nationalism and political unification of Italy that began after the French Revolution of 1789 and consolidated in the period 1860–1870.

6. It is not clear why the the neologism *dottora* was preferred to the Italian feminine noun *dottoressa*, although it most probably refers to a linguistic twist of her lower-class patients. Later, it might have been kept for its emphasis on Kuliscioff's radical ideas and anarchic attitude toward gender.

7. Giovanni Giolitti was a five-time premier of Italy (1892-1893, 1903-1905, 1906-1909, 1911-1914, and 1920-1921).

8. For an assessment of the period called *Il Novecento*, or twentieth century, and the modifications in Italian literature it implies, see Brand and Pertile (1999).

9. For a historical study on fascism, see Morgan (1995). For a comprehensive feminist study on fascism, see De Grazia (1992).

10. I discuss the discipline of male bodies during fascism in chapter 3.

11. I elaborate on the representation of homosexuality in this film in chapter 6.

12. In February 1929, the Italian government and the Vatican signed a treaty that reasserted the political power and diplomatic standing of the Catholic Church, which had been lost with the unification of Italy and the annexation of Rome in 1870.

13.By 1968, literacy rates had increased to 20 percent for both sexes in some regions; school-leaving age was raised to the age of fourteen for both sexes, and nineteen million Italians could read (Lumley, 1996).

14.The marriage of the victim and the offender.

15.Small groups of leftist feminists who would meet regularly in private homes to share experiences under the motto "the personal is the political."

16.I am aware that while some readers might find these statistics indicative of the unchallenged strength of marriage, others might read them as indicators of an impressive change in attitudes toward matrimony. In either case, my main concern is to show the relationships between the legal and symbolic contexts.

17.For example, divorce first became legal in France on September 20, 1792; it was abolished in 1816, and re-established in 1884 under the Third Republic.

18.A style of European architecture containing both Roman and Byzantine elements, prevalent especially in the eleventh and twelfth centuries.

19.A humorous account of this tradition appears in Pietro Germi's sardonic comedy *Divorzio all'Italiana* (Divorce, Italian Style, 1961). Marcello Mastroianni interprets Ferdinando Cefalú, a married Sicilian man who falls in love with Angela (Stefania Sandrelli). He hates his wife and is determined to get a divorce from her—the only problem being that divorce was illegal at the time. The protagonist then realizes that the law justifies the killing of a wife if she is caught during the adulterous act, and so he tries to set his wife up in an affair with a family acquaintance. After killing his wife, he can finally marry Angela. Ironically, though, she is now unfaithful to him.

20.Indeed, another reading of Petrignani's story is possible. The tale can represent the disillusionment of leftist Italians with grand politics during the crisis of communism—but before the fall of the Berlin Wall (the story dates back to 1984). In this sense, notice the similarity between Petrignani's story and Nanni Moretti's film *Palombella Rossa,* which also takes place in a swimming pool (see chapter 3).

Chapter 3

1.Interestingly, Braidotti states that the English term *gender* does not have a correlate in Romance languages; she notes that the corresponding French word, *genre*, does not parallel the uses of the English term. The same point can be made about the Italian *genere*, which can be used in a universalistic way to designate, for instance, humanity as a whole—*il genere umano*.

2.With these terms, Lapassade conceptualized the dialectic interchange of forces between what has been established as the norm in any social domain and what becomes disruptive of it, hence forcing individuals and groups to recognize the limits of any *norm* and appreciate the continuous change and stability of the social order.

3.Paragraph 175 was a provision of the German Criminal Code from 1871 to 1994 that made homosexual acts between males a crime and compared it to bestiality.

4.To avoid confusion, I will distinguish between Mario and Aldo Mieli using both first and last names.

5.One example of this retroactive look at fascism is seen in Rossellini's classic film *Roma Città Apperta* (Rome Open City, 1945), where partisans are representatives of heteronormativity, while Nazi officers are homosexuals.

6.In the official version, teenage hustler Giusepe (Pino) Pelosi killed Pasolini in a deserted parking lot in Ostia. However, in May 2005, Pelosi confessed on public television that in fact the murder was committed by a gang of three people with political and religious connections.

7. Friulian is a dialect characteristic of an area in the northeastern part of Italy, spoken in the provinces of Udine, Pordenone, and Gorizia (in the region of Friuli Venezia Giulia) and in Trieste.

8. The expression *atto impuro* remains a way of referring to homosexuality. It is also the name of Pasolini's novel, posthumously published in 1982.

9. For a comprehensive analysis of Italian literature and homosexuality, see Gnerre (2000).

10. Unfortunately, in some cases sociopolitical circumstances conspired against these movements. To cite an example particularly interesting to me, the first Argentine homosexual association—Nuestro Mundo (Our World), dating back to 1969–was comprised of homosexual railway workers who were politically committed to communist "syndicalism." In 1972, Nuestro Mundo was converted into the Frente de Liberación Homosexual (Homosexual Liberation Front) by Néstor Perlongher, who incorporated Trotskian radical politics into the association until it was dissolved under the repression of the 1976 coup d'état, when several of its members permanently disappeared through abduction or were tortured (see Rapisardi, 2003a).

11. Pride and Pride Parade are also English terms that usually remain without translation in Italy.

12. This slogan mirrored Mieli's schizophrenic politics by incorporating and transforming the well-known Latin American political jingle, "el pueblo unido jamás seá vencido."

13. There is no translation for this. The name of the play simply plays with onomatopoeic words.

14. The form of therapeutic writing assumed by Mario Mieli can be related to certain stylistic approaches in Italian literature following World War II, which emphasized the location of the self within the narrative. This is particularly clear in authors like Primo Levi and Pier Paolo Pasolini, and in most feminist writers. On the use of the self in Italian gay literature, see Giartosio (2004).

15. For a complete analysis of this novel, see Pustianaz (2004).

Chapter 4

1. Earlier in this book, I followed Giovanni Dall'Orto (2004a; 2004b) in his historical analysis of communal silence as a repressive mechanism, particularly clear in the libertarian period of *Risorgimento* and fascism, both of which implied the imaginary grandeur of the Italian nation, albeit in different ways. Dall'Orto's viewpoints are very much applicable here as well.

2. Mario Mieli brilliantly termed the effects of institutionalized education *educastration*.

3. When both boys disappeared, Galatola's father denounced Agatino for the suborning, kidnapping, and corruption of minors (Suicidio su commissione, 2005).

4. I borrow this explanatory model from the seminars at the Department of Psychology, Ethics, and Human Rights at the University of Buenos Aires, Argentina, and in particular the classes given by Gabriela Salomone, Carlos Gutierrez, and Juan Jorge Michel Fariña.

5. The word *de-gaying* was coined by activists Ben Schatz and Eric Rofes to refer to the strategies of the United States's gay movement during the 1980s (Vaid, 1995). Urvashi Vaid (1995) sees no naïveté in *de-gaying* when she argues: "We chose to focus on AIDS rather than on homophobia and racism, even though these were the causes of the governmental and societal paralysis. . .the degaying of AIDS was a conscious political choice made by gay organizers" (p. 75).

6. On June 12, 2005, only 25.9 percent of Italians voted in a referendum on Assisted Reproductive Technology (ART), and no change was introduced into the current law against ART. Pope Benedict XVI personally asked Italians to boycott the referendum. Arcilesbica and Arcigay repudiated this position and asked queers not to abstain from voting.

7. The name *Tangentopoli* (Kickbackville) derives from the Italian word for kickback (*tangente*) and alludes to subterranean roots spreading spatially or conceptually.

Chapter 5

1. In particular, France, Italy, and Spain. Canada and England are particular cases, for they both share their philosophical and political traditions not only with continental Europe but also with the United States: "Canada, Britain, and especially the United States have a very pronounced civil-society tradition for opposing voluntary association to the state. (This may be another reason why queer politics works in Anglo-American nations but has not much caught on in countries with stronger conceptions of socialist democracy)" (Warner, 2002, pp. 213-214).

2. I am citing the most memorable book by Altman, from 1982. However, similar ideas are developed in more recent articles. See Altman (1996).

3. Discussions on monogamy in Italy are necessary to deconstruct interrelated dominant ideologies of sexual identity, ethnicity, and gender. Valerie Lehr suggests that "[i]deologically, monogamy is the preferable form of human sexual relationship because within a monogamous relationship human beings learn to control their desires and direct their energy into useful social purposes. In fact, the social privileging of heterosexual monogamy was part of an early twentieth-century attempt to control and civilize European immigrants, and to control and encourage the development of private family life, a life away from the public space of the street. By performing such isolated family units, men would be influenced by the pro-social desires and needs of their wives; workers would be more hesitant to strike, both because they would be less connected to one another and because they would feel greater responsibility to their wives and children; ideal consumer units would be created; and parents would be able to support their increasingly costly children" (Lehr, 1999, p. 57).

4. Although I cannot develop this topic any further here, I think that the invention of a complete new language to name queer relationships is problematic for it implies the acknowledgment of the symbolic framework of heterosexuality as the real, legitimate Other. In this light, queerness is structurally performed as a "weak" or "funny" or "foreign" version of the "real" legitimate language of straights.

5. This is an ironic nickname: *Nilla* is an allusion to the Italian singer Nilla Pizzi, popular during the 1960s, and also known as La regina della musica italiana (the queen of Italian music).

6. Households of wealthy families with farmlands and families of servants living under one roof.

7.Although I will be using demographic trends in the following short sections, I do not intend to construct an objective picture of the Italian family. Rather, I use demographics to further illustrate the different contexts that underlie the current plea for civil unions in Italy. For this reason, I will take liberties and refer only to a small number of sociological sources.

8.As early as 1973, sociologist Chiara Saraceno explained that "The concept of the nuclear family as applied to contemporary family structure in industrialized societies is problematic. The nuclear family is not a recent phenomenon; it has always been the family pattern of dependent classes who owned no property. The cultural and social value attached to the nuclear family by bourgeois society and now by capitalistic industrial society is what constitutes its novelty. . . .The ideological pattern of the contemporary nuclear family is empirically evidenced in studies showing that it is neither isolated nor reduced to a private and affective function; a kin network, functioning on the affective and social levels, exists. This network. . .(1) is more efficient and functional to the needs of a[n]. . .occupational system, within which it has flexible structure and is based on choice, (2) has a more solidaristic function. . .and (3) is more exposed to the risk of disruption since its members have less material and cultural means to communicate" (p. 1).

9.Average number of children per woman.

10.People from Buenos Aires.

11.I will be focusing on one of the two main characters of the movie: the relationship between the two married adults. I do not include the drama of their teenage children, which deserves a discussion that exceeds the limits of this chapter.

12.In this film, the magnificent splendor of a southern island frames the drama of a woman searching for freedom. High cliffs, deep blue waters, and immense skies represent this liberty and are shown in plain contrast with the domestic space of the household unit where she lives.

13.In comparison, despite being an international production by one of Italy's most famous *auteurs,* Bernardo Bertolucci's *I Sognatori* (The Dreamers) in the same year made €4,866,737.08, with an audience of 817,308 spectators (Della Casa, 2004).

14.In psychoanalytic theory, all love is transference love insofar as all love implies fantasy. However, here I am overemphasizing the fictional, almost ridiculous characteristics of Giulia's fascination with the director.

15.This metaphorical use of mirrors is evocative of Fellini's *Amarcord* and *Giulietta degli Spiriti* (Juliet of the Spirits), two of the films in which the director was most concerned with oppressive gender relations (Bondanella, 2003).

16.For a discussion about enjoyment and consumption from a Lacanian-Marxist perspective, see Žižek (1999).

17.There are many cases, particularly during a psychoanalytic treatment, when the relations between the subject and the object of desire coexist with relations framed in terms of enjoyment.

18.When I first saw this film, I could not help but think of the similarities between its ending and Concetta and Michele's marriage, preserved despite Michele's infidelity.

Chapter 6

1.In this chapter I also use the term *genderqueer*, which I take from activist Ricky Wilchins (2004). This signifier stresses the centrality of gender in queer theory.

2.In other words, that there is no "natural," instinctual, or predetermined knowledge about sexuality.

3.In the following films: *Anche i Commercialisti Hanno un'Anima* (1994), *Il Branco* (1994), *La Scorta* (1993), *Ultrà* (1990), *Il Maestro del Terrore* (1988, TV), *Il Volpone* (1988), *Noi Uomini Duri* (1987), *Il Tenente dei Carabinieri* (1986), *Sono Contento* (1983), and *Scusate il Ritardo* (1982).

4.To understand the particular space of the hamam depicted in two of the films directed by Özpetek, see Nina Cichocki's (2005) discussion of permanence and change in the meaning of bathing culture in Istanbul, and her analysis of the perception of the hamam by foreign and Turkish visitors in times of global tourism.

5.For a psychoanalytic analysis of Özpetek's films in the context of Middle East/European relations, see Diken and Laustsen (2001).

6.The Lacanian formula *ne pas céder sur son désir*, difficult to translate into English (roughly stated, it means "do not give up/succumb/yield to one's desire"—which can also be thought of as "don't succumb to what you do not know" or "do not give up your position as a subject of desire"), can be regarded as characterizing human subjectivity around a desire that is articulated but cannot be defined.

7.This is a question that, according to Lacanians, characterizes the discourse of hysteria. For a complete analysis of neurotic structures in Lacanian theory, see Fink (1995).

8.I thank Pat Gill for this suggestion.

9.To be totally faithful to Lacanian theory, one should say that there is no same-sex relation insofar as there is no sex relation.

10.Later on in the teaching of Lacan, however, the letter is situated in the register of the real, not destined to be read or interpreted by any Other. It is on this late conceptualization of the letter that I base my claim that these films encode desire as impersonal, and identity as queer.

Conclusion

1.It is popularly believed that Saint Sebastian is the protector of gays, mostly because of the erotic art and iconography regarding this saint in Renaissance Italy.

❧ Filmography ❧

Adriatico, A. (Director). (2004). *Il Vento, di Sera*. [Videotape]. Bologna, Italy: Teatro di Vita.

Almodóvar, P. (Director). (1999). *All about My Mother*. [DVD]. Madrid: El Deseo.

————. (Director). (2002). *Talk to Her*. [DVD]. Madrid: El Deseo.

Barnett, D. (Director). (1910). *Il Trovatore*. [Videotape]. London: Animatophone Syndicate.

Bava, L. (Director). (1988). *Il Maestro del Terrore* [TV]. Rome: Reteitalia.

Beaumont, H. (Director). (1929). *The Broadway Melody*. [DVD]. Warner Home Video.

Bertolucci, B. (Director). (1970). *Il Conformista* [DVD]. Rome: Mars.

Borgnetto, L.R., & Pastrone, G. (Directors). (1911). *La Caduta di Troia*. [Videotape]. Turin, Italy: Museo Nazionale del Cinema.

Bragaglia, C. (Director). (1970). *Figaro Qua. . .Figaro Là*. [Videotape]. Turin, Italy: Museo Nazionale del Cinema.

Capuano, A. (Director). (1996). *Pianese Nunzio, Quattordici Anni a Maggio*. [DVD]. Picture This.

Cavani, L. (Director). (1977). *Al di là del Bene e del Male*.

Crialese, E. (Director). (2003). *Respiro*. [DVD]. Sony Pictures.

De Sica, C. (Director). (2003). *Uomini Uomini Uomini*. [DVD]. Ensemble Film.

Demme, J. (Director). (1993). *Philadelphia*. [Videotape]. Sony Pictures.

Fellini, F. (Director). (1961). *La Dolce Vita*. [DVD]. Koch Lorber Films.

Fosse, R. (Director). (1972). *Cabaret*. [Videotape]. Warner Home Video.

Friedkin, W. (1980). *Cruising*. [Videotape]. Warner Home Video.

Germi, P. (1961). *Divorzio all'Italiana*. [DVD]. Criterion Collection.

Guazzoni, E. (Director). (1912). *Quo Vadis?* [Videotape]. Rome: Italiana Cines Production.

Grimaldi A. (Director). (2002). *Un Mondo d'Amore* (A World of Love) [Videotape]. Toronto International Film Festival.

Hogan, P.G. (Director). (1997). *My Best Friend's Wedding*. [DVD]. Sony Pictures.

Hytner, N. (Director). (1998). *The Object of My Affection*. [DVD]. Twentieth-Century Fox.

Lautner, G. (Director). (1985). *La Cage aux Folles III. "Elles" se Marient*. [DVD]. MGM.

Lean, D. (Director). (1965). *Doctor Zhivago*. [DVD]. Turner Home Entertainment.

Levingston, J. (Director). (1990). *Paris Is Burning*. [DVD]. Miramax.

Martoglio, N. (Director). (1914). *Sperduti nel Buio*. [Videotape]. Turin, Italy: Museo Nazionale del Cinema.

Mastrocinque, C. (1961). *Totòtruffa '62*. [Videotape]. Turin, Italy: Museo Nazionale del Cinema.

Molinaro, E. (Director). (1979). *La Cage aux Folles I*. [DVD]. MGM.

————. (Director). (1981). *La Cage aux Folles II*. [DVD]. MGM.

Moretti, N. (Director). (1989). *Palombella Rossa*. [Videotape]. Fox Lorber/Wellspring.

Muccino, G. (Director). (1999). *Come te Nessuno Mai*. [DVD]. Warner.

————. (Director). (2001). *L'Ultimo Bacio*. [DVD]. Walt Disney Video.

————. (Director). (2004). *Ricordati di Me*. [DVD]. Roadside Attractions.

Neuroni, B., & Serena, G. (Directors). (1915). *La Signora delle Camelie*. Turin, Italy: Museo Nazionale del Cinema.

Özpetek, F. (Director). (1997). *Hamam*. Rome: Medusa Films.

———. (Director). (1999). *Harem Suaré*. Rome: Medusa Films.

———. (Director). (2001). *Le Fate Ignoranti*. Rome: Medusa Films.

———. (Director). (2003). *La Finestra di Fronte*. Rome: Medusa Films.

———. (Director). (2005). *Cuore Sacro*. Rome: Medusa Films.

———. (Director). (2007). *Saturno Contro*. Rome: Medusa Films.

Palermi, A. (Director). (1939). *Napoli che non Muore*. [Videotape]. Turin, Italy: Museo Nazionale del Cinema.

Pasolini, P. (Director). (1962). *Mamma Roma*. New York: Criterion Collection.

———. (Director). (1962). *La Ricotta*. New York: Criterion Collection.

———. (Director). (1963). *La Rabbia*. New York: Criterion Collection.

———. (Director). (1963-1964). *Sopralluoghi in Palestina per il Vangelo Secondo Matteo*. New York: Criterion Collection.

———. (Director). (1964). *Comizi d'Amore*. New York: Criterion Collection.

———. (Director). (1968). *Accattone*. New York: Water Bearer Films, Inc.

———. (Director). (1968). *Teorema*. New York: Water Bearer Films, Inc.

———. (Director). (1976). *Salò o le 120 Giornate di Sodoma*. Les Productions Artistes Associés, Produzioni Europee Associati (PEA).

Ponzi, M. (Director). (1983). *Sono Contento*. [TV]. Rome: Reteitalia.

———. (Director). (1986). *Il Tenente dei Carabinieri*. [Videotape]. Rome: C.G. Silver Film.

———. (Director). (1987). *Noi Uomini Duri*. [DVD]. Rome: Cecchi Gori Home Video.

———. (Director). (1988). *Il Volpone*. Rome: Cecchi Gori Group Tiger/Maura International Film.

———. (Director). (1994). *Anche i Commercialisti Hanno un'Anima*. [Videotape]. Rome: Multivision.

Risi, M. (Director). (1994). *Il Branco*. [Videotape]. Rome: Cecchi Gori Group.

Rossellini, R. (Director). (1945). *Roma Città Aperta*. [DVD]. London: British Film Institute.

———. (Director). (1949). *Germania Anno Zero*. [Videotape]. London: British Film Institute.

Samperi, S. (Director). (1979). *Ernesto.*

Schlesinger, J. (Director). (2000). *The Next Best Thing*. [DVD]. Paramount.

Scola, E. (Director). (1977). *Una Giornata Particolare*. [DVD]. Jeff Films, Inc.

Scott, T. (Director). (1997). *The Hunger*. [DVD]. MGM.

Steno. (Director). (1952). *Totò a Colori*. [Videotape]. Turin, Italy: Museo Nazionale del Cinema.

———. (Director). (1963). *Totò Contro I 4*. [Videotape]. Turin, Italy: Museo Nazionale del Cinema.

Tognazzi, R. (Director). (1990). *Ultrà*. [DVD]. Rome: Italy, Numero Uno / Raidue.

———. (Director). (1993). *La Scorta*. [DVD]. Rome: Blue Underground.

Troisi, M. (Director). (1982). *Scusate il Ritardo*. [DVD]. Rome: Cecchi Gori Group.

Visconti, L. (1943). *Ossessione*. [Videotape]. Turin, Italy: Museo Nazionale del Cinema.

———. (1969). *La Caduta degli Dei*. [Videotape]. Turin, Italy: Museo Nazionale del Cinema.

———. (1971). *Morte a Venezia*. [DVD]. Warner Home Video.

———. (1972). *Ludwig*. [Videotape]. Turin, Italy: Museo Nazionale del Cinema.

References

Aaron, M. (2004). *New queer cinema.* New Brunswick, NJ: Rutgers University Press.

Abelove, H. (1993). Freud, male homosexuality, and the Americans. In H. Abelove, M.A. Barale, & D.M. Halperin (eds.), *The lesbian and gay studies reader* (pp. 381-396). New York and London: Routledge.

Adorno, T., & Horkheimer, M. (1947/2002). *Dialectic of enlightenment. Philosophical fragments.* Stanford, CA: Stanford University Press.

Agamben, G. et al. (1993). *Politica.* Napoli, Italy: Cronopio.

Allan, J. (2004, May). *And baby makes three. . ..: Gay men, straight women and the parental imperative in film and television.* Paper presented at the International Communication Association convention, New Orleans, LA.

Allen, B., & Russo, M. (1997). *Revisioning Italy. National identity and global culture.* Minneapolis and London: University of Minnesota Press.

Allum, P. (2003). Catholicism. In Z. Baranski & R. West, (eds.), *The Cambridge companion to modern Italian culture* (pp. 97-112). Cambridge, UK: Cambridge University Press.

Altman, D. (1982). *The homosexualization of America, the Americanization of the homosexual.* New York: St. Martin's Press.

————. (1996). Rupture or continuity? The internationalization of gay identities. *Social Text,* 48, 74-94.

————. (2002). *Sex, politics, and political economy.* Chicago: University of Chicago Press.

Amoia, A. (1996). *20th-century Italian women writers. The feminine experience.* Carbondale, IL: Southern Illinois University Press.

Anderlini-D'Onofrio, S. (2004). Bisexual games and emotional sustainability in Ferzan Özpetek's queer films. *New Cinemas: Journal of Contemporary Film,* 2, 3, 163-174.

Anzaldúa, G. (1987/1999). *Borderlands=La frontera.* San Francisco: Aunt Lute Books.

Arcigay (2003). *Holy Dictionary vs. Lexicon.* Retrieved March 31, 2004, from http://www.arci gay.it/show.php?560.

————. (2005). See the site's homepage and related links with information about the organization. Retrieved March 31, 2005, from http://www.arcigay.it/presentazione/.

Arendt, H. (1959). *The human condition.* New York: Doubleday Anchor Books.

Ariès, P. (1987). *Sexualidades occidentales.* Buenos Aires: Paidós.

Aulagnier Spairani, P. (1967). *Le désir et la perversion.* Paris: Seuil.

Balbo, L. (1978). La doppia presenza. *Inchiesta,* VIII, 32, 3-6.

Ballarin, P., Euler, C., Le Feuvre, N., & Raevaara, E. (2004). *Women in the European Union.* Retrieved May 6, 2004, from http://www.helsinki.fi/science/ xantippa/wee/wee20.html.

Baranski, Z., & West, R. (2003). *The Cambridge companion to modern Italian culture.* Cambridge, UK: Cambridge University Press.

Barbagli, M. (1984). *Sotto lo stesso tetto. Mutamenti della famiglia in Italia dal XV al XX secolo.* Bologna, Italy: Il Mulino

Barbagli, M., & Colombo, A. (2001). *Omossessuali moderni. Gay e lesbiche in Italia.* Bologna, Italy: Il Mulino.

Barker, C. (2004). *Cultural studies. Theory and practice.* London: Sage.

Basoli, A.G. (2004). *Rekindling our love of Italian cinema: Moma's second act series. The neo-realists did what they wanted, regardless of the market.* Retrieved March 9, 2004, from www.moviemaker.com/issues/39/italian-cinema.html.

———. (2005). *A true Italian now, caught in a "beautiful trap."* Retrieved September 20, 2005, from http://travel2.nytimes.com/mem/travel/articlepage.html?res=9D01E0DD123 CF930A35755C0A9679C8B63.

Bech, H. (1997). *When men meet: Homosexuality and modernity.* Chicago: University of Chicago Press.

Beck-Gernshein, E. (2003). *La reinvención de la familia.* Buenos Aires: Paidós.

Bennet, B.A., & Wilkins, D.G. (1984). *Donatello.* Oxford: Phaedon.

Berlant, L., & Warner, M. (2002). Sex in public. In M. Warner (ed.), *Publics and counterpublics* (pp. 187-208). New York: Zone Books.

Bernstein M., & Reimann R. (eds.). (2001). *Queer families, queer politics.* New York: Columbia University Press.

———. (2001). Queer families and the politics of visibility. In M. Bernstein & R. Reimann (eds.), *Queer families, queer politics* (pp. 1-17). New York: Columbia University Press.

Bersani, L. (1995). *Homos.* Cambridge, MA: Harvard University Press.

———. (2002). Sociability and cruising. *Umbr(a)*, 1, 9-24.

Bertelli, P. (2002). *Cinegay. L'omosessualità nella lanterna magica.* Rome: Croce Libreria.

Bertone, C., Casiccia, A., Saraceno, C., & Torrioni, P. (2003). *Diversi da chi? Gay, lesbiche, transessuali in un'area metropolitana.* Milan: Guerini e Associati.

Bhaba, H. (1994). *The location of culture.* New York: Routledge.

Biasin, G.-P. (2001). Narratives of self and society. In Z. Baranski & R. West (eds.), *The Cambridge companion to modern Italian culture* (pp. 151-171). Cambridge, UK: Cambridge University Press.

Biersted, R. (1959). The human condition. *American Sociological Review*, 24(1), 113-114.

Bilton, T. (1996). *Introductory sociology.* London: Macmillan.

Blake, N. (2004). "What does mother want?" Pedro Almódovar's "All about My Mother." *Aesthethika*, 1, 1, 1-11.

Bonaccorso, M. (1994). *Mamme e papà omosessuali. Primo saggio italiano sulla famiglila omosessuale.* Roma: Editore Riuiti.

Bondanella, P. (2003). *Italian cinema.* New York: Continuum.

Boswell, J. (1994). *Same-sex unions in premodern Europe.* New York: Villard.

Bourcier, M.-H. (2001). *Queer zones. Politiques des identités sexuelles, des représentations et des savoirs.* Paris: Balland.

Bowman, M. (2000). *The significance of psychoanalysis in modern thought.* Retrieved February 24, 2004, from http://www.psychoanalysis.org.uk/bowman.htm.

Bozett, F.W. (1989). *Homosexuality and the family.* New York: Harrington Park Press.

Braidotti, R. (1994). *Dissonanze. Le donne e la filosofia contemporanea.* Milan: La Tartaruga Edizioni.

———. (1994). *Nomadic subjects.* New York: Columbia University Press.

Braidotti, R., & Griffin, G. (eds.). (2002). *Thinking differently. A reader in European women's studies*. New York: Zed Books.

Brand, P., & Pertile, L. (1996). *The Cambridge history of Italian literature*. London: Cambridge University Press.

Brennan, T. (ed.). (1989). *Between feminism and psychoanalysis*. London: Routledge.

Brown, W. (1991). Feminist hesitations, postmodern exposures. *Differences* 3, 1, 63-84.

————. (1995). *States of injury: Power and freedom in late modernity*. Princeton: Princeton University Press.

Brunetta, P. (1991). *Cent'anni di cinema italiano*. Rome: Laterza.

Bruni, F. (2002, December 26). *Persistent drop in fertility reshapes Europe's future*. Retrieved October 27, 2004, from http://query.nytimes.com/gst/abstract.html?res=F30 C1EFB3B580C758EDDAB0994DA404482&incamp=archive:search.

Bruno, G. (1993). *Streetwalking on a ruined map: Cultural theory and the city films of Elvira Notari*. Princeton, NJ: Princeton University Press.

Burston, P. (1995). Just a gigoló? Narcissism, nellyism and the "new man" theme. In P. Burston & C. Richardson (eds.), *A queer romance. Lesbians, gay men and popular culture* (pp. 111-122). London and New York: Routledge.

Buss, R. (1989). *Italian films*. London: B.T. Batsford.

Butler, J. (1990). *Gender trouble: Feminism and the subversion of identity*. New York: Routledge.

————. (1993). *Bodies that matter*. New York and London: Routledge.

————. (1997a). *Excitable speech. A politics of the performative*. New York: Routledge.

————. (1997b). Feminism by any other name. Interview. In E. Weed & N. Schor (eds.), *Feminism meets queer theory* (pp. 31-67). Bloomington and Indianapolis: Indiana University Press.

————. (2002). Is kinship always already heterosexual? *Difference: A Journal of Feminist Cultural Studies* 13, 1,14-44.

Cadoret, A. (2003). *Padres como los demás*. Barcelona: Gedisa.

Calhoun, C. (1997). Plurality, promises and public spaces. In C. Calhoun and J. McGowan (eds.), *Hannah Arendt and the meaning of politics*. Minneapolis: University of Minnesota Press.

Carey, J. (1989). A cultural approach to communication. In *Communication as culture: Essays on media and society* (pp. 13-36). Boston: Unwin Hyman.

Cavagna, C. (2005). Profile & interview: Gabriele Muccino. Retrieved June, 6, 2005, from http://www.aboutfilm.com/features/muccino/muccino.htm.

Cavallini, G. (2002). La dolcezza della vita e il sentimento del crepuscolo nei Sillabari di Goffredo Parise. *Otto/Novecento, 26*, 2, 71-89.

Cavarero, A. (1987). Per una teoria della differenza sessuale. In A. Cavarero et al. (eds.). *Diotima. Il pensiero della differenza sessuale*. Milan, Italy: La Tartaruga Edizioni.

————. (1999). *Il pensiero femminista, un approccio teoretico*. Milan: Feltrinelli.

Cecchi Paone, A. (2004). *Solo per amore. Famiglia, sessualità e procreazione nel nuovo mondo globale*. Milan, Italy: Il Saggiatore.

Cento Bull, A. (2001). Social and political cultures in Italy from 1860 to the present day. In Z. Baransky & R. West (eds.), *The Cambridge companion to modern Italian culture* (pp. 35-62). Cambrdge, UK: Cambridge University Press.

Cestaro, G.P. (2004). Queer Italia: Same sex desire in Italian literature and film. In *Queer Italia* (pp. 1-18). New York: Palgrave Macmillan.

Chodorow, N. (1992). The psychodynamics of the family. In S. Saguaro (ed.), *Psychoanalysis and woman, a reader* (pp. 108-127). New York: New York University Press.

Cichocki, N. (2005). Continuity and change in Turkish bathing culture in Istanbul. *Turkish Studies*, 6, 1, 93-112.

Cixous, H. (1981). Castration or decapitation? In S. Saguaro (ed.), *Psychoanalysis and woman, a reader* (pp. 231-244). New York: New York University Press.

Clark, K. (1956). *The nude. A study in ideal form.* New York: Pantheon.

Clifford, J. (1998). *The predicament of culture.* Cambridge, MA: Harvard University Press.

Cole, C. (1999). Bettino Craxi Italian Socialist Leader. Retrieved April 15, 2005, from http://www.uwgb.edu/galta/333/BIOS98/CRAXI.HTM.

Comunicato Stampa. Ratzinger papa: ha vinto la Chiesa più retriva. *Arcigay.com.* Retrieved April 20, 2005, from http://www.arcigay.it/ show.php?1377.

Consoli, M. (1991). *Homocaust.* Milan: Kaos.

————. (2000). *Independence gay. Alle origini del gay pride.* Bolsena (VT), Italy: Massari Editore.

Copjec, J. (2003). *Imagine there's no woman: Ethics and sublimation.* Cambridge, MA: MIT Press.

Crofts Wiley, S.B. (2004). Rethinking nationality in the context of globalization. *Communication Theory*, 14, 1, 78-96.

Crompton, L. (2003). Homosexuality and civilization. Cambridge, MA, and London: The Belknap Press of Harvard University Press.

CulturaGay. (2005). Cuore Sacro. Retrieved July 12, 2005, from www.culturagay.it/cg/recensione.php?id=10982.

Cunningham, D. (2003). Queer cinema since 1997. In L. Daniel & C. Jackson (eds.), *The bent lens. A world guide to gay and lesbian film* (pp.10-13). Los Angeles: Alyson Books.

Dall'Orto, G. (1986). Per il bene della razza. Al confino il pederasta. Retrieved March 15, 2005, from http://www.giovannidallorto.com/saggistoria/fascismo/bb/confino1.html.

————. (1989). "Socratic love" as a disguise for same-sex love in the Italian Renaissance. In *The pursuit of sodomy: Male homosexuality in Renaissance and Enlightenment Europe* (pp. 33-66). New York: Harrington Park Press.

————. (1994). Omosessualità e razzismo fascista. In Il Centro Furio Jesi (ed.), *La menzogna della razza: documenti e immagini del razzismo e dell'antisemitismo fascista* (pp. 139-144). Bologna, Italy: Grafis.

————. (1999). Il paradosso del razzismo fascista verso l'omosessualità. In A. Burgio (ed.), *Nel nome della razza: il razzismo nella storia d'Italia 1870-1925* (pp. 515-528). Bologna, Italy: Il Mulino.

————. (2004a). "Nature is a mother most sweet": Homosexuality in sixteenth and seventeenth-century Italian libertism. In G. Cestaro (ed.), *Queer Italia* (pp. 83-104). New York: Palgrave Macmillan.

————. (2004b). *Ricchioni, Femmenelle e Zamel: L'"omosessualità mediterranea."* Retrieved January 20, 2004, from http://www.giovannidallorto.com/cultura/medit/medit.html.

Daniel, L., & Jackson, C. (eds.). (2003). *The bent lens. A world guide to gay and lesbian film.* Los Angeles: Alyson Books.

Danna, D. (1997). *Matrimonio omosessuale.* Rome: Erre Emme.

————. (1999). *Lesbian mothers in contemporary Italy.* Paper presented at the conference Women's World 99, Tromsø, Norway, August 1999. Retrieved March 15, 2005, from www.danieladanna.it/ Microsoft percent20Word percent20--percent20lesbian percent20mothers.pdf.

———. (2004). Beauty and the beast: Lesbians in literature and sexual science from the nineteenth to the twentieth centuries. In G. Cestaro (ed.), *Queer Italia* (pp. 117-132). New York: Palgrave Macmillan.

Davis, G. (2004). Camp and queer and the new queer director: Case study—Gregg Araki. In M. Aaron (ed.), *New queer cinema* (pp. 53-67). New Brunswick, NJ: Rutgers University Press.

de Clementi, A. (2002). The feminist movement in Italy. In R. Braidotti & G. Griffin (eds.), *Thinking differently. A reader in European women's studies* (pp. 332-340). New York: Zed Books.

de Grazia, V. (1992). *How fascism ruled women: Italy, 1922-1945*. Berkeley: University of California Press.

de Lauretis, T. (1988). Displacing hegemonic discourses: Reflections on feminist theory in the 1980s [electronic version]. *Inscriptions*, 3-4. Retrieved May 24, 2005, from http://humwww.ucsc.edu/CultStudies/PUBS/Inscriptions/vol_3-4/delauretis.html.

———. (1989). *Technologies of gender. Essays on theory, film and fiction*. London: Macmillan.

———. (1993). Upping the anti [sic] in feminist theory. In S. During (ed.), *The cultural studies reader* (pp. 307-319). New York: Routledge.

———. (1994). *The practice of love*. Bloomington: Indiana University Press.

———. (1999). *Soggetti eccentrici*. Milan, Italy: Feltrinelli Editore.

De Melis, F. (1995). Pasolini poeta offeso. Retrieved November 2, 2005, from www.pasolini.net/manifesto15.htm.

Dean, T. (1997). Two kinds of otherness and their consequences. *Critical Inquiry*, 23, 910-920.

———. (2000). *Beyond sexuality*. Chicago: University of Chicago Press.

———. (2003). Lacan and queer theory. In J.M. Rabaté (ed.), *The Cambridge companion to Lacan* (pp. 238-252). Cambridge, UK: Cambridge University Press.

Dean, T., & Lane, C. (eds.). (2001). *Homosexuality and psychoanalysis*. Chicago: University of Chicago Press.

Delfino, S. (1998). Desigualdad y diferencia. *Doxa. Cuadernos de Ciencias Sociales*, 9, 123-145.

Della Casa, S. (2004). *Cinema Italiano. Annuario 2004*. Milan, Italy: Il Castoro.

Della Casa, S., Manera, P., and Paolicchi, A. (2004). I lungometraggi dell'anno. In S. Della Casa (ed.), *Cinema Italiano. Annuario 2004* (pp. 29-85). Milan, Italy: Il Castoro.

Delmas, J. (1977). Comizi d'Amore. *Jeune cinema*, 101 n/p. Retrieved November 2, 2006, from http://www.cineforum.bz.it/pellicola/archivio/film/schede/comizi percentd'amore/.

D'Emilio, J. (1993). Capitalism and gay identity. In H. Abelove, M.A. Barale, & D. Halperin (eds.), *The lesbian and gay studies reader* (pp. 467-479). New York and London: Routledge.

Denzin, N. (1978). *The research act*. New York: McGraw-Hill.

———. (1992). *Symbolic interactionism and cultural studies. The politics of interpretation*. Oxford, UK, and Cambridge, MA: Blackwell.

———. (1997). *Interpretive ethnography. Ethnographic practices for the 21st century*. Thousand Oaks, CA; London; and New Delhi: Sage Publications.

———. (2001). *Interpretive iteractionism*. 2nd ed. Thousand Oaks, CA; London; and New Delhi: Sage Publications.

Derrida, J. (1982). *Margins of philosophy*. Chicago: University of Chicago Press.

Dickie, J. (1996). Imagined Italies. In D. Forgacs & R. Lumley (eds.), *Italian cultural studies. An introduction* (pp. 19-33). Oxford: Oxford University Press.

————.The notion of Italy. In Z. Baranski & R.J. West (eds.), *The Cambridge companion to modern Italian culture* (pp. 17-33). Cambridge, UK: Cambridge University Press.

Diken, B., & Laustsen, C.B. (2001). Postal economies of the Orient. *Millennium: Journal of International Studies*, 30, 3, 761-784.

Dogliani, P. (1999). *L'Italia fascista*. Milan, Italy: Sansoni.

Dolto, F. (1981). *Hommes et femmes*. Retrieved March 23, 2003, from http://www.sospsy.com /Bibliopsy/Biblio9/biblio022.htm.

Dombroski, R.S. (2003). Socialism, communism and other "isms." In Z. Baranski & R. West (eds.), *The Cambridge companion to modern Italian culture* (pp. 113-130). Cambridge, UK: Cambridge University Press.

Donahue, D. (2000). *Lesbian, gay, bisexual, and transgender rights. A human rights perspective*. Minneapolis: University of Minnesota Press.

Doty, A. (1998). Queer theory. In *Oxford guide to film studies* (pp. 148-157). London and New York: Oxford University Press.

Doumanis, N. (2001). *Italy. Inventing the nation*. London: Arnold.

Due. (2005). *Interview with Ferzan Özpetek*. Due, 87, March, April 2001. Retrieved September 18, 2005, from http://claweb.cla.unipd.it/home/eduso/cinema/intervista_opzetek.htm.

Duncan, D. (2004). Secret wounds: The bodies of fascism in Giorgio Bassani's *Dietro la porta*. In G. Cestaro (ed.), *Queer Italia* (pp. 187-206). New York: Palgrave Macmillan.

During, S. (1993). Introduction. In S. During (ed.), *The cultural studies reader* (pp. 1-30). New York: Routledge.

Dyer, R. (2002). *The matter of images: Essays on representation*. London: Routledge.

Ebert, R. (2002, August 30). The last kiss. *Chicago Sun-Times*. Retrieved June 7, 2005, from http://rogerebert.suntimes.com/apps/pbcs.dll/article?AID=/20020830/REVIEWS/208300 302/1023.

————. (2004, February 13). The dreamers. *Chicago Sun-Times*. Retrieved February 7, 2005,   from http://rogerebert.suntimes.com/apps/pbcs.dll/article?AID=/20040213/REVIEWS/4 02130302/1023.

Ergas, Y. (1982). 1968-1979. Feminism and the Italian party system: Women's politics in a decade of turmoil. *Comparative Politics*, 14, 3, 253-279.

Eribon, D. (1999). *Réflexions sur la question gay*. Paris: Fayard.

————. (2003). *Dictionnaire des cultures gays et lesbiennes*. Paris: Larousse.

Espin, O. (1997). *Crossing borders and boundaries: The life narratives of immigrant lesbians*. London: Sage Publications.

Eurispes: Cattolici favorevoli ai Pacs (2006, September 29). *City*, section *Fatti*, p. 4.

Eve, M. (1996). Comparing Italy: The case of corruption. In D. Forgacs & R. Lumley (eds.), *Italian cultural studies. An introduction* (pp. 34-51). Oxford: Oxford University Press.

Falassi, A. (1980). *Folklore by the fireside. Text and context of the Tuscan Veglia*. London: Scholar Press.

Fariña, J.J.M. (1999). *Ética, un horizonte en quiebra*. Buenos Aires: EUDEBA.

Fernbach, D. (1980). Introduction. In M. Mieli (ed.), *Homosexuality and liberation: Elements of a gay* critique (pp. 7-17). London: Gay Men's Press.

Fink, B. (1995). *The Lacanian subject. Between language and jouissance*. Princeton, NJ: Princeton University Press.

————. (2004). *Lacan to the letter. Reading écrits closely.* Minneapolis: University of Minnesota Press.

Fisher, D.D. (2003). L'adoption du PACS: "Exception française," "communautarisme" et symbolique identitaire. *Contemporary French Civilization*, 27, 2, 211-230.

Forgacs, D. (1997). Twentieth-century culture. In G. Holmes (ed.), *The Oxford illustrated history of Italy* (pp. 290-319). London: Oxford University Press.

Forgacs, D., & Lumley, R. (1996). *Italian cultural studies. An introduction.* New York: Oxford.

Foucault, M. (1971/1984). Nietzsche, genealogy, history. In P. Rabinow (ed.), *The Foucault reader* (pp. 76-100). New York: Pantheon Books.

————. (1976/1984). *Histoire de la sexualité.* Paris: Gallimard.

————. (1977/1994). *Dits et écrits*, Vol. 3. Paris: Gallimard.

————. (1986). *Care of the self* (vol. 3 of *The history of sexuality*) (trans. Robert Hurley). New York: Random House.

————. (1993). Space, power and knowledge. In S. During (ed.), *The cultural studies reader* (pp. 134-145). New York: Routledge.

————. (1997). Friendship as a way of life (R. de Ceccaty, J. Danet, & J. Le Bitoux, Interviewers; J. Johnston, trans.). In *Ethics: Subjectivity and truth* (pp. 135-140). New York: New Press.

Frankel, C. (1959). Man and crisis; human condition. *Political Science Quarterly*, 74 (3), 420-422.

Freire, H. (2004). *Cine "gay."* Retrieved March 15, 2004, from http://www.topia.com.ar/arti culos/21gay.htm.

Freud, S. (1905). Three essays on the theory of sexuality. *SE Vol. VII* (pp. 123-245). New York: Norton.

————. (1905/1963). *Jokes and their relation to the unconscious.* New York: Norton.

————. (1910/1974). Leonardo da Vinci and a memory of his childhood. *SE Vol. XI* (pp. 57-137). New York: Norton.

————. (1912/1986). *Totem and Taboo: Some points of agreement between the mental lives of savages and neurotics.* New York: Norton.

————. (1912/1974). The dynamics of transference. *SE Vol. XII* (pp. 97-108). New York: Norton.

————. (1916/1966). *Introductory lectures on psychoanalysis.* New York: Norton.

————. (1921/1975). *Group psychology and the analysis of the ego.* New York: Norton.

————. (1930/1989). *Civilization and its discontents.* New York: Norton.

Gabb, J. (2004). Critical differentials: Querying the incongruities within research on lesbian parent families. *Sexualities*, 7, 2, 167-182.

Gamson, J. (2001). Talking freaks: Lesbian, gay, and transgender families on daytime talk TV. In M. Bernstein & R. Reimann (eds.), *Queer families, queer politics* (pp. 68-86). New York: Columbia University Press.

Gatt-Rutter, J. (1996). The aftermath of the Second World War (1945-56). In P. Brand & L. Pertile (eds.), *The Cambridge history of Italian literature* (pp. 533-606). London: Cambridge University Press.

Gerber, D. (2005). Muerte en Venecia. La belleza como límite. Retrieved September 20, 2005, from

http://www.islaternura.com/ARINCONES/FILMOGRAFIA/ARTICULOS/CINEarticulo
BellezaLimiteVenecia.htm.

Giartosio, T. (2004). *Perché non possiamo non dirci: Letteratura, omosessualità, mondo.*
Milan, Italy: Feltrinelli.

Giddens, A. (1992). *The transformation of intimacy. Sexuality, love and eroticism in modern
societies.* Stanford, CA: Stanford University Press.

Gill, P. (2003). Taking it personally: Male suffering in 8MM. *Camera Oscura*, 52, 18, 1, 157-
187.

Ginsborg, P. (2003). *Italy and its discontents. Family, civil society, state: 1980-2001.* New
York: Palgrave Macmillan.

Giusti, M. (2004). Pubblicità d'autore 2003. In S. Della Casa (ed.), *Cinema Italiano. Annuario
2004* (pp.193-194). Milan, Italy: Il Castoro.

Gnerre, F. (2000). *L'eroe negato. Omosessualità e letteratura nel novecento italiano.* Milan,
Italy: Baldini & Castaldi.

Golini, A., & Silvestrini, A. (1995). Cambiamenti familiari e relazioni generazionali: una
lettura demografica. In P.P. Donati (ed.), *Quarto rapporto CISF sulla famiglia in Italia, q.
v.* (pp. 89-126). Milan, Italy: San Paolo.

Gomez, P., & Travaglio, M. (2004). *Regime.* Milan, Italy: Libri S.p.A.

Gramolini, M.C. (2000). Arcilesbica perché. In M. Consoli, *Independence gay. Alle origini
del gay pride* (appendix, pp. 115-127). Volsena, Italy: Massari Editore.

Greenberg, D.F. (1988). *The construction of homosexuality.* Chicago: University of Chicago
Press.

Grillini, F. (1990). Apdendix: La via italiana all'orgoglio gay. In M. Consoli (ed.), *Stonewall.
Quando la rivoluzione é gay* (pp. 113-121). Rome: Casa Editrice Roberto Napoleone.

Gross, L. (2005). The past and future and gay, lesbian, bisexual, and transgender studies.
Journal of Communications, 55, 3, 508-528.

————. (1995). *Contested closets. The politics and ethics of outing.* Minneapolis and
London: University of Minnesota Press.

Grossberg, L., Nelson, C., & Treichler, P. (eds.). (1992). Cultural studies: An introduction. In
L. Grossberg, C. Nelson, & P. Treichler (eds.), *Cultural studies* (pp. 1-22). New York:
Routledge.

Hall, S. (1983). The narrative construction of reality: An interview with Stuart Hall. *Southern
Review* 17, 3-17.

————. (1996). The question of cultural identity. In S. Hall, D. Held, & K. Thompson
(eds.), *Modernity* (pp. 595-634). Malden, MA: Blackwell.

Hanson, E. (1999). *Out takes. Essays on queer theory and film.* Durham, NC, and London:
Duke University Press.

Hawley, J. (2001). Introduction. In J. Hawley (ed.), *Post-colonial, queer. Theoretical
intersections* (pp. 1-18). Albany: State University of New York Press.

Held, D. (1980). The changing structure of the family and the individual: Critical theory and
psychoanalysis. In D. Held, *Introduction to critical theory: Horkheimer to Habermas* (pp.
11-147). Berkeley: University of California Press.

Herdt, G. (1997). *Same-sex, different cultures: Gays and lesbians across cultures.* Boulder,
CO: Westview Press.

Hine, D. (1997). Italy since 1945. In G. Holmes (ed.). *The Oxford illustrated history of Italy*
(pp. 320-347). London: Oxford University Press.

Hocquenghem, G. (1978). *Homosexual desire.* London: Allison & Busby.

Iaculo, G. (2002). *Le identità gay. Conversazioni con noti uomini gay ed un saggio introdutti- vo sul processo di coming out.* Rome: Fabio Croce Editore.

ILGA-Europe (2004). *Equality for lesbians and gay men.* (See specially the section by E. Biagini, G. Bertozzo, & M. Ravaioli.) Retrieved March 16, 2004, from http://www.steff.suite.dk/report.htm#ITALY.

Irigaray, L. (1985). This sex which is not one. In S. Saguaro (ed.), *Psychoanalysis and woman, a reader* (pp. 261-268). New York: New York University Press.

ISTAT (2004, October 27). *Le strutture familiari. Media 2002-2003.* Retrieved June 6, 2005, from http://www.istat.it/Societ-/Strutture-/index.htm.

————. (2006a, September 25). *Rilevazione sulle forze di lavoro.* Retrieved September 25, 2006, from http://www.istat.it/salastampa/comunicati/in_calendario/forzelav/20060920 _00/.

————. (2006b, September 24). *La popolazione straniera residente in Italia per classi di età.* Retrieved September 24, 2006, from http://www.istat.it/salastampa/comunicati/non_calen dario/20060330_00/.

————. (2006c, September 25). *Bilancio demografico nazionale.* Retrieved September 25, 2006, from http://www.istat.it/salastampa/comunicati/in_calendario/bildem/20060710 _02/.

————. (2006d, September 25). *La vita di coppia.* Retrieved September 25, 2006, from http://www.istat.it/dati/catalogo/20060821_00/.

Jacques, C. (2004). *Talking about marriage.* Retrieved March 8, 2004, from http://www.gay.com/families/article.html?sernum=403.

Jagose, A. (1996). *Queer theory: An introduction.* New York: New York University Press.

Jameson, F. (1998). The political unconscious: Narrative as a socially symbolic act. In *The Norton anthology of theory and criticism* (pp. 1937-1960). New York: Norton.

Jones, C. (1996). Lesbian and gay cinema. In Jill Nelmes (eds.), *An introduction to film studies* (pp. 308-344). London and New York: Routledge.

Kehr, D. (2002, August 16). Film review: Love, Italian style, but, oh, such complications. *New York Times*, section E, 16:2.

Kertzer, D., & Saller, R. (eds.). (1991). *The family in Italy. From antiquity to the present.* New Haven, CT: Yale University Press.

————. (1991). Historical and anthropological perspectives on Italian family life. In D. Kertzer & R. Saller (eds.), *The family in Italy. From antiquity to the present* (pp. 1-22). New Haven, CT: Yale University Press.

Kirsch, M.H. (2000). *Queer theory and social change.* London and New York: Routledge.

Kitzinger, C., & Wilkinson, S. (2004). The re-branding of marriage: Why we got married instead of registering a civil partnership. *Feminism & Psychology*, 14, 1, 127-150.

Klein, M. (1928). Early stages of the Oedipus conflict. In Shelley Saguaro (ed.), *Psychoanaly- sis and woman, a reader.* New York: New York University Press.

————. (1961). *Narrative of a child analysis: The conduct of the psychoanalysis of children as seen in the treatment of a ten year old boy.* London: Hogarth Press.

Koff, S., & Koff, S. (2000). *Italy. From the first to the second republic.* London: Routledge.

Kristeva, J. (1980). Place names. In *Desire in language*, L. Roudiez, trans. New York: Columbia University Press.

Lacan, J. (1933/1988). Motives of a paranoiac crime: The crime of the Papin sisters. *Critical Texts* (J. Anderson, trans.), 5, 3, 7-11.

————. (1933/1988). The problem of style and the psychiatric conception of paranoiac forms of experience. *Critical Texts* (J. Anderson, trans.), 5, 3, 4-6.

————. (1938/1988). The family complexes. *Critical Texts* (C. Asp, trans.), 5, 3, 13-29.

————. (1948/2002). Aggressiveness in psychoanalysis. In *Écrits: A selection* (B. Fink, trans.) (pp. 10-30). New York: Norton.

————. (1949/2002). The mirror stage as formative of the *I* function, as revealed in psychoanalytic experience. In *Écrits: A selection* (B. Fink, trans.) (pp. 3-9). New York: Norton.

————. (1953/2002). The function and field of speech and language in psychoanalysis. In *Écrits: A selection* (B. Fink, trans.) (pp. 30-106). New York: Norton.

————. (1953/1979). Le mythe individuel du névrose. *Ornicar*, 17/18, n/p.

————. (1957/2002). The instance of the letter in the unconscious, or reason since Freud. In *Écrits: A selection* (B. Fink, trans.) (pp. 138-168). New York: Norton.

————. (1958/2002). The directions of the treatment and the principles of its power. In *Écrits: A selection* (B. Fink, trans.) (pp. 215-270). New York: Norton.

————. (1958/2002). The signification of the phallus. In *Écrits: A selection* (B. Fink, trans.) (pp. 271-280). New York: Norton.

————. (1959-1960/1992). *Seminar VII. The ethics of psychoanalysis*. New York: Norton.

————. (1960/2002). Subversion of the subject and dialect of desire in the Freudian unconscious. In *Écrits: A selection* (B. Fink, trans.) (pp. 281-312). New York: Norton.

————. (1965-1966). *Seminar XIII, L'objet de la psychanalyse*. Unpublished.

————. (1969-1970). *Seminar XVII, L'envers de la psychanalyse*. Paris: Seuil.

————. (1972-1973). *Le Séminaire, Livre XX: Encore*. Paris: Seuil.

Lacquer, T. (1990). *Making sex: Body and gender from the Greeks to Freud.* Cambridge, MA: Harvard University Press.

Landy, M. (1986). Culture and politics in the work of Antonio Gramsci. *Boundary* 2, 14, 3, 49-70.

————. (2000). *Italian film*. New York: Cambridge University Press.

Lapassade, G. (1967). *Groupes, organisations, et institutions*. Paris: Gauthier-Villars.

Lapsley, R., & Westlake, M. (1988). *Film theory: An introduction*. Manchester, UK: Manchester University Press.

Laviosa, F. (2003). Archibugi's cinematic representations. *Italica*, 80, 4, 540-549.

Lazere, A. (2004). The wind, in the evening. Retrieved November 2, 2005, from http://www.culturevulture.net/Movies9/Wind.htm.

Le Fur, A. (2004). ¿Adoptar o adaptar? In J. H. Raíces Montero & E. Giberti (eds), *Adopción. La caída del prejuicio*. Buenos Aires: Del Puerto Editores.

Lehr, V. (1999). *Queer family values: Debunking the myth of the nuclear family*. Philadelphia: Temple University Press.

Lévi-Strauss, C. (1949/1992). *Las estructuras elementales del parentesco*. Buenos Aires: Planeta Agostini.

————. (1968). *Antropología estructural*. Buenos Aires: EUDEBA.

Lexicon (2003). Retrieved March 8, 2004, from http://www.agedo.org/press10.html.

Livi Bacci, M. (1997). *A concise history of world population*. Malden, MA: Blackwell.

Llamas, R. (1999). *Homografías*. Madrid: Espasa Calpe.

Lonzi, C. (1974). *Sputiamo su Hegel. La donna clitoridea e la donna vaginale*. Milan, Italy: Rivolta femminile.

Luepnitz, D. (2003). Beyond the phallus: Lacan and feminism. In J.M. Rabaté (ed.), *The Cambridge companion to Lacan* (pp. 221-237). Cambridge, UK: Cambridge University Press.

Lumley, R. (1996). Peculiarities of the Italian newspaper. In D. Forgacs & R. Lumley (eds.), *Italian cultural studies. An introduction* (pp. 199-215). Oxford: Oxford University Press.

Luongo, M. (2002). Rome's world pride. Making the eternal city an international gay tourism destination. *GLQ,* 8:1-2, 167-181.

Mackinnon, C. (1987). *Feminism unmodified. Discourses on life and law.* Cambridge, MA, and London: Harvard University Press.

Mancini, E. (1985). *Struggles of the Italilan film industry during fascism, 1930-1935.* Ann Arbor, MI: UMI Press.

Martel, F. (2000). Gay rights and civil unions. *Dissent,* Fall, 20-23.

Mattone, S., & Ruggiano, M.G. (1977). L'intervento del giudice nella famiglia. *Democrazia e Diritto,* 1, 197-203.

Mauro, F. (2001). *Analisi del film Le Fate Ignoranti.* Retrieved September 20, 2005, from http://www.gianniromoli.it/fate.html.

McCarthy, C. (2003). *All consuming identities.* Paper presented at the Center for Democracy in a Multicultural Society colloquium, April 11, 2003, University of Illinois at Urbana-Champaign.

———. (2004). *The work of art and the postcolonial imagination.* Paper delivered at the 2004 Crossroads in Cultural Studies conference, June 30, 2004, University of Illinois at Urbana Champaign.

McCarthy, P. (1997). *The crisis of the Italian state: From the origins of the cold war to the fall of Berlusconi and beyond.* New York: St. Martin's Press.

McRobbie, A. (1996). More!: New sexualities in girls' and women's magazines. In J. Curran, D. Morley, & V. Walkerdine (eds.), *Cultural studies and communications* (pp. 172-194). London: Arnold.

Menniti, A., Palomba, R., & Sabbadini, L.L (1997). Italy: Changing the family from within. In F.-X. Kaufmann, A. Kuijsten, H.-J. Schulze, & K. Strohmeier (eds.), *Family life and family policies in Europe, V. I. Structures and trends in the 1980s* (pp. 225-252). Oxford: Clarendon Press.

Merlini, F. (1977). *Io, omosessuale.* Milan, Italy: La Salamandra.

Metz, C. (1977/1982). *The imaginary signifier.* Bloomington: Indiana University Press.

Michalczyk, J. (1986). *The Italian political filmmakers.* Cranbury, NJ: Associated University Presses.

Michalik, R. (2001). The desire for philosophy—Interview with Judith Butler. *Lola Press,* 2. Retrieved November 20, 2002, from http://www.lolapress.org/elec2/artenglish/butl_e.htm.

Mieli, M. (1980). *Homosexuality and liberation: Elements of a gay critique.* London: Gay Men's Press.

Mitchell, J. (1984). *The question of femininity and the theory of psychoanalysis.* In S. Saguaro (ed.), *Psychoanalysis and woman, a reader* (pp. 128-141). New York: New York University Press.

———. (2003). *Sibilings.* London: Polity.

Mocchi, P. (2004). *La "dottora" dei poveri e la rivoluzionaria.* Retrieved November 2004, from http://www.cronologia.it/storia/biografie/annakuli.htm.

Mohr, R. (2005). *The long arc of justice.* New York: Columbia University Press.

Moliterno, G. (2003). *Pier Paolo Pasolini*. Retrieved March 15, 2004, from http://www.sens esofcinema.com/contents/directors/02/pasolini.html.

Moon, M. (1993). Introduction. In G. Hocquenghem, *Homosexual desire*. London: Allison & Busby.

Morgan, P. (1995). *Italian fascism, 1919-1945*. New York: St. Martin's Press.

Murray, S.O. (2000). *Homosexualities*. Chicago: University of Chicago Press.

Nardi, P. (1998). The globalization of the gay & lesbian socio-political movement: Some observations about Europe with a focus on Italy. *Sociological Perspectives*, 41, 3, 567-586.

Nicholson, L. (1995). Interpreting gender. In L. Nicholson & S. Seidman (eds.), *Social postmodernism*. Cambridge, UK: Cambridge University Press.

Norton, R. (1997). *The myth of the modern homosexual. Queer history and the search for cultural unity*. London and Washington: Cassell.

Oakley, A. (1974). *Housewife*. London: Allen Lane.

PACS proposal (2005). Retrieved June 12, 2005, from http://www.unpacsavanti.it/download/index.htm.

Pallota, A. (2002). Book review: Women in Italian cinema. *Symposium,* 56, 2, 113-116.

Parise, G. (1999). *Italia*. In N. Roberts (ed.), *Short Stories in Italian—Racconti in Italiano* (pp. 15-28). New York: Penguin.

Parker, S. (1996). Political identities. In D. Forgacs & R. Lumley (eds.), *Italian cultural studies. An introduction* (pp. 112-128). Oxford: Oxford University Press.

Passerini, L. (1996). Gender relations. In D. Forgacs & R. Lumley (eds.), *Italian cultural studies. An introduction* (pp. 144-159). Oxford: Oxford University Press.

Pavese, C. (1967). *Prima che il gallo canti*. Turin, Italy: Einaudi.

Petrella, F. (1998). History of Italian psychoanalysis. *Newsletter, International Psychoanalytic Association*, 7, 2. Retrieved November 22, 2004, from http://eseries.ipa.org.uk/prev/newsletter/98--2/G6.htm.

Petrignani, S. (1999). *Donne in piscina*. In N. Roberts (ed.), *Short stories in Italian—Racconti in Italiano* (pp. 95-108). New York: Penguin.

Petrosino, D. (1996). Traditori della stripe. Il razzismo contro gli omosessuali nella stampa del fascismo. In A. Burgio & L. Casali (eds.), *Studi sul razzismo italiano* (pp. 89-107). Bologna: Clueb.

Peyrefitte, R. (1967). *Eccentrici amori*. Milan, Italy: Longanesi.

Pezzana, A. (1996). *Dentro e fuori*. Milan, Italy: Sperling and Kupfer.

Pieroni Bortolotti, F. (1991). *Alle origini del movimento femminile in Italia (1848-1892)*. Turin, Italy: Einaudi.

Pireddu, N. (2001). The anthropological roots of Italian cultural studies. In G. Parati & B. Lawton (eds.), *Italian cultural studies* (pp. 66-88). Boca Raton, FL: Bordighera Press.

Pitkin, D. (1985). *The house that Giacomo built. History of an Italian family, 1898-1979*. Cambridge, UK: Cambridge University Press.

Plummer, K. (1992). Speaking its name: Inventing a lesbian and gay studies. In K. Plummer (ed.), *Modern homosexualities: Fragments of lesbian and gay experience* (pp. 2-25). London: Routledge.

Porn in the United States (2004, September 5). *CBS News*. Retrieved May 26, 2005, from http://www.cbsnews.com/stories/2003/11/21/60minutes/main585049.shtml.

Preciado, B. (2003). *Performance, performatividad y prótesis*. Paper delivered at the conference "Retóricas del género. Políticas de identidad," Universidad Internacional de

Andalucía, March 17-23, 2003. Retrieved May 1, 2004, from http://www.unia.es/art-pen/estetica/estetica01/frame.html.

Prono, L. (2001). Gay pride, Italian style. *Scope: An Online Journal of Film Studies*, 34, n/p.

Pustianaz, M. (2004). Transitive gender and queer performance in the novels of Mario Mieli and Vittorio Pescatori. In G. Cestaro (ed.), *Queer Italia* (pp. 207-235). New York: Palgrave Macmillan.

Queer View (1997). *Pianese Nunzio, fourteen in May*. Retrieved March 10, 2004, from home.snafu.de/fablab/queerview/277pianesenunzio/english277.html.

Rabinovich, D. (2003). What is a Lacanian clinic? In J.M. Rabaté (ed.), *The Cambridge companion to Lacan* (pp. 208-220). Cambridge, UK: Cambridge University Press.

Rambach, A., & Rambach, M. (2003). *La culture gaie et lesbienne*. Paris: Fayard.

Rapisardi, F. (2003a). La educación como práctica de la libertad. In P. Agosto & R. Longo (eds.), *Taller sexualidades, géneros, subjectividades. Cuadernos de educación popular* (pp. 83-94). Buenos Aires: Universidad Popular Madres de Plaza de Mayo.

————. (2003b). Regulaciones políticas: Identidad, diferencia y desigualdad. Una crítica al debate contemporáneo. In D. Mafia (ed.), *Sexualidades migrantes. Género y transgénero* (pp. 97-116). Buenos Aires: Feminaria.

Roberts, N. (1999). *Short stories in Italian—Racconti in Italiano*. New York: Penguin.

Robertson, R. (1992). *Globalization*. London and Newbury Park, CA: Sage.

Rocchio, V. (1999). *Cinema of anxiety. A psychoanalysis of Italian neorrealism*. Austin: University of Texas Press.

Rocke, M. (1996). *Forbidden friendships: Homosexuality and male culture in Renaissance Florence*. New York: Oxford University Press.

Roman, D. (2003). Book review: In the forbidden city: An anthology of erotic fiction by Italian women. *European Legacy*, 8, 1, 91-136.

Romano, P. (1999). Judith Butler y la formación melancólica del sujeto. *Economía, Sociedad y Territorio*, 2, 6, 313-327

Rosaldo, R. (1993). *Culture & truth: The remaking of social analysis*. Boston: Beacon Press.

Rossi Barilli, G. (1999). *Il movimento gay in Italia*. Milan, Italy: Universale Economica Feltrinelli.

Roth, C. (1993). On equal treatment of lesbians and gay men in the EC. Preliminary draft report. Retrieved March 22, 2005, from http://www.france.qrd.org/texts/roth.html.

Roudinesco, E. (1997). *Jacques Lacan*. New York: Columbia University Press.

————. (2002). *La familia en desorden*. Buenos Aires: Fondo de Cultura Económica.

Rubin, L.B. (1994). *Families on the fault line*. New York: Harper Perennial.

Ruby Rich, B. (1993). Homo pomo: The new queer cinema. Reprinted in P. Cook & P. Dodd (eds.), *Women and film: A sight and sound reader* (pp. 164-166). Philadelphia: Temple University Press.

Rushing, R. (2003). The real of desire: travel/detection/Hitchcock/Antonioni. *Communication Review*, 6, 4, 313-326.

Russo, V. (1987). *The celluloid closet*. New York: Harper & Row.

Saéz, J. (2004). *Teoría queer y psicoanalisis*. Madrid: Síntesis.

Said, E.W. (1979). *Orientalism*. New York: Vintage.

Sapegno, M.S. (2002). Psychoanalysis and feminism: A European phenomenon and its specificities. In R. Braidotti & G. Griffin (eds.), *Thinking differently. A reader in European women's studies* (pp. 110-123). New York: Zed Books.

Saraceno, C. (1973). The nuclearity of the contemporary family: A problematic axiom. *Quaderni di Sociologia,* 22, 2, 145-170.

————. (1991). The Italian family: Paradoxes of privacy. In A. Prost & G. Vincent (eds.), *A history of private life, V, Riddles of identity in modern times.* Cambridge, MA: The Belknap Press of Harvard University Press.

Scalise, D. (1996). *Cose dell'altro mondo. Viaggio nell'Italia gay.* Milan, Italy: Zelig.

Schérer, R. (2005). L'enfer de l'hédonisme. *Multitudes.* Retrieved November 2, 2006, from http://multitudes.samizdat.net/article.php3?id_article=1586.

Schinardi, R. (2003). *Cinema gay, l'ennesimo genero.* Florence, Italy: Cadmo.

Sedgwick, E. (1993). Epistemology of the closet. In H. Abelove, M.A. Barale, & D.M. Halperin (eds.), *The lesbian and gay studies reader* (pp. 45-61). New York and London: Routledge.

————. (1994). *Tendencies.* London and New York: Howard Fertig.

Settembrini, L. (2001). *I Neoplatonici.* Palermo, Italy: Sellerio.

Siciliano, E. (1982). *Pasolini: A biography.* New York: Random House.

Smith, A.M. (2001). Words that matter: Butler's excitable speech. *Constellations,* 8, 3, 390-399.

Smith, C. (1995). The transgressive sexual subject. In P. Burston & C. Richardson (eds.), *A queer romance. Lesbians, gay men and popular culture* (pp. 123-146). London and New York: Routledge.

Spivak, G. (2001). Can the subaltern speak? In *The Norton anthology of theory and criticism* (pp. 2197-2207). New York: Norton.

Stacey, J. (1996). *In the name of the family: Rethinking family values in the postmodern age.* Boston: Beacon Press.

Stacey, J., & Davenport, E. (2002). Queer families quack back. In D. Richardson & S. Seidman (eds.), *Handbook of lesbian and gay studies.* London: Sage.

Stajano, C. (1996). *La cultura Italiana del novecento.* Rome and Bari, Italy: Laterza.

Stavrakakis, J. (1999). *Lacan and the political.* London: Routledge.

Stephenson, A. (2005). The provoking philosophy of Jacques Derrida. Retreived November 1, 2006, from http://www.bups.org/bups-dis.w3archive/0506/msg00000.html.

Stoddard, T. (1992). Why gay people should seek the right to marry. In S. Sherman (ed.), *Lesbian and gay marriage: Private commitments, public ceremonies.* Philadelphia: Temple University Press.

Stychin, C.F. (2005). Being gay. *Government and Opposition,* 40, 1, 90-109.

Suicidio su commissione. (2005). Retrieved June 16, 2005, from http://www.arcigaymodena.org/default.asp?mnu=rassegna_stampa&id=198.

Testa, C. (2002). *Italian cinema and modern European literatures.* Westport, CT: Praeger.

Thompson, J. (2002). *Mommy queerest.* Amherst and Boston: University of Massachusetts Press.

Turner, W.B. (2000). *A genealogy of queer theory.* Philadelphia: Temple University Press.

Vaid, U. (1995). *Virtual equality.* New York: Anchor Books.

Van Watson, W. (2002). Lucchino Visconti's (homosexual) *Ossessione.* In J. Reich and P. Garofalo (eds.), *Re-viewing fascism. Italian cinema, 1922-1943.* Bloomington and Indianapolis: Indiana University Press.

Vaticano: unioni gay nocive, è peccato legalizzarle. (2003). Retrieved October 27, 2005, from http://www.arcigay.it/show.php?685.

Viano, M. (1993). *A certain realism: Making use of Pasolini's film theory and practice.* Berkeley: University of California Press.

Viazzo, P.P. (2003). What's so special about the Mediterranean? Thirty years of research on household and family in Italy. *Continuity and Change,* 18, 1, 111-137.

Vogel, J. (2003). The family. *Social Indicators Research,* 64, 3, 393-435.

Wagstaff, C. (1996). Cinema. In D. Forgacs & R. Lumley (eds.), *Italian cultural studies. An introduction* (pp. 216-232). Oxford: Oxford University Press.

Ward, T.N., & Larner, M. (2003). *Living, studying and working in Italy.* New York: Henry Holt and Company.

Warner, M. (1999). *The trouble with normal. Sex, politics, and the ethics of queer life.* New York: The Free Press.

————. (2002). *Publics and counterpublics.* New York: Zone Books.

Waugh, T. (2000). *The fruit machine. Twenty years of writing on queer cinema.* Durham, NC and London: Duke University Press.

Webster, F. (2000). The politics of sex and gender: Benhabib and Butler debate on subjectivity. *Hypatia,* 15, 1. Retrieved March 22, 2005, from http://iupjournals.org/hypatia/hyp15--1.html.

Weeks, J. (1978). Preface. In G. Hocquenghem, *Homosexual desire.* London: Allison & Busby.

Weeks, J., Heaphy, B., & Donovan, C. (2001). *Same-sex intimacies. Families of choice and other life experiments.* London: Routledge.

Weston, K. (1991). *Families we choose.* New York: Columbia University Press.

Wilchins, R. (2004). *Queer theory, gender theory. An instant primer.* Los Angeles: Galyson Books.

Williams, G. (2001). Film review: The last kiss. *Sight & Sound* 14, 4, 56-57.

Williams, R. (1989). Culture is ordinary. In R. Gable (ed.), *Resources of hope. Culture, democracy, socialism.* London: Verso.

Winnicott, D.W. (1951). *Transitional objects and transitional phenomena. Playing and reality.* New York: Pelican Books.

White, S.K. (1998). Excitable speech. A politics of the performative; The psychic life of power: Theories in subjection. *The Journal of Politics,* 60, 3, 881-884.

Wood, S., & Farrell, J. (2001). Other voices: contesting the status quo. In Z. Baranski & R.J. West (eds.), *The Cambridge companion to modern Italian culture* (pp. 131-149). Cambridge, UK: Cambridge University Press.

World history of male love. (2005). Retrieved August 31, 2005, from http://www.androphile.org/preview/Museum/Rome/ficoronicist.htm

Zafiropoulos, M. (2002). *Lacan y las ciencias sociales. La declinación del padre (1938-1953).* Buenos Aires: Nueva Visión.

Zanatta, A.L. (1997). *Le nuove famiglie.* Bologna, Italy: Il Mulino.

Zaretsky, E. (1994). Identity theory, identity politics: Psychoanalysis, marxism, post-structuralism. In C. Calhoun (ed.), *Social theory and the politics of identity* (pp. 198-215). Oxford: Blackwell.

Zelizer, V.A. (1985). *Pricing the priceless child: The changing social value of children.* New York: Basic Books.

Žižek, S. (1989). *The sublime object of ideology.* London: Verso.

————. (1998). Multiculturalismo. In E. Gruner (ed.), *Estudios culturales. Reflexiones sobre el multiculturalismo* (pp. 92-134). Buenos Aires: Paidós.

————. (1992). *Everything you always wanted to know about Lacan (but were afraid to ask Hitchcock)*. New York: Verso.

————. (1999). *The ticklish subject: The absent centre of political ontology*. New York: Verso.

————. (2001a). *Did somebody say totalitarianism?* New York: Verso.

————. (2001b). *Welcome to the desert of the real*. Retrieved April 5, 2004, from http://www.theglobalsite.ac.uk/times/109zizek.htm.

Intersections in Communications and Culture

Global Approaches and Transdisciplinary Perspectives

General Editors: Cameron McCarthy & Angharad N. Valdivia

An Institute of Communications Research, University of Illinois Commemorative Series

This series aims to publish a range of new critical scholarship that seeks to engage and transcend the disciplinary isolationism and genre confinement that now characterizes so much of contemporary research in communication studies and related fields. The editors are particularly interested in manuscripts that address the broad intersections, movement, and hybrid trajectories that currently define the encounters between human groups in modern institutions and societies and the way these dynamic intersections are coded and represented in contemporary popular cultural forms and in the organization of knowledge. Works that emphasize methodological nuance, texture and dialogue across traditions and disciplines (communications, feminist studies, area and ethnic studies, arts, humanities, sciences, education, philosophy, etc.) and that engage the dynamics of variation, diversity and discontinuity in the local and international settings are strongly encouraged.

LIST OF TOPICS

- Multidisciplinary Media Studies
- Cultural Studies
- Gender, Race, & Class
- Postcolonialism
- Globalization
- Diaspora Studies
- Border Studies
- Popular Culture
- Art & Representation
- Body Politics
- Governing Practices
- Histories of the Present
- Health (Policy) Studies
- Space and Identity
- (Im)migration
- Global Ethnographies
- Public Intellectuals
- World Music
- Virtual Identity Studies
- Queer Theory
- Critical Multiculturalism

Manuscripts should be sent to:

Cameron McCarthy OR Angharad N. Valdivia
Institute of Communications Research
University of Illinois at Urbana-Champaign
222B Armory Bldg., 555 E. Armory Avenue
Champaign, IL 61820

To order other books in this series, please contact our Customer Service Department:
(800) 770-LANG (within the U.S.)
(212) 647-7706 (outside the U.S.)
(212) 647-7707 FAX

Or browse online by series:
www.peterlang.com